Inside Magazine Publishing

David Stam and Andrew Scott

 Routledge
Taylor & Francis Group

LONDON AND NEW YORK

First published 2014
by Routledge
2 Park Square, Milton Park, Abingdon, Oxon OX14 4RN

and by Routledge
711 Third Avenue, New York, NY 10017

Routledge is an imprint of the Taylor & Francis Group, an informa business

British Library Cataloguing in Publication Data
A catalogue record for this book is available from the British Library

Library of Congress Cataloging in Publication Data
Inside magazine publishing / edited by David Stam and Andrew Scott.
pages cm
Includes index.
1. Periodicals--Publishing--Great Britain. 2. English periodicals. 3. Publishers and publishing--Great Britain. I. Stam, David, 1953- editor of compilation. II. Scott, Andrew, 1966- editor of compilation.
Z326.I57 2013
070.5'720941--dc23
2013030318

ISBN: 978-0-415-82711-9 (hbk)
ISBN: 978-0-415-82712-6 (pbk)
ISBN: 978-1-315-81852-8 (ebk)

Typeset in Scala
by Saxon Graphics Ltd, Derby

Contents

Figures and tables

FIGURES

TABLES

Photos

Acknowledgements

The publisher would like to thank the following companies and individuals for permission to reproduce the following illustrations:

Page 12, *The Spectator* (1828); pages 14, 17, 20, 23, 25, 26 and 34, IPC Media; page 15, University of Reading, Special Collections; page 22, Immediate Media (*Radio Times*); page 28, *Private Eye* magazine www.private-eye.co.uk; page 57, Ken Moreton of *Stylist* magazine; page 61, Blue Publishing; page 85, Hearst Magazines UK; page 89, Future plc; page 101, Alfol; page 106 and 112, Bauer Consumer Media; page 108, Future plc; page 115, *New Statesman*; page 122, Immediate Media; pages 140, 141 and 162, IPC Media; page 149, Reed Business Information; page 172, WH Smith and National Federation of Retail Newsagents; page 207, DHP and The Carp Den; page 216, Hearst Magazines UK; page 249, Polestar.

Preface

The idea behind *Inside Magazine Publishing* came from a chance meeting in January 2012. Both of us had worked for competitive publishing businesses for many years but more recently our lives had gone their separate ways. One thing we still had in common was teaching and training young people who were about to embark on careers in the world of publishing. Sipping piping hot coffee on a freezing cold day in London's Holborn, we came to the conclusion that there was a clear need for a contemporary general magazine publishing textbook but that there may be good reasons why we should not write it.

Two objections were foremost in our minds. First, the magazine industry is changing incredibly rapidly. Could we commit our ideas to paper in such a timely fashion that the book would be as fresh when it hit bookseller's shelves as it was on the day it was written? Secondly, our backgrounds and disciplines were principally commercial and 'old media'; we were certainly not academics.

An author who writes in the media studies area put us in touch with Routledge and they were surprisingly positive. The concept was put out for peer review and came back with a resounding 'go ahead'. Vibes from colleagues at Oxford Brookes and Harlow College were upbeat.

What of our two concerns? To address the issue of timeliness we set ourselves a tough and exhausting timeframe to publish the book as quickly as was practical. The multi-disciplinary approach required was solved by 'putting a band together' to write the history, editorial and digital chapters and additional essays. We are incredibly grateful to the contributors and essayists listed on pages xv and xvi. They are industry-leading writers who have given up their time. We could not have done it without them.

Inside Magazine Publishing will give you an insider's view of magazine publishing – an important part of the UK media scene. It has largely been written by a team who have spent their working lives in the business or teaching its future practitioners. It is as up-to-date as we can make it. As we moved into the final editing process we had to draw a line in the sand concerning statistics. By the time the book appears there will be new trends available which may possibly run counter to our material. If that is the case we apologise in advance and crave your indulgence.

Magazines are people businesses and there are countless individuals to thank for checking a fact here or suggesting an idea there. Specific case study acknowledgements are made at the end of each chapter. In addition we acknowledge the following for their contribution: John Ashfield, Jamie Bill, James Brown, Marius Cloete, Tim Ewington, Patrick Fuller, Steve Goodman, Brian Grant, Joe Haines, David Hall, Reid Holland, Adrian Hughes, Simon Kippin, Alan Lewis, Chris Llewellyn, Conor McNicholas, Angie O'Farrell, Angus Phillips, Paul Phillips, Alistair Ramsay, Hugh Sleight, Mike Soutar, Julian Thorne, Alan Weaver, Matt Winsor, Carola York. Also, Steve Grayson-Healey for producing the graphics in Chapter 5. We also wish to thank everyone at Routledge who has worked on the project.

In particular a major thank you must go to Christine Stam. She tirelessly navigated the (to us) strange worlds of publisher house style and referencing to ensure that consistency and accuracy were maintained. In addition, she tackled the unenviable task of compiling the index. Without her efforts the exacting deadline we set ourselves would not have been met.

Finally, there is a large group who deserve applause. The people who work in magazine publishing are facing tremendous upheaval in what they do and how they do it. As readers will discover, the dual effects of technology and recession have been hugely disruptive but there are now arguably more opportunities than threats on the publishing horizon. There are a lot of people out there working very hard and creatively to ensure that UK magazine publishing continues to lead and inspire the world with its creative content and commercial acumen. As we lay down our pens on *Inside Magazine Publishing* we salute you all.

We invite feedback, comments and ideas to be sent to us at info@insidemagazinepublishing.com and will forward to any contributing author as you may request.

David Stam and Andrew Scott
London, 15 July 2013

Authors and contributors

CHAPTER AUTHORS

David Stam joined Thomson Magazines in 1976 after graduating from the
University of Bath. Moving through a succession of roles in advertising,
publishing and circulation he was appointed as Managing Director within
Reed Business Information in 1993 and of the market leading distributor
Marketforce (UK) in 1995. In this role he also served as a Board Director of
IPC Media. Since 2006 David has developed an active consultancy career
working for blue chip magazine publishers including TSL Education, *The
Economist*, DC Thomson and *The Spectator*. He has served as an ABC Council
Member and advises PPA. David is a guest lecturer and member of the
Publishing Industry Advisory Board at Oxford Brookes University.

Andrew Scott graduated from the University of Birmingham and joined the
Sunday Correspondent as a graduate trainee. From that title he joined the
research department of Associated Newspapers. In 1992 Andrew joined the
Magazine Marketing Company working his way up to Managing Director – a
position he held for seven years. Since then Andrew has been teaching and
lecturing on the Business of Magazines to NCTJ, BA and MA students at
Harlow College and City University.

Richard Sharpe is a Senior Lecturer at the University of East London and co-
founder of editorial training consultancy ContentETC. After leaving the
University of Kent he joined the computing industry. Shortly afterwards,
Richard jumped ship to become a journalist and rose to become Editor of
Computing. Richard is a major figure in industry training – as well as his
academic work he designs and leads courses for a variety of magazine
publishers.

Dr Christine Stam graduated from Bath University in 1976 and spent the first
years of her working life as a pharmacist, before the marketing bug took hold.
After more than 20 years working in the Pharmaceutical Industry and as a
consultant, she took to academia and studied for an MA in Intercultural
Communication with International Business at Surrey University. A PhD in
English Literature followed closely behind in 2009. She has been married to
David since 1978 and they have two grown up children: Peter (an economist)
and Sarah (a teacher).

Jim Bilton is a graduate of the University of Oxford and set up Wessenden Marketing in 1992 and BrandLab in 2000. These companies have an enviable client register and provide information, consultancy, research and training mainly in the area of supply chain and circulation sales. Jim also writes and edits the monthly *Wessenden Briefing* – an essential read for all magazine publishing executives.

ESSAY CONTRIBUTORS

Dr Andrew Calcutt is a Principal Lecturer in Journalism at the University of East London. In this role he leads both BA and MA courses. Before entering academia, Andrew worked as a journalist for 25 years in print, broadcasting and online. His range of media covered *Arena, Living Marxism*, Clarke TV and Channel Cyberia. Recent publications include: *London after Recession: fictitious capital* (Ashgate, 2012) and *Journalism Studies: a critical introduction* (Routledge, 2011).

Leander Reeves is a Senior Lecturer in Publishing at Oxford Brookes University and Subject Coordinator for their Publishing Media Undergraduate Programme. She is a graduate of Oxford Brookes and holds an MA in Electronic Media. She also spent time as a print and interactive designer in London and New York. Leander's principal teaching interests are in magazine publishing. Her research interests include trash culture and the hyperreal.

Please contact any author or contributor at info@insidemagazinepublishing.com

Introduction

Inside Magazine Publishing is written at a time of great change within the UK magazine publishing industry. Since 2008 this important business sector has experienced two seismic shifts and a trading pattern far removed from normal cyclical activity.

First, and most important, the innovation of new digital platforms and how they interact with readers is dominating strategic planning for all publishers. The energy and scope of transformation will vary between business sectors and indeed between companies themselves – it has generated both disruptive threats and massive new opportunities. The pace of these changes creates a challenge in itself for any textbook to track, despite the best endeavours of its editors and contributors.

Websites, iPads and other tablets are causing traditional business and financial models to be re-evaluated. This would have been a tough enough task in normal trading conditions. Enter the second change dynamic – the severe post 2008 recession. This has forced both circulation and advertisement revenues into decline. Publishers have had to make huge investments in order to survive, at the same time as profitability from their traditional brands came under crushing pressure. The magazine industry joined the book publishing world, the music business and some elements of UK retail in having to deal with major disruption when it was least welcome.

> it has generated both disruptive threats and massive new opportunities

DISRUPTIVE ELEMENTS

In the last twenty years there has been a revolution in the way people work and communicate. There are three areas which have had profound effects on business in general and the magazine industry in particular. They are:

- access to unlimited information
- opportunity to voice opinions
- ability to buy direct by cutting out the 'middleman', consequently expanding consumer choice.

These three separate but connected trends have become benchmarks for so many aspects of our culture. They seem to underpin everything – from the government's latest attempts to reform the education sector, to becoming the rationale behind new(ish) businesses like tripadvisor or moneysupermarket.com. All three provide a direct challenge to the position of magazine publishers.

Unlimited information

The democratisation of information ushered in by the digital age has undermined a key aspect of the job traditionally performed by magazines. This was to bring to an audience's attention new 'stuff', in other words, to break stories. This has become immeasurably more difficult as developing events appear instantly in social media. Moreover, very few people are prepared to pay for basic news, which has become a commodity item. Your daily newspaper rarely pretends that it is informing you of something for the first time and now has an increased focus on supplements and features.

If the sheer weight of information available online has mushroomed to overwhelming proportions, perhaps the job of editing it into digestible and meaningful chunks is becoming even more important? In a culture where time is at a premium, everyone needs some navigational help and a reliable editor is an asset. In business terms this combination quickly becomes a *brand* which people *trust*. The key aspiration for publishing companies is to create or maintain these brands which are relied upon and can survive any media format – and do so profitably.

Voicing opinions

Meanwhile, readers are no longer passive consumers who might occasionally write a letter to the editor. The comments section, the forum, the radio phone-in, social media and the blog have given the public endless opportunities to give their view. This can be regardless of the level of authority, knowledge or wit involved. Look at the number of posts at the end of a story on the website of a political weekly or news title – they can run into hundreds. It's a deafening chorus of opinions in search of an audience. Every organisation now expects such feedback from its customers, from local councils to the smallest retailer. 'Rate us!' 'Your opinion really matters to us!' 'How was your experience of using our service?' Every purchase is followed by the questionnaire to gauge customer satisfaction.

Seemingly, our opinions are really valuable and important, or so the marketing department would have us believe. This is perhaps even more challenging for magazine publishers. The phrase 'everyone is on our turf' is one which nicely sums up how many publishers feel about blogs. Note the possessive. It was 'our turf' but now it is just common ground. The power that came from having the platform of a magazine has been largely eroded as search engines determine which voices are heard loudest and longest. Is this democratising, as advocates of the web proclaim? Or do Google's Adwords and their ever changing algorithms actually reduce the range of debate?

Cutting out the mediator

If it is becoming difficult for magazine journalists and editors to keep their heads above water and their voices above the braying crowd, then what of the magazine business model itself? Consumers now easily deal direct. They know it will be cheaper if they can cut out the middleman. Hence the success of eBay and other trading sites. Businesses also know this. For example, why pay to advertise a job vacancy in a magazine when your own business has a website with massive traffic? Traditionally, a reader of a magazine saw a product advertised and then waited until an opportunity presented itself to buy that product at retail or by conventional mail order. Online there is no gap between these experiences.

Choice is also a great clarion call of our era. Patients can choose their doctor, parents can choose their child's school, supermarkets offer scores of options even for staple items. What are the prerequisites? First, a resourced and informed public who turn to digital media instinctively for information and need help to navigate it. Second, a global organisation that has delivered a vast and highly imaginative vision.

> it is becoming difficult for magazine journalists and editors to keep their heads above water and their voices above the braying crowd

CUE GOOGLE

Google, with its loose structures and 'anti-corporate' corporate culture, has eclipsed rivals Microsoft, IBM and Yahoo to become the dominant technology business. In 2012 its revenues topped \$50 billion[1], a similar number to that of the entire US TV industry's advertisement sales. It has been the embodiment of the winner-takes-all culture which seems to be the end game in mature online markets.

The internet, for a medium which purports to democratisation, has been very successful at creating players with gigantic market shares. This differs from the culture of magazine sales. With print, as each element of the market matures, a plethora of titles will jockey for position behind a market leader, which every so often is supplanted by a major new introduction. *Glamour* launched in the UK in 2001 and has become the number one women's monthly title but *Cosmopolitan* and *Marie Claire* are also large selling brands. In the UK search market, however, Google is seven times larger than all the other engines combined, despite well reported unfavourable publicity surrounding tax and privacy. This model of a market, dominated by one player, paints a scary futuristic picture for magazine publishers, used to operating with strong brand leaders and many profitable also-rans.

The rise of search engines and of Google as an advertising medium may be a subdivision of the seismic shift that technology has wrought on the magazine industry, but it is so significant that it almost warrants its own category of causality.

> The internet... has been very successful at creating players with gigantic market shares

ALWAYS LOOK ON THE BRIGHT SIDE ...

From the outside perspective, magazine publishers could have fared a lot worse in the last five years. They still have unique advantages that other industries covet. *Inside Magazine Publishing* will extoll many of these advantages but to nominate six:

- The industry benefits from a legacy of iconic brands, many of which are household names.
- Magazines have remarkably loyal customers, called subscribers, who can be persuaded to buy a product up to a year in advance, at a price set by the publisher.
- The UK benefits from a diverse retail infrastructure ranging from corner newsagent to superstore served by a cost effective supply chain.
- UK value added tax exemption on printed copies is still in place.
- Advertisers still buy space in magazines to a greater level than the share of consumer's time devoted to the medium suggests they should. Overall media consumption is still rising.
- Creatively, the UK magazine business is the envy of the world and is well-placed for international expansion.

... publishers are survivors

There is no doubt that many aspects of the magazine publishing world have had a torrid time since 2008, but publishers are survivors. Ask industry gurus the question: did they expect to see more title closures in that period than have actually occurred? The answer will be: yes they did. So how does this compare to other media industries? Should magazine publishers thank their lucky stars when comparing their woes to those of music and book colleagues?

Gazing over the garden wall

In the music industry digital downloads initially created havoc. How the music industry adapted to a digital world is a subject for a book in its own right – and a long one at that. Suffice to say, it has had to innovate to survive, as its basic business model was destroyed by sites offering music free of charge. Now the development of high quality and trusted sites such as i-tunes, Spotify and Last FM has resulted in 2012 being the first year of growth in the industry since 1999[2]. The business has learned how to monetise the digital marketplace in the face of arguably greater barriers than the magazine industry faces. Licensed music services rate highly on customer satisfaction surveys and music drives the digital economy. People buy devices to play music and the most popular celebrities on social media sites are music artists. Seven of the ten most followed people on Twitter, for example, are pop stars. The traditional record companies have expanded into music management, merchandising, organising tours and gigs.

The music industry is still facing a major problem from pirate sites offering illegal but free content. The magazine industry is also aware of this threat but it is currently small – as digital editions remain modest income generators – but it may become a problem in time. Publishers must seek innovative solutions to keep customers honest.

It is certainly instructive to see how the free music model, which looked to have won the battle in the early part of the 2000s, has been pushed back by licensed sites which charge for downloads. Legislation has played its part here, as has morality. Most people do not really believe that music should be free.

In publishing, free is here to stay. It is unlikely that we will see the BBC and others ceasing to offer free to access news. Pay and no-pay have to co-exist – sometimes within the same domain with tiered levels of users enjoying different access rights. But it can be frustrating when one sees a historically workable business model being whittled away. Publishers do have to make a profit and individuals have to pay the rent.

This is brought home by the story of a magazine journalist who sold a feature idea to a market-leading football magazine. He told recently of how his idea was undermined by a poorly (in his view) researched but similar feature which appeared on a national newspaper website. This attracted much traffic and many comments and resulted in the football editor cancelling his commission. Would anyone have paid to read this piece in a national newspaper environment? Probably not but it was free to access, so therefore widely read.

The book publishing industry has obvious parallels with magazines and faces similar dilemmas concerning digitally-based formats. It also appears to be at a comparable phase of development with 12 per cent of sales made digitally in 2012[3]. The current difference lies in the fact that with books, the growth in digital is more than compensating for any decline in print sales. In the magazine industry digital formats are not yet taking up the slack.

What is clear is that the magazine industry – in all its various guises – has to come up with a response to the challenge of a digital world. The false dawn of giving away content and hoping to sell the audience on 'portals' to advertisers will be exposed in Chapter 2. It was just that, false. A more sophisticated solution is required.

Many talented people are working extremely hard to find the answer or answers and we will look at a number of them. Will magazines survive? Even if they do, will the traditional publishers survive with them? What is the future of print? How is the industry structured and what will be its shape in the future? Can publishers in the UK escape from a dependency on shrinking retail sales? To answer these questions it is necessary to go back to basics and look at how this important industry was formed and how it is structured today.

Celebrate success

Amid the hand wringing and sheer hard graft of working daily in a market under pressure, it is especially important to analyse and celebrate successes. We are pleased to examine parts of the industry which are growing. We look at the free distribution model in some detail in the fiercely competitive mass market consumer arena. The emergence of the content marketing industry – previously known as customer publishers – has altered the magazine landscape. This is especially the case when partnering with major supermarkets to publish the largest circulation magazines in the UK. How the UK's leading business to business (B2B) publishers have positioned themselves as information providers, regardless of format, provides stimulating case study material. They demonstrate real entrepreneurial flair and true grit.

WHO IS HIRING?

These opportunities are important for students to note. Universities and colleges train young people to enter the industry who in turn often have an extensive portfolio of work from their own blogs, internships and work experience. Everyone needs a first job. It is therefore essential that sectors of the industry provide the necessary new shoots of growth to offset decline elsewhere. It is no longer a given that a good young journalist or business studies graduate will find a full-time job with a major media organisation. It is really important that young people seek out and target who is really in a position to hire (and pay a salary) and ensure they have the required skills to impress.

A senior editor, who was interviewed as background research for this book, commented that young journalists often have pieces of work several months old in their portfolio. He is only interested in their latest work. What did they write yesterday? There is no longer a need to wait to be asked to be a contributor as young journalists blog and tweet everyday. This networking is essential for any aspiring writer.

This book is not intended as a road map to entering the magazine industry. It will, however, provide media students, trainee journalists and newcomers with a contemporary and detailed insight of how the business of magazines in the UK is currently organised, with all of its preoccupations and idiosyncrasies. We also hope our text will be of interest to those who have been in the industry for some years and who now wish to take a broader perspective.

When this book was conceived it was possible to imagine that we would be able to assess the industry in the light of an economy coming out of recession. It is now widely assumed by most economists that this is unlikely as the UK economy is predicted to oscillate around very low growth numbers for the foreseeable future. The key focus of most publishers today revolves around how to harness the plethora of opportunities open to them. Most businesses have more ideas than they can resource and so (digital) activity must be prioritised to deliver the vital growth required to offset the decline of print. The relationship between historic and new brands and their delivery format is critical to the future of the industry.

Many publishers are looking at international markets for growth in their core print business and at emerging digital revenues at home. These twin drivers are combining to instil confidence in the future. Magazines which have become brands look very well placed to survive and even thrive, in the next few years.

> Magazines which have become brands look very well placed to survive and even thrive ...

WHAT'S IN STORE?

In the chapters which follow we seek to discuss all aspects of the important business of publishing magazines in the UK, in a detailed and thought-provoking manner. We make extensive use of practical examples and case studies.

The writing, printing and selling of magazines has a rich and varied history which is explored in Chapter 1. Titles have always been at the forefront of reflecting social change and of taking advantage of technological innovation. This chapter traces the development of the consumer industry from the late seventeenth century through to the millennium. It is immediately followed by a micro-essay which discusses the legacy of Princess Diana on the genre of celebrity magazines.

Chapter 2 brings us right up to the present day with a detailed analysis of today's industry, focussing particularly on the main challenges facing consumer publishing and the transformation of the B2B sector. In particular the development of a 'perfect storm' over the industry is traced. The chapter includes brief biographies of a number of leading publishers.

To set the financial scene, the third chapter has a detailed examination of how business models are changing and the importance of launches, international business and reader events. It includes a number of case studies to highlight these developments.

Using a catch phrase borrowed from estate agents, there is a saying in magazine publishing that the three most important criteria for success are content, content and content. Therefore two chapters are devoted to this important area. Chapter 4 covers the importance of setting an editorial vision which appeals both to the heads and the hearts of readers – it also covers editorial management. Chapter 5 focusses on the detailed practices of how to create excellent content, whether through design or by words. The importance of covers is highlighted. This chapter is illustrated by a number of useful graphics.

Sandwiched between these two editorially-focussed chapters is a stimulating micro-essay – What is a magazine? The role of the medium as a mediator is discussed from the 1700s to the present.

The two traditional and main revenue streams for magazine publishers are, of course, circulation and advertisement sales; these are described in detail in Chapters 6 and 7. The first of these covers retail and subscription supply chains and introduces the concept of 'lifetime value' when assessing circulation profitability. The importance of having the right distribution strategy for individual titles is discussed and the key methods of marketing a consumer magazine brand highlighted.

Chapter 7 argues that the buying and selling of advertisement space has scientific type properties. The key readership and circulation verification metrics are detailed. How a magazine advertising schedule is bought is demonstrated and the mechanics of different types of advertisements in magazines – present and future – outlined. There is a useful discussion of how to avoid 'crossing the line' of editorial independence.

The need to understand the newly emerging digital platforms is threaded through the whole book – there is no 'new media section' per se within *Inside Magazine Publishing*. It is a theme that is woven into all the contemporary chapters. The final chapter pulls together a number of these themes into a comprehensive review. In particular it focuses on the need to understand emerging businesses and structures, as well as learning the skills necessary to take traditional companies into the brave new world of digital. In addition there is a description of the various digital newsstands available – particularly Apple.

Inside Magazine Publishing concludes with two useful and factual appendices. The first suggests how best to select a printer and choose the right paper, while the second gives a brief review of legal issues. To supplement the notes at the end of each chapter we have added a list of further information resources and a glossary.

A successful magazine is greater than the sum of its parts. Commercial teams in circulation and advertisement sales interact with editorial colleagues bouncing ideas off each other to generate new content – this in turn grows sales and readership and brings new advertisers on board. For practical reasons the journey through *Inside Magazine Publishing* may resemble a linear path, however each chapter stresses the holistic nature of this unique and exciting medium.

NOTES

1. Google Investor Relations: 2013 financial tables available at http://investor. google.com/financial/tables.html (Accessed 13 June 2013.)
2. IFPI Digital Music Report 2013 available at 20132012http://www.ifpi.org/ content/section_resources/dmr2013.html (Accessed 13 June 2013.)
3. Flood, A., 'Fifty Shades of Grey boosts book trade' *Guardian*, 1 May 2013 available at http://www.guardian.co.uk/books/2013/may/01/fifty-shades-of-grey-boosts-book-trade?INTCMP=ILCNETTXT3487 (Accessed 13 June 2013.)

CHAPTER 1

A short history of British magazine publishing

Christine Stam

In these early years of the twenty-first century colourful magazines are everywhere. We see them in newsagents, in supermarkets, on buses, trains, aeroplanes and anywhere readers have spare time to enjoy them. They entertain us, enlighten us, challenge us (occasionally), sometimes anger and frustrate us. Printed weeklies, monthlies and quarterlies make a popular contribution to the culture of Britain today; many would argue that a world without print-on-paper magazines would be a dull place indeed, whatever the trend towards digital editions might bring.

> ...a world without print-on-paper magazines would be a dull place indeed, whatever the trend towards digital editions might bring

King William III and his wife Mary were on the throne in 1693 when *The Ladies Mercury,* the very first weekly 'periodical' aimed specifically at women was introduced. Printed in London on two sides of a single sheet of paper, it promised to address the issues of 'love, marriage, behaviour, dress and humour of the female sex, whether virgins, wives, or widows'. It lasted four weeks but began an industry that expanded rapidly in the nineteenth century, thrived in the twentieth century then began its diversification in the twenty-first century. Today, in the age of digital publishing and the internet, the printed publication might be considered a dying artefact. Will the reign of a future King William see the end of magazines as we currently know them?

This chapter investigates the evolution of magazines during the eighteenth, nineteenth and twentieth centuries and aims to show how such an inexpensive, everyday item affected the sociocultural makeup of a nation. In turn, magazines themselves are heavily influenced by the society of the day. It will show how a publication which starts to become out-of-date as soon as it leaves the printing press, by necessity, must foreground the social and cultural ethos of the moment. We will see how the development of transport and communication systems impacted on distribution channels and how technological developments have consistently affected the industry.

In simple terms, the UK magazine market may be divided into three areas:

- consumer
- business (also known as trade, professional or B2B)
- customer (contract or custom).

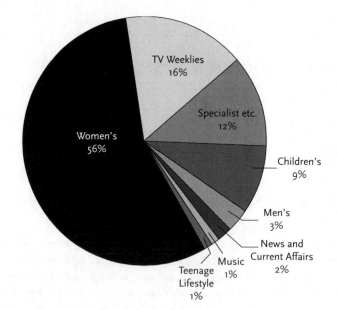

Figure 1.1 Consumer magazines: revenue market share

Source: Adapted from Marketforce ABC Market Summary Report (Jan–June 2012)

Suffice to say here that consumer, or mass publishing holds by far the greatest market share today: women's titles being the dominant source of revenue. The tradition of these reaches farthest back into the past and therefore this chapter will be dominated by the magazines that the general public read. Although B2B and customer publishing are included, their significance is discussed in greater detail elsewhere in this book.

IN THE BEGINNING (1731–1838)

Although various forms of printing onto paper and material have been around for thousands of years, the German Johannes Gutenberg is credited with the invention of the first workable, movable type, printing press in the 1440s. William Caxton brought the technology to England in 1476, setting up a printing press in Westminster and producing the first mass copies of books such as Chaucer's *Canterbury Tales*. It took a further 250 years, however, before the first printed magazine appeared. *The Gentleman's Magazine* was founded in London by Edward Cave in 1731, surviving for almost 200 years, until it finally closed in 1922. Cave coined the nomenclature 'magazine' for his publication after the French *magasin*, meaning 'warehouse' (originating from the Arabic *makhazan*) and, unknowingly, generated the modern industry of today. His was a monthly digest of commentary and news on any topic in which the educated public might be interested: from parliamentary debates to 'select pieces of poetry'. Prior to his innovative and perhaps accidental introduction, specialised journals and transitory periodicals, such as *The Ladies Mercury*, had existed but had failed to capture the imaginations of the public at large.

THE

Gentleman's Magazine:

OR,

Monthly Intelligencer.

For the Year 1734.

CONTAINING,

I. Proceedings and Debates in PARLIAMENT.

II. ESSAYS, *Controverfial, Humorous*, and *Satirical*; *Religious, Moral*, and *Political*: Collected chiefly from the *Publick Papers*.

III. Select Pieces of POETRY.

IV. A fuccinct Account of the moft *remarkable Tranfactions* Foreign and Domeftick.

V. *Births, Marriages, Deaths, Promotions*, and *Bankrupts*.

VI. The Prices of Goods and Stocks, Bill of Mortality.

VII. Regifter of Books

With proper INDEXES.

VOL. IV.

By SYLVANUS URBAN, *Gent.*

Prodeffe & delectare.   *E Pluribus Unum.*

LONDON:

Printed, and fold at *St John's Gate*, by *F. Jefferies in Ludgate ftreet*, and moft Bookfellers.

Photo 1.1 Edward Cave's eighteenth century *The Gentleman's Magazine* was the first printed publication to use the term 'magazine'

During this period, one of the most significant advances in printing technology became available. Lithography was developed in Germany by Alois Senefelder in 1796 and the basic principles of this 200-year-old method are still used today in the production of most magazines (see Appendix 1). Other examples of the deep-rooted historical nature of the magazine industry may be seen in the titles introduced in the eighteenth century. In 1709 Richard Steele founded a literary and society journal, calling it *The Tatler*. Two years later, after the closure of this enterprise, Steele went on to co-found another periodical, *The Spectator* which catered to the emerging middle classes. While neither of these august publications are the direct ancestors of today's titles through uninterrupted lineage, they are good examples of how magazines decline and die, only to metamorphose and evolve in future generations.

During the latter half of the eighteenth century the 'magazine' format, with its miscellany of content and consistency of availability, became more widely adopted. Women's periodicals adapted to the changes and their numbers increased, with more than a score of these new types of publications appearing before the end of the century. The most notable of these were *The Lady's Magazine* (1770–1837) and *The Lady's Monthly Museum* (1798–1832); two publications upon which many of the early Victorian women's periodicals were modelled.

Photo 1.2 Three hundred years of *The Spectator* magazine. Richard Steele and Joseph Addison's original version of 1711 and a recent cover from the modern publication (2011)

Photo 1.2 Three hundred years of *The Spectator* magazine. Richard Steele and Joseph Addison's original version of 1711 and a recent cover from the modern publication (2011)

The Spectator

- Co-founded by Richard Steele and Joseph Addison, the first title by that name appeared in 1711. Published six days a week (excluding Sunday) it offered comment and opinion on matters of the day. It ran for 555 issues until December 1712. Each copy was about 2,500 words and it had a print run of approximately 3,000 but a readership in the region of 60,000, due to its popularity in the London coffee houses. (Today's online blog, *Coffee House*, harks back to the early history of the magazine.) The magazine was aimed mainly at the interests of England's tradesmen and merchants. While claiming to be politically-neutral, it did, in fact, espouse Whig (predecessors of the Liberal Party) values.
- The title was revived for six months in 1714.
- On 5 December 1828 Robert Rintoul, a liberal-radical, launched the modern *The Spectator* insisting, as editor, on having total power over its content. Thus began the tradition of the paper's editor and proprietor being one and the same person; an arrangement that lasted into the twentieth century.
- *The Spectator* is now the oldest continuously published magazine in the English language. It is published weekly and has a circulation of about 64,000[1]. (Not so very different to the original readership in 1711.)
- Over the years the political leaning of the magazine has been influenced by the editor/proprietor. In the latter half of the nineteenth century it gradually became more conservative; then reverted to liberalism in the early twentieth century. Editors in the latter half of the twentieth century indicate the political direction the magazine took: Ian Gilmour (1954–59), Ian Macleod (1963–65), Nigel Lawson (1966–70), Boris Johnson (1999–2005), all prominent Conservative Members of Parliament during their careers.

THE EARLY VICTORIANS (1839–55)

One of the most notable controversies expounded in the early days of *The Spectator* magazine occurred when it included a hostile review of Charles Dickens' *Bleak House*. In 1853 the magazine held the popular author in contempt; the anonymous contributor commenting that the novel 'would be a heavy book to read through at once ... But we ... found it dull and wearisome as a serial'[2]. This observation highlighted the unusual method by which the novels of Charles Dickens reached the general public at the time. The journals that serialised most of his works, such as *Bentley's Miscellany* (*Oliver Twist*), *Master Humphrey's Clock* (*The Old Curiosity Shop* and *Barnaby Rudge*) and *Household Words* (*Hard Times*) are long forgotten. In the mid-nineteenth century, however, these weekly and monthly magazines, containing the author's latest episodes, were widely anticipated by his adoring public. Dickens was the master of the 'cliff-hanger' at the end of each episode; a technique employed regularly today in television serials and soap operas. Publishing his stories in instalments in magazines brought his works to a wider audience, especially to those who could ill-afford to buy the novel in its expensive book format. It was also a genius stroke of self-marketing; a precursor of today's celebrity techniques. (Indeed, Dickens himself was the owner, editor and chief contributor of the journals, thus using them as vehicles for self-promotion while reaping the pecuniary benefits of a high volume circulation. Proprietors of today's magazines could learn much from this eminent Victorian.)

As the British Empire expanded in the nineteenth century, so magazines aimed at the male reader flooded the market: advertising in many such publications clearly defined the target audience as masculine. Most of these magazines were relatively short-lived but *Punch* (1841), *The Economist* (1843) and *The Field* (1853) are three titles that have stood the test of time. Indeed, *The Field* can claim to be the world's longest established field sports magazine, never being out of production since its introduction in the mid-nineteenth century. Appealing to the burgeoning class of Victorian industrialists with their new-found wealth and increased leisure time, as the current editor claims on the magazine's website: 'the magazine was founded for those who loved shooting, fishing, hunting and could sniff out a decent claret at 1,000 paces. It's still like that today.'

For women, perhaps the most significant introduction was made by Samuel Beeton (husband of the ubiquitous Mrs Beeton) in 1852. The content of magazines of the 1830s had predominantly consisted of romantic fiction, providing women with an alternative to the unsuitably 'serious' content of the daily newspapers. By the 1850s women's magazines had become more practical in content and even, in some cases, edged towards the political. Samuel Beeton's *The Englishwoman's Domestic Magazine* (1852–77) was the title that did most to change the attitudes and social aspirations of a generation of women. Aimed at the middle classes, with a cover price of only twopence (2d), it included recipes (Mrs Beeton's), an 'agony column', the first paper dress patterns, gardening hints and practical tips on such topics as how to destroy bed bugs. The fiction was relevant and the political commentary treated the reader as an intelligent member of society. The magazine was a phenomenal success, recording monthly sales of 50,000 copies within its first three years[3]. The era of the woman's magazine as we know it today had begun.

Photo 1.3
Neville Chamberlain
appears on the
front cover of the
9 September 1939
issue of *The Field*

Two closely related events that probably had more impact on the exponential growth of magazine readership in the nineteenth century had nothing to do with the printing processes, the editorial policy or, indeed, the fame of magazine contributors. The expansion of the railways in mid-century and, more importantly, the placing of bookstalls on the platforms by an equally expansive and innovative company known as WH Smith may claim to be the catalysts that facilitated the explosion. The rapid development of the railway network throughout Britain meant that newspapers and magazines could reach the provincial cities swiftly and reliably, opening up new markets for their publishers. In addition, passengers needed entertainment on their journeys and who better to fulfil this need than a provider of suitable reading material?

Having taken advantage of the public's new-found mania for railway travel, WH Smith went on to build a distribution network that included warehouses in Dublin, Liverpool, Manchester and Birmingham. (Their virtual monopoly of bookstalls on station platforms came to an end in 1905, when a dispute with the railway companies over rents prompted them to close many of their sites. WH Smith retaliated rapidly with yet another inspired and aggressive act; within three months they opened 150 of their own retail outlets near to the stations.) Today WH Smith is one of the UK's top retailers and (the now separate company) Smiths News is the leading newspaper and magazine wholesaler and distributor.

The growth in magazine sales during the mid-nineteenth century was further compounded by the abolition of the crippling Stamp Duty in 1855; a tax that had been levied on printed newspapers and periodicals since 1712. At the same time, the prohibitive cost of paper, previously manufactured using an ever-diminishing supply of rags, was reduced significantly by the transfer to production using wood pulp. These factors, combined with an increase in capital investment and the beginning of the technological revolution that characterised the second half of the nineteenth century, precipitated the boom years of magazine production and readership. From a high base level – several cheap newspapers and periodicals could already claim readerships in excess of 100,000 before 1855 – the second half of the nineteenth century saw circulation figures comparable to today's top sellers. In 1858 sales of three fiction magazines totalled 895,000 with an estimated readership of at least three million people[4].

Photo 1.4 Blackpool North Railway Station WH Smith Bookstall, 1896

THE VICTORIAN BOOM YEARS (1856–1901)

In 1861 the Parliamentary Act demanding high levels of excise duty payments on paper was finally repealed, significantly reducing the cost of this vital element of magazine production. In addition, the print process itself took several dramatic leaps forward during the latter decades of the century, with the introduction of the high speed rotary printing presses (printing on huge rolls of paper rather than single sheets) and the development of the mechanical typesetting process.

Photography was also making huge technical advances, allowing the use of illustrations and reproductions that were unimagined by a previous generation.

These innovations heralded the true beginning of the production of cheap, mass-circulation magazines and created opportunities for publishers to tap into the vast numbers that made up the lower and middle classes. In addition, the Elementary Education Act of 1870 and subsequent extensions over the next few years brought basic schooling to the lower classes and thus improved literacy for generations to come. Magazine publishers happily exploited this new market of customers, dropping their cover prices and providing suitable content to appeal to the masses.

For the first time, the sales potential of the growing numbers of literate children was also recognised. The Religious Tract Society introduced a penny weekly for boys in 1879, following in 1880 with a similar paper for girls. While these story papers were intended to encourage children to read and to instil Christian morals, they became hugely successful, lasting well into the second half of the twentieth century. *Boys Own Paper* and *Girls Own Paper* probably averaged sales in the region of 200,000 copies each every week during the latter decades of the nineteenth century[5], demonstrating the massive potential of this market. Indeed, Alfred Harmsworth introduced the first comic book in 1890, costing only a halfpenny. *Comic Cuts* was initially aimed at adults but was rapidly taken up by youngsters and was soon selling 300,000 copies a week. It is claimed that by the first decade of the twentieth century this had risen to half a million[6].

In the first half of the nineteenth century, cover prices for magazines were high as they were aimed at the upper classes who could easily afford a shilling a copy. By the middle of the century, the less sophisticated but far more popular magazines were selling for one-sixth of the price (2d.) While *Punch* (aimed at the upper- and middle-class reader) sold 40,000 copies, *London Journal*, with its mass appeal, sold almost half a million copies. In 1873 alone, 630 different consumer magazines were published in the UK[7]. Three men emerged during this period who were to revolutionise the publishing world in Britain: George Newnes, Alfred Harmsworth (later Lord Northcliffe) and Arthur Pearson. All were connected at some stage with *Tit-Bits* (1881–1984) which typified the direction in which many of the new magazines were heading. It was filled with snippets of interesting facts, odd stories, anecdotes, jokes and material that required little concentration from the reader, accompanied by plentiful illustrations. This was described as ' ... reading matter ... to keep their eyes busy while their brains took a rest'.[8] By the end of the nineteenth century Newnes was claiming circulation figures of 600,000 copies a week for *Tit-Bits*[9]. (George Newnes was the progenitor of the company that was to become part of the IPC Media empire. Alfred Harmsworth became one of the most successful newspaper publishers in the history of the British press, founding both the *Daily Mirror* and the *Daily Mail* and transforming *The Times* into the modern newspaper of today. Arthur Pearson became a newspaper magnate, most noted for founding the *Daily Express*.)

Magazines, however, were not aimed exclusively at mass audiences; two highly successful introductions were made towards the end of the nineteenth century, designed to satisfy the aspirations of the more well-heeled members of society. In 1897 George Newnes launched a limited circulation, highly pictorial quality magazine which celebrated the rural homes and pastimes of Britain's

'... reading matter ... to keep their eyes busy while their brains took a rest.'

Photo 1.5 First issue of *Country Life*, January 1897

upper classes. Known initially as *Country Life Illustrated* this lucrative publication dropped the 'Illustrated' from its masthead in later years, becoming one of the iconic brands of luxury lifestyle publishing which still thrives today.

A few years before, in 1885, Thomas Gibson Bowles founded a women's magazine that was intended to be practical, while enjoyable to read. He named it *The Lady*. Priced at sixpence, it attracted a limited audience until 1894 when a new, female editor introduced classified advertisements for nannies, domestic staff, holiday lets and similar into its pages. Aimed at intelligent women, it captured the imagination of the growing numbers of 'new women'. *The Lady* went on to become Britain's longest surviving magazine for women. With a current circulation of about 28,000[10] it remains to this day in private hands.

Towards the end of the century, the potential of a new mass audience began to be suspected and capitalised upon. As the population became more mobile with the expansion of the railways, both nationally and with the opening of the London Underground system, so the novel concept of suburban living was born. As men found work at a distance from their homes, their wives remained more and more within the domestic sphere. In the last two decades of the nineteenth century no fewer than 48 new titles for women were introduced[11]. Magazines that cost only a penny and were full of practical advice for the home-loving housewife were soon selling 200,000 copies each, becoming the precursors of today's *Woman* and *Woman's Own*. This new army of middle-class housewives was the willing target of advertising on a grand scale, as the range of consumer goods escalated.

Although newspapers and periodicals had contained advertisements for hundreds of years, the real growth in the advertising industry began towards the end of the nineteenth century. As the numbers and circulation figures of magazines escalated, so did the manufacturing and distribution costs. Just as in the present day, the sales price did not cover the final costs of production. Advertising subsidised each issue and ultimately made magazines highly profitable for publishers. The withdrawal of the duty on advertising in 1853 had contributed to the expansion of the trade but by the end of the century advertisements had become the life blood of publishers.

As the nineteenth century faded and the twentieth century dawned, publishers began to experiment, particularly with their magazines for women. In addition to the plethora of home management and domestic papers, specialist journals began to emerge, catering to the needs of women who cycled, motored, gardened, painted, used cameras and travelled abroad amongst many other activities previously unthought-of by their mothers and grandmothers.

INTO THE TWENTIETH CENTURY

After the revolutionary social changes of the nineteenth century, the magazine-reading habits of the twentieth century settled into the sort of pattern with which we are familiar today. That is not to say that startling events and radical advances did not take place during the century, merely that these were, in the main, continuations of trends already in place during the Victorian era. Cheap, domestic women's weeklies, established in the 1890s, formed the dominant market by 1910 and remained the most important genre of magazines in terms of sales throughout the twentieth century. Indeed, the formula adopted in these papers was not so very different to that introduced in the 1850s by Samuel Beeton.

Pre-war (1910s)

In 1910 the small, family-run publisher DC Thomson introduced a magazine for women called *My Weekly*. Having successfully acquired *The People's Friend* (1869–), a family weekly paper with a predominantly working-class readership, the Dundee firm became one of the least likely publishing giants of the time. (Some would argue even of today.) *My Weekly* was aimed specifically at the working classes and it became a phenomenon, creating the mould for popular women's magazines which is still used in the twenty-first century. Appealing directly to its audience (hence the *My* in the title) the editorial was cosy and gossipy while remaining defined within the domestic sphere. Several elements were essential:

- romantic fiction (short story or serialised)
- knitting and dressmaking patterns
- cookery features
- household hints
- problem page
- childcare
- competitions
- gossip.

Where *My Weekly* differed from its rival penny papers was in its deliberate policy to appear old-fashioned and conservative. It contained few illustrations and certainly no fashion-plates, eschewing any attempt to include features on fashion, appearance or social aspirations. The editor (ironically, a man for the introductory issues) spoke directly to readers, appealing to a brand of feminity that would have appalled the suffragettes. Indeed, the aggressive campaign for women's suffrage that took place in Britain during the early years of the twentieth century had little impact upon the magazine publishing industry. Even at its height, few articles advocating a woman's right to vote appeared, except in the short-lived journals specifically printed by organisations dedicated to the cause, such as *Votes for Women* (1907–18) and *The Suffragette* (1912–15).

Most editors and publishers ignored the social unrest generated by the feminists and maintained their hegemonic stranglehold on their readers' expectations of their magazines. Even those papers specifically aimed at the suffragettes, written and published by militant organisations such as the Womens' Social and Political Union, still pandered to the feminine aspirations of their readers and employed commercial journalistic techniques. Articles were lively, pictures were included and advertising, such as that for hair dye, copies of Paris fashions and Debenham and Freebody's sale bargains, helped to fund the publication. On the political front, perhaps the most significant introduction came in 1913 with the launch of *New Statesman* by Sidney and Beatrice Webb. Working with Bernard Shaw and other members of the Fabian Society, it aimed to indoctrinate educated and influential people (men) with socialist ideology. From an initial circulation in 1913 of about 3,000, it now boasts weekly sales figures in excess of 20,000[12] and maintains its centre-left political stance.

As so often is the case when a highly successful magazine such as *My Weekly* is launched, a rival publisher will introduce a 'lookalike' within a matter of months. In 1911, Alfred Harmsworth launched *Woman's Weekly* and was claiming sales of half a million for the first issue[13]. Both magazines went on to survive two world wars and intense competition from glossy rivals, continuing to thrive well into the twenty-first century. (ABC audited average weekly circulation figures of 113,528 for *My Weekly* and 316,869 for *Woman's Weekly* during the first half of 2012.)

> ...a rival publisher will introduce a 'lookalike' within a matter of months

As the number of magazines, newspapers and publishers grew during the early twentieth century, so the need arose for a professional body that could advise on issues such as unionisation, distribution and material suplies. In 1913 the Society of Weekly Newspapers and Periodical Proprietors Limited was formed by a group of publishers who were already meeting regularly for lunch to discuss such matters. From this evolved the Professional Publishers Association (PPA) which, today 'represents the interests of the UK's consumer and business media publishing sector' and is 'dedicated to promoting, protecting and advising'[14] its members. It represents more than 200 companies in all three sectors of the magazine publishing market.

As war broke out in Europe in 1914, there were about fifty women's magazines on the newsstands in Britain[15]. Many of these failed to survive the conflict and the austere social climate of war years would seem an inappropriate time for the launch of a luxury glossy magazine. Against all the odds, however, Condé Nast, an American publisher, chose to introduce *Vogue* to the British

market in 1916. Priced at one shilling, its 120 glossy pages of high fashion, society news, literary and cultural articles boosted the morale of those that could afford to read it. Today *Vogue* remains the archetypical glossy, high fashion magazine with a circulation well in excess of 200,000[16]. As such, it was able to take advantage of the significant improvements to the quality of reproduction afforded by the new rotogravure printing process.

While the three major technological developments of the nineteenth century (automation of composition, increased mechanisation of printing and new graphical techniques) represented huge advances, the practical implementation of the gravure process in the early twentieth century marked a further quantum leap. Although expensive to set up initially, the process allows high speed printing onto less expensive paper with superior image reproduction. As such, it has historically been reserved for magazines, such as *Vogue,* which require high quality colour reproduction and long print runs.

Post-war (1920s)

The radical economic and social changes brought about by the First World War had an enormous impact on the magazine industry. The pre-war years had seen the marketplace dominated either by expensive, high-class magazines or, at the other end of the spectrum, cheap, mass circulation papers that appealed to the working classes. After the war, society had changed beyond recognition: many of the upper class families lost their wealth, while those in the lower classes had become more affluent, resulting in an expanding new social class in the 'middle'. The excess of single women, no longer content to remain in domestic service, added to the realignment of the social classes during the 1920s. This, together with the first radio transmission in Britain by the British Broadcasting Company (BBC) in 1922, heralded a watershed in the cultural evolution of the country. Publishers responded accordingly, launching magazines that catered for the burgeoning middle and lower-middle classes. Many of these journals became household names and remain in print today: the monthlies *Homes and Gardens* (1919), *Ideal Home* (1920), *Good Housekeeping* (1922) and *Woman and Home* (1926) all still have respectable circulation figures.

Advertisers adopted the new, middle-class magazines with enthusiasm, realising that the collective buying power of these readers was greater than those of the expensive glossies. Many 'quality' journals thus fell by the wayside and closed, leaving *Vogue* and *Harper's Bazaar* (launched in 1929 as a direct competitor to *Vogue*) to satisfy the aspirations of the upper classes.

Table 1.1 Women's monthly journals introduced 1916–29

	Publisher	Average Monthly Circulation Print (digital)
Good Housekeeping (1922)	Hearst	409,326 (3,378)
Woman and Home (1926)	IPC	352,586 (800)
Vogue (1916)	Condé Nast	203,356 (3,703)
Ideal Home (1920)	IPC	190,481 (726)
Homes and Gardens (1919)	IPC	127,489 (1,554)
Harper's Bazaar	Hearst	111,353 (5,524)

Source: ABC (July–Dec 2012)

Surprisingly, the potential for comics deliberately aimed at children was not realised until well into the twentieth century when James Henderson and Sons (later part of Alfred Harmsworth's Amalgamated Press) launched *The Rainbow* (1914–56). In the 1920s DC Thomson became aware of the untapped market of schoolboys aged 9–12 and launched their first juvenile magazine *Adventure* (1921–61). Its success generated other boys' storypaper launches:

- *Rover* (1922–61)
- *Wizard* (1922–63)
- *Skipper* (1930–41)
- *Hotspur* (1933–59).

These became known as the 'big five'. Almost identical in format they hit the newsstands on different days of the week, spreading the work for compositors, allowing economy of use of the printing presses and repeat purchases by the same readers. Launches for girls followed some decades later: *Bunty* (1958–2001), *Judy*

The demise in 2012 of the print version of *The Dandy* ... still brings sentimental tears to the eyes of generations of 'grown up' school boys

(1960–91), *Mandy* (1967–91) and *Twinkle* (1968–99). As cartoon strips became increasingly popular, DC Thomson introduced their highly successful and iconic *The Dandy* (1937–2012) and *The Beano* (1938–) comics. Today only *The Beano* remains in its original format. The cultural importance of this market should not be underestimated: *Comic Cuts* (Amalgamated Press, 1890–1953) held the record for the most issues of a British comic weekly (3006) until *The Dandy* overtook it in 1999. (The demise in 2012 of the print version of *The Dandy* in favour of an online version still brings sentimental tears to the eyes of generations of 'grown up' school boys.)

Only one other significant magazine launch took place in the 1920s but it was one of overwhelming importance and happened almost by accident. Aggrieved by the demands of the Newspaper Publishers' Association for a large fee to allow radio listings in their publications and the subsequent embargo, the then Director-General of the BBC, John Reith, decided to publish his own listings magazine. *Radio Times* was born. The first edition, 'the official organ of the BBC', reached the newsstands on 28 September 1923. Initially a joint venture with George Newnes Ltd, the BBC took over editorial control in 1925 and became totally independent by 1937. By the end of the 1920s, published weekly and costing just twopence (2d), the *Radio Times* had the second highest circulation of all magazines in the UK. (Only *John Bull* outstripped it during this decade.) By the 1930s it was selling nearly two million copies a week and in the 1940s this leapt to just under two and a half million[17]. By 1950 the *Radio Times* was selling eight million copies a week; with sales still in the region of 900,000 copies[18], despite the deregulation of TV listings in 1991, the *Radio Times* remains one of the all-time success stories of the magazine publishing industry.

Photo 1.7
Radio Times.
The first issue
(28 September 1923)
and one of the issues
from 1950 that sold
8 million copies

THE WAR YEARS AND THE DAWN OF CELEBRITY WATCHING (1930–60)

Pre-war (1930s)

The 1930s saw the significant impact of the gravure process of printing on the magazine market. Apart from *Vogue,* almost all other magazines had historically been printed using letterpress with its associated dull and colourless appearance. In 1937 Odhams' Press launched its weekly magazine *Woman* as a rival to the highly successful *Woman's Own* (1932, George Newnes Ltd.) and *Woman's Illustrated* (1936, Amalgamated Press). By printing the entire magazine using the rotogravure process, at a stroke, *Woman* introduced vibrant colours, together with superior quality printing in a twopenny magazine aimed at lower-middle-class readers. Its competitors could only follow suit and, together, they captured the market and sounded the death knell for those that could not keep up with their technological advance. To maintain their viability, however, they had to attract massive circulation figures and advertising revenue on a major scale. The gamble paid off: advertisers were attracted by the high volume print runs and the quality of the colour printing. While the glossy shilling monthlies bemoaned the impertinence of domestic servants and the difficulty in finding good staff, the almost-as-glossy weeklies, selling at a fraction of the price, included articles on cookery, knitting, babycare, problem pages and true-to-life fiction. *Woman* and *Woman's Own* became the publishing phenomena of the twentieth century, going

Photo 1.8 First issue of *Woman* magazine, 5 June 1937

on to achieve enormous circulation figures[19] and massive profits for their
publishers. (By 1939 *Woman* was selling more than three-quarters of a million
copies every week; in the 1950s this rose to more than three and a half million[20].)

These magazines contributed little to the feminist cause, appealing openly to
the traditional homemaking values of women within the domestic sphere. It was
almost as if the advances made by women during the war years had been
annihilated in favour of a return to Victorian patriarchy. Indeed, attempts made by
the editor of *Woman* to include articles concerning social problems were met with
a downturn in sales of 30 per cent and the experiment was soon abandoned[21].
It took another war before women began to yield sufficient social influence to
affect the content of their reading matter.

War and post-war (1939–59)

The Second World War was a watershed in British magazine development.
Titles that had endured for decades failed to survive the harsh reality of a changing
society, while others took advantage of the high demand for pictorial exposition
and expanded rapidly. Coverage of the events of the war both at home and
overseas was provided by the newly introduced picture paper, *Picture Post*
(1938–57, Hulton Press). With its emphasis on high quality journalism and
photography, the first issue sold out almost immediately and circulation figures of
nearly two million a week were commonplace.

Perhaps the most significant factor for magazine publishers during the war
was paper rationing, forcing them to cut the size of their editions in both page
content and, in some cases in physical dimension as well. (*Good Housekeeping*
changed its format three times during the war and eventually became pocket-sized
in order to maintain a substantial number of pages[22].) There was little spare room
for advertisements as space was at a premium if readers' insatiable demands for
entertainment, news and gossip were to be satisfied. Reading material was scarce
and every magazine flew off the newsagents' shelves as soon as it appeared, to be
read over and over by several different people. Priority was given to government
advertising campaigns leading to the ironic situation of advertisements
demanding readers should use less of a product, not more. Many magazines
closed and there was no opportunity for new ones as they were not eligible for any
paper allocation. When paper rationing finally ended for magazines in 1950,
Woman's Own celebrated with a bumper issue of 48 pages. (*Woman* and *Woman's
Own* both increased their number of pages, from 20 in 1946 to around 40
in 1951[23].)

After the war, the ever-expanding publishing conglomerates thrived by
providing what the reading public, and in particular women, wanted. By the 1950s
readers had become more sophisticated and demanding, expecting quality
products for their money. These were the boom days of Harold Macmillan's 'never
had it so good' era; rationing had ended and consumer goods were flooding the
markets. Advertisers responded to the expanding buying power of women by
dramatically increasing their spend in magazines, further fuelling the profits of
the large publishing houses. Colourful photographs began to replace line
drawings and advertisements became more appealing to readers. As White
observed:

> After the war,
> the ever-
> expanding
> publishing
> conglomerates
> thrived by
> providing what
> the reading
> public, and in
> particular
> women,
> wanted

Before the war, money had been short while goods were plentiful. After it, people had money to spend but the shops were empty. Now, for the first time, production matched spending power, and manufacturers and consumers were eager to make contact through the medium of advertising.[24]

In the ever-expanding world of media, the introduction of commercial television in 1955 brought with it golden opportunities for both advertisers and the broadcasting companies. Prior to this date, the BBC had held a monopoly on television viewing and the *Radio Times* had exclusive rights for television and radio listings. Now a new magazine was needed to inform the public of what was available to view on the Independent Television (ITV) channel broadcasting in their region of the country. In September 1955 the new television companies launched *TV Times* which, by 1960 was selling nearly four million copies a week, compared with *Radio Times* at about seven million[25]. (Although traditionally regarded as competitor magazines, until the deregulation of TV listings in 1991, each offered different information appropriate to their own channels so should perhaps be regarded as complementary rather than opponents until that date.)

Photo 1.9 First issue of *TV Times*, 22 September 1955

One other important social event had significant impact on the cultural development of Britain in the post-war period: in 1947 Princess Elizabeth married Prince Philip of Greece, an event that, above all others, marked the dawn of the age of 'celebrity watching' as we know it. Not to say that prior to this date the public at large hadn't been fascinated by the comings and goings of the famous; photographs of film stars on covers of magazines were almost guaranteed to increase circulation figures from the 1920s onward. Indeed, as a child, Princess Elizabeth had featured in an article in *Woman's Friend* in the 1930s, extolling the virtues of her Harris Tweed coat. Brian Braithewaite, the elder statesman of the publishing world and a contemporary observer commented:

> The wedding, and the birth of the children, began the popular magazines' love affair with the royals. A new industry was created, and it saturated the magazines for decades with photographs and text about every aspect of the royal family. Both editors and readers had an insatiable appetite for the subject.[26]

Scandal came in 1950 when the royal nanny, Marion Crawford ('Crawfie') published a book sharing harmless details of the childhood days of the young princesses. These were subsequently serialised in *Woman's Own*. Mild though

Photo 1.10 One of many 'royal' covers of the 1950s

these revelations were, compared with the intimate details that are on public
display today, the publication heralded the end of privacy for royalty and public
figures at large. The trivia of other people's family lives became public possession
and magazine readers lapped it up.

THE YEARS OF SEXUAL AND TECHNOLOGICAL REVOLUTION (1960–2000)

The decade of vibrant change (1960s)

With its emphasis on high circulation numbers in order to satisfy the economic
demands of the advertisers and print shops, it was inevitable that the fragmented
magazine industry would have to consolidate in order to survive. By 1963, thanks
to amalgamations, takeovers and closures at the end of the previous decade, many
of the major players had been united to form the appropriately nicknamed
'ministry of magazines', otherwise known as the International Publishing
Corporation (IPC). Most of the long-established houses were no more: gone were
Odhams, Amalgamated Press (Fleetway), George Newnes and Hultons, all folded
into the IPC empire. The other major magazine publishing groups of the time
were Condé Nast, the National Magazines Company (a UK subsidiary of the
American Hearst Corporation), the Canadian-owned Thomson Publication (UK)
and, not to be confused with, the Scottish DC Thomson publishing house.
Waiting in the wings, however, was the East Midland Allied Press (EMAP), a
company successfully producing several local newspapers. In 1953 the printing
presses in Peterborough lay idle for part of the week and the decision was taken to
start a magazine division and to buy a weekly fishing publication, *Angling Times*.
This was quickly followed in 1956 by the purchase of *Motor Cycle News*. These
specialist magazines were to form the foundation of a highly competitive
publishing business that lasted into the twenty-first century.

The 1960s was the decade that the 'teenager', if not actually invented, was at
least recognised and became the magazine publisher's dream. Here was a market
of over seven million people, who were spending £3 million a day[27]. Publishers
queued up to make the most of this opportunity with magazines such as *Honey*
(1960–86, Fleetway), *Jackie* (1962–93, DC Thomson), *Petticoat* (1966–75, IPC)
and *19* (1968–2004, IPC). Their era was short-lived although the reasons
attributed to the decline in sales are complicated and often speculative. Teen
magazines have come and gone since their initial heyday in the 1960s and 70s
but almost certainly, inconsistency in the market can be put down in part to the
fickleness of the age group, the advent of computers and the trend for children to
grow up, with associated expectations, at a far earlier age than perhaps they did a
generation before.

The 'swinging sixties' was a decade that also saw the rise of satire generally
and in the magazine world in particular: conventional news and current affairs
journalism was subverted when *Private Eye* launched in 1961. Events of the time,
such as the Profumo scandal, leant themselves to this irreverent style of reporting,
which captured the *zeitgeist* at the tired end of the Macmillan years. The recently
developed offset-lithography printing method facilitated the introduction of

'specialist' magazines for publishers who couldn't afford the high costs of set up involved with the other processes available at the time. *Private Eye*, a small-scale, predominantly black-and-white paper, was the first real competitor to the long-established *Punch* (1841–2002) magazine. Begun by a group of undergraduates from Oxford University as an extended 'in-house magazine', the original schoolboy humour soon hardened into the uncompromising satire with which we are familiar today. Edited until 1986 by Richard Ingrams and since then by Ian Hislop, *Private Eye*'s irreverent approach to the world through controversial and combative journalism has led to numerous libel cases. Perhaps the most famous were those brought by Sir James Goldsmith in the 1970s and Robert Maxwell in the 1980s. The magazine continues to thrive on controversy to this day and enjoys sales of over 200,000 every fortnight[28].

The sixties was also the era of rapid expansion of supermarkets, with Sainsbury's, Tesco and Safeway all vying for customer footfall. International Thomson Publishing capitalised on this new trend by introducing first *Family Circle* (1964–2006) and then *Living* (1967–95) which had exclusive distribution through this retail channel. At its peak in the 1960s, *Family Circle* sold a million copies from its privileged position beside the checkouts. (Sales were 625,000 in 1988 when IPC bought it, together with *Living*. One of the main strategic reasons for this purchase was IPC's desire to learn more about supermarket distribution in order to facilitate a launch into the area with their own magazines.) The precariousness of depending on the supermarket giants as sole distribution channel was demonstrated when Sainsbury's introduced its own in-house

Photo 1.11 Robert Maxwell on the cover of *Private Eye*, November 1986

magazine for customers in 1994. This, together with the introduction of large-scale newsagent sections opening within first Tesco, then all the other supermarket chains, accounted for the downward trend of sales of *Family Circle*. (Sales had plummeted to less than 120,000 per issue when it finally closed in 2006[29].) In the 1960s *Family Circle* had embodied the image of most women's magazines of the time: the domestic female. All that was to change in the following decades.

The Cosmo era (1970s)

Social history will report the 1970s as the decade of dissent and strife: the three-day week, the miners' strike, IRA terrorism in mainland Britain, the oil crisis, not to mention currency decimalisation, joining the European Economic Community and Margaret Thatcher becoming the first female Prime Minister. In the magazine world the 1970s will be remembered, however, for an event that was to make an impact on a similar scale. In March 1972 National Magazines launched the first international version of *Cosmopolitan* in the UK, a title that had been published in the USA since 1886.

Across the Atlantic, Hearst Magazines decided to take a risk and, in 1965, handed the editorship of their ailing family magazine, *Cosmopolitan* over to the enthusiastic and charismatic Helen Gurley Brown (1922–2012). Already a published author with her (then) risqué and controversial book, *Sex and the Single Girl*, Brown almost singlehandedly reversed the fortunes of the magazine and created a worldwide, iconic brand. As Braithewaite (the launch publisher of *Cosmopolitan* UK) observed:

> Hearst saw a golden opportunity. Here was a bright, articulate, exciting new editor with celebrity status and a bestselling book to back her ideas. ... The overwelming success of the magazine was undoubtedly due to the persona of Helen Gurley Brown and her dedicated belief that 'out there' were millions of girls looking for self-improvement, self-confidence, interesting employment, good relations with a man and a better sex life.[30]

Cosmopolitan became the jewel in Hearst's crown and it wasn't long before they were looking to other countries to exploit their success. National Magazines (their UK subsidiary) had already demonstrated expertise in transferring US titles such as *Harper's Bazaar* and *Good Housekeeping* to the UK market and British *Cosmopolitan* was launched with great fanfare in 1972.

The timing of the launch could not have been better. The 1960s had been a decade of increasingly liberal attitudes; the pill was available, abortion and homosexuality were legalised in 1967 and in 1969 divorce became easier to achieve. The women's magazine market was relatively static in the early 1970s and National Magazines judged that it was ripe for this new, brash title that had already taken the US by storm. The UK launch was arguably the most sensational and successful magazine introduction ever: Saatchi & Saatchi, a newly-formed advertising agency, took on the television advertising campaign which contributed in no small measure to the overwhelming success of the magazine in its early days. The 45-second commercial and 16-sheet posters in the London Underground

... arguably the most sensational and successful magazine introduction ever ...

were regarded as extravagant for the time but the initial print run of 350,000 sold out by lunchtime on the first day, justifying the expenditure. The second issue, thanks in part to its attendant publicity generating rumours (not fulfilled) of a full-frontal male nude featuring within its pages, sold all 450,000 copies within two days. Ironically, the highly effective PR campaign for *Cosmopolitan* served to regenerate interest in women's magazines generally and its competitors benefited substantially from its efforts.

The introduction was a considerable success, despite the fact that National Magazines had got their market research (the little they did) completely wrong. *Cosmopolitan* in the US was aimed at middle-class women aged 25–40 and the company had assumed that the UK version would appeal to a similar class and age group. In reality, the readership turned out to be single women with the peak reading age of just eighteen, with class and level of education being less significant than marital status. What made *Cosmopolitan* such a phenomenon was its blatant approach to all matters sexual and its openhanded treatment of the subject. As one researcher commented:

> *Cosmopolitan* put female sexuality right out there on the front page, where everyone could see it at the grocery store ... People could no longer pretend that it didn't exist.[31]

Cosmopolitan went on to become the UK's biggest monthly women's glossy magazine until the launch of *Glamour* by Condé Nast in 2002. Encouraged by its incredible achievement, National Magazines took the brave decision to launch a new title that, to all intents and purposes, appeared to compete directly with their own blockbuster. In 1978 they launched *Company*, with similar fanfare and an even larger advertising expenditure, profiling it directly at the 18–24 female market but with careful editorial distinctions. The first issue sold 300,000 copies and National Magazines dominated this market in such a way that their publishing rivals gave up any attempts to compete. (Ironically, Condé Nast had contemplated launching a UK version of their US title *Glamour* at this time but changed their mind when *Company* arrived.) The overwhelming success of National Magazine launches in the 1970s contributed significantly to the change in balance of power amongst magazine publishers that was to take place in the following decade.

Domestic expansion and foreign invaders (1980s)

The 1980s may be regarded as the decade that saw a huge number of new magazines come and go. On the domestic front, East Midland Allied Press were building on their expertise in the specialist magazine market with the launch of titles aimed at younger readers. Their introduction of *Smash Hits* in 1978 had taken the youth market by storm and encouraged the company to expand within specific sectors. In 1986, now renamed EMAP, it published 38 consumer magazines in three main markets: youth, hobbies and outdoor pursuits as well as 53 business to business publications.

The women's magazine sector was experiencing one of its 'most inventive periods ... [with] ... some brilliant and enduring hits and some doleful failures'[32]

Business to business (B2B) publishing

Arguably the first B2B publication was *Lloyd's List*, first introduced in 1734, providing London weekly shipping news to merchants' agents and insurance underwriters. It still exists today, providing daily information both online and (Monday to Friday) in print. About 75 per cent of its 3,500 issue sales are to subscribers[33].

In 1840 the Penny Post was introduced, replacing its expensive forerunner. (Prior to this the cost of sending a letter had been calculated on distance and charges had been many times the new standard rate.) *Post Magazine*, based just off London's Fleet Street, was the first publication to take advantage of this postal revolution. Sending out 5,000 copies weekly to the insurance industry it became the first postal subscription B2B title. Today's circulation is in the region of 4,000 print copies, of which over 70 per cent is on subscription.

In 1862 William Reed published his first issue of *The Grocer* magazine providing information on a weekly basis to the grocery business. Its objective was to target the growing number of shopkeepers serving Victorian society. William Reed Business Media remains a family-run business and still trades 150 years later. The magazine today has a circulation of over 30,000 per issue of which approximately half is on subscription and half sold through newsagents[34]. This was perhaps the first of a range of publications introduced towards the end of the nineteenth century aimed at specific industries, for example, *Engineering, Architectural Review*. Many of these continue to thrive to this day.

Similarly, *Farmers Weekly* was introduced in 1934, providing news and articles for farmers and the agricultural industry. Its average circulation of about 60,000 is also split fairly evenly between sales and subscriptions[35]. At the end of the twentieth century the two main B2B publishers were Reed Business Information and EMAP. Many titles were free to readers – known as controlled circulation titles.

Today there are estimated to be approximately 4,400 B2B titles covering such diverse subjects as computing, medicine and law. As will be seen in Chapter 2, this magazine sector is fast moving away from traditional print on paper. Today's B2B publishers see themselves as the providers of high value business information and are also heavily engaged in organising conferences and exhibitions.

In the early years of the twenty-first century the controlled circulation sector has come under immense pressure – with the migration of many advertisement revenue streams to digital products. Unfortunately closures of print titles are not uncommon.

during the 1980s. Of 34 launches, 12 titles died within the decade and only 14 survive to this day. A significant number of these – including several of the most successful ones – having their origin in the startling invasions from across the Channel in the second half of the decade.

Until 1986 the British market had been satisfied with home-grown magazines or by anglicised versions of glossies from across the Atlantic such as *Vogue, Good Housekeeping* and *Cosmopolitan*. This complacent attitude, with its associated assumptions, was shattered when a powerhouse of magazine publishing from Germany, Gruner+Jahr, decided to enter the British market. The launch of *Prima* in September 1986 was explosive, expensive and took the British publishers completely by surprise. On paper such a launch looked commercial suicide: the domestic market was already saturated and women were supposedly flocking to read magazines such as *Cosmopolitan* which rejected the cosy image of family and home. How could a foreign magazine full of recipes, articles about childcare, health and beauty and gardening, which even included a paper pattern in every issue, possibly hope to survive in such a climate?

> ... explosive, expensive and took the British publishing companies completely by surprise

The initial advertising expenditure was £1.5 million[36] (ten times that of *Cosmopolitan*) and included television commercials that emphasised, and did not disguise, the homely nature of the product. The free paper pattern (worth more than the cover price of the magazine itself) was an instant success and the first two issues sold out completely with print runs well in excess of half a million. (Much has been made of the novelty of the free paper pattern and its contribution to attracting purchasers; commentators forget that Samuel Beeton had used this sales tactic 134 years earlier in *The Englishwoman's Domestic Magazine*, proving once again that there is seldom anything truly innovative in marketing.) A year after launch *Prima* broke the million copies a month barrier and in August 1987 Gruner+Jahr added to their success with the launch of *Best*, a weekly magazine that profiled itself as a lightweight, chatty magazine that was classless, fun and cheap at only 35 pence. Within a year it too was selling over a million copies a week[37].

While publishers, traditionally, had taken at least six months to arrange the launch of a new magazine, Gruner+Jahr gave their advertisers and the news trade only two weeks' notice before introducing *Best*. These surprise tactics were also used by their own German rival, Bauer when they launched a direct competitor *Bella*, in the same year, undercutting *Best*'s price by six pence. Soon Bauer were claiming sales of a million copies a week for their own title and the British (in the shape of IPC) felt obliged to react to the German invasion of their home territory. In February 1988 *Essentials* was launched with an introductory budget of a staggering £2.5 million, directly challenging *Prima* for readers. The new monthly was moderately successful and was soon selling in the region of 750,000 copies. The complacency of the bureaucratic 'ministry of magazines' was no longer appropriate in this climate of aggressive competition; in the 1980s IPC was finally forced to change its working practices and, with it, its culture. All of these magazines survive to this day although sales figures will almost certainly never again reach the levels they did in the 1980s.

In May 1988 the Spanish followed in the footsteps of their German counterparts when, by launching *Hello!*, they threatened the British market still further. Once again, the likelihood of success seemed improbable for such a venture at that time: the Spanish version, *¡Hola*, was owned by a private family company without the enormous publicity budgets of the Germans or of IPC, the magazine itself was weekly and priced at 75 pence and, worst of all, it was set to appeal to the voyeuristic nature of celebrity and royal watchers. Nothing in this profile was to suggest that *Hello!* would be anything but a niche product. How wrong. Weekly sales soared to over 400,000 by 1993 and the reticent, respectful image of the British stereotype was shattered. Braithewaite describes the phenomenon:

> The over-the-top voyeurism of the rich, famous and infamous captured an immediate and passionately devoted readership in this country. *Hello!* is a feast for the curious and the prying, a banquet for armchair peeping-toms.[38]

(*Hello!* thrived for nearly five years without any real competition until Richard Desmond and Northern and Shell, launched *OK!* in 1993. See Chapter 4, page 113.)

Encouraged by the success of other Europeans, finally the French decided to try their hand at attacking the British market. More cautious than their predecessors, Group Marie Claire chose to form a partnership with IPC for the UK launch in September 1988 of its highly successful French women's monthly, *Marie Claire*. The first issue of the British version was a staggering 252 pages of glossy fashion and beauty; it was successful in its own right and remains a popular title to date. By the early 1990s it was rivalling *Cosmopolitan* as the top woman's monthly. Indeed, the magazine has probably received more awards and prizes for its editorial and content than any other similar product.

Table 1.2 Successful women's magazine launches of the 1980s

	Frequency	Publisher (2012)	Launched	Average Issue Circulation Print (digital)
Hello!	Weekly	Hello!	1988	305,567 (2,860)
Yours	Fortnightly	Bauer	1984	272,040 (N/A)
Prima	Monthly	Hearst	1986	256,053 (676)
Marie Claire	Monthly	IPC/European Magazines	1988	255,333 (905)
Best	Weekly	Hearst	1987	236,430 (175)
Bella	Weekly	Bauer	1987	218,340 (N/A)
Elle	Monthly	Hearst	1985	194,253 (7,070)
Essentials	Monthly	IPC	1988	117,594 (N/A)

Source: ABC (July–Dec 2012)

The challenge laid down by the European invaders in the mid-1980s was perhaps one of the most significant occurrences in the UK women's magazine market in the twentieth century. The Germans, French and Spanish publishers stirred a flaccid industry into directions it would not otherwise have considered. This was good for the market, for readers, advertisers and newsagents and gave a number of companies, particularly IPC, the much needed jolt that would stimulate them into actions that were rewarded with ever-greater profits.

The decade of TV listings, lads' mags and customer magazines (1990s)

On 1 March 1991 the overall monopoly for printing seven-day programme guides enjoyed by *Radio Times* and *TV Times* came to an end and many new titles flooded the highly lucrative TV listings market. As deregulation took place, the large publishing houses lined up to launch new magazines that would attack the stranglehold of these two, well-established titles. First on the scene in March were IPC, the publishers of *TV Times*, with *What's on TV* (1991–) and Bauer with the appropriately named *TV Quick* (1991–2010). Competition in the market was intense, as newspapers could also now carry the seven-day listings where before they had only been allowed to print the same day's programmes (two on Saturdays). Some, such as the *Sunday People* with *TV First!*, chose to provide their readers with free colour magazine supplements to rival the magazines on sale in the newsagents and supermarkets. Bauer followed their initial entry into the market with *TV Choice* in 1999, to rival IPC's highly successful *What's on TV* at

Photo 1.12 *Marie Claire*, still a top selling title in 2013

the budget end of the market. Although *Radio Times* was never again to reach the dizzy heights of sales it experienced in previous decades, it, together with *TV Times,* continues to record respectable sales and readership figures to date. (See Table 4.1, page 121.)

The 1990s was also the era of customer publishing. Magazines distributed specifically to patrons of, for example, a particular store, manufacturer or travel company was not a new phenomenon in the 1990s. British Airways had given their passengers an in-flight magazine, *High Life* (Premier magazines; Cedar Communications) since 1973. Indeed, Harrods and Selfridges had sold copies of their own magazines (free to account customers) while the National Trust had sent copies of their newssheet to subscribers since 1932. Numerous other organisations such as British Rail (*Intercity*), the Automobile Association (*AA Magazine*) and American Express (*Expressions*) have also served their customers with quality magazines for decades. Agencies such as Cedar and Redwood exploited this niche market for publications and became extremely successful outside the giant publishing houses. What changed in the 90s was the extraordinary success supermarkets' own brand of magazine experienced. Placed conveniently by check-outs and often given away free or competitively priced, these glossy magazines looked like their expensive counterparts in the newsagents with high quality journalism and features. The overt promotion of its own brands and suppliers was an acceptable face of the publication in the eyes of consumers. Sainsbury's launched *The Magazine* (now *Sainsbury's Magazine*) in 1994 and in the twenty-first century almost every significant retail outlet has followed suit. Circulation figures in 2012 are remarkable: Tesco and Asda give away nearly two million copies of every issue of their magazines; Redwood claims a circulation of 1.6 million for *Boots Health and Beauty* and nearly a million for Marks and Spencer's *Your M&S*. These are impressive numbers for print magazines and, needless to say, all are backed up with skilfully produced, lively websites. Indeed, figures provided by the National Readership Survey (NRS) for 2012 claim that *Tesco Magazine* has an average readership of over 7.1 million – almost one in six women in Britain – reaching more people than all other newspapers and magazines, including the *Sun*.

As this chapter has shown, the development of magazine publishing in the last three centuries has been a series of significant events, both socially and technologically, each followed by periods of evolution and expansion. For every significant introduction, imitators jump into the fray to capture their own share of the market. Women's magazines probably started the trend three centuries ago but throughout that time the publication of magazines aimed specifically at the opposite sex has been a relative failure. Right up until the 1990s the idea of general interest men's magazines was regarded, at best, as niche and at worst a recipe for disaster. The market for men's magazines consisted of specialist titles devoted to masculine pursuits such as cars or football and mainstream pornography, the latter titles being banished to the top shelves in newsagents. By the mid-1980s, however, the concept of a 'lifestyle' magazine for the growing numbers of 'new men' who were seen to be expressing interest in fashion, grooming and relationships, was being explored. Born in the 60s and 70s, these young people were the first cohort to grow up alongside new technology such as computers and the internet. Stereotyped as 'Generation X' (the name popularised by Douglas Coupland's 1991 novel), the potential for these readers was even more appealing as men stayed single longer and had more cash in their pockets than ever before.

The major publishers remained sceptical and it was Nick Logan's small company, Wagadon who took the brave step in 1986 of launching *Arena* (1986–2008). Building on his experiences with *The Face*, the style magazine for the under-25s he had introduced in 1980, Logan turned his attention to older male readers. With little introductory fanfare, *Arena* was soon selling 65,000 copies a month and others sat up and took note. Condé Nast launched *GQ* in 1989 and National Magazines followed with *Esquire* in 1991. Editorial on all of these titles was carefully managed to avoid being perceived as either pornographic or gay and issues seldom featured women on their covers. The aim was to have newsagents place them alongside upmarket, political journals such as *The Spectator* and *The Economist*.

What followed in May 1994 was to turn the traditional processes of magazine launches on their head. From out of nowhere a whole new genre of magazines was created when IPC launched *Loaded*, aimed at young, heterosexual males. Gill defined them as 'pursuing women, alcohol and football ... Anti-aspirational, inept, optimistic and self-deprecating'[39] and as the editor, James Brown put it in the first issue: 'the man who believes he can do anything, if only he wasn't hungover'. Seen variously as a backlash against feminism and the *Cosmo* ethos of women or as a rebellion against the male stereotype of 'breadwinner' and family man, the laddish culture seemed to provide escapism for those who really didn't care for traditional male responsibilities or image. The era of the lads' mags had arrived and others soon jumped on this bandwagon. Within a year EMAP had revamped their recently-acquired men's fashion title, *For Him* and relaunched it as *FHM* and Dennis Publishing introduced *Maxim* (1995–2008). By the end of the century, these three titles contributed three-quarters of the men's market by sales, having expanded this sector from a total of a mere 250,000 copies in 1990 to 2.3 million in 1998[40]. As the market became increasingly competitive the titles became more sexually blatant in the quest to chase sales, moving away from the initial *Loaded* concept as a lifestyle magazine. Developments of this sector in the twenty-first century have been both controversial and dynamic, with the launch of similar weekly magazines such as *Nuts* (2003; IPC) and *Zoo* (2004; EMAP now Bauer). In circulation terms, *Loaded* and *FHM* are now shadows of their former selves and their long-term prospects do not look encouraging. Few would dispute, however, that the launch of *Loaded* was one of the influential events of the twentieth century.

... the launch of *Loaded* was one of the influential events of the twentieth century

Magazine publishing in the second millennium is a very different world to that of the preceding three centuries. Despite this, the rich heritage of its ancestry in Britain has shaped and formed the current industry. Technology has progressed to such an extent that readers of the pre-internet generation would hardly recognise today's publications. A magazine without a website is unthinkable and circulation figures are now audited with digital copies included in the totals alongside the more conventional print versions. Indeed, some 'old-timers' such as DC Thomson's iconic comic *The Dandy* only exist online as 'virtual magazines'. While circulation figures for individual magazines may continue to decline, the market itself remains healthy and, to paraphrase Mark Twain, rumours of its demise have been greatly exaggerated.

NOTES

1.　ABC (Jan–June 2012) average net weekly circulation *The Spectator* 63,619.
2.　Brimley, 1853 p 924.
3.　Braithewaite, 1995 p 12.
4.　The *Family Herald*, the *London Journal* and *Cassell's Family Papers*. Altick, 1998 p 357.
5.　Drotner, 1988 p 115.
6.　Reed, 1987 p 92.
7.　Altick, 1998 p 361.
8.　Ibid: p 364.
9.　Reed, 1987 p 91.
10.　ABC (June–Dec 2012) average circulation per issue *The Lady*: 27,694.
11.　White, 1970 p 58.
12.　ABC (Jan–Dec 2012) average circulation per issue *New Statesman*: (print) 24,910; (digital) 224.
13.　Braithewaite, 1995 p 26.
14.　See the PPA website at www.ppa.co.uk.
15.　Braithewaite and Barrell, 1979 pp 10–11.
16.　ABC (July–Dec 2012) average circulation per issue *Vogue*: (print) 203,356; (digital) 3,703.
17.　Reed, 1987 p 178.
18.　ABC (July–Dec 2012) average circulation per issue *Radio Times*: 893,512.
19.　Both magazines are now owned by IPC Media Ltd. Weekly circulation figures at the end of 2012 were: *Woman* 261,170; *Woman's Own* 222,571. Source ABC (July–Dec 2012.)
20.　White, 1970 p 97.
21.　Ibid: p 112.
22.　Braithewaite, 1995 p 58.
23.　White, 1970 p 138.
24.　Ibid: p 157.
25.　Reed, 1987 p 223.
26.　Braithewaite, 1995 p 63.
27.　Braithewaite, 2009 p 33.
28.　ABC (Jan–Dec 2012) average circulation per issue *Private Eye*: 224,796.
29.　ABC (July–Dec 2005) average circulation per Issue *Family Circle*: 112,597.
30.　Braithewaite, 1995 pp 96–7.
31.　Kim and Ward, 2004.
32.　Braithewaite, 2009 p 62.
33.　ABC (Jan–Dec 2012) average circulation per issue *Lloyd's List*: (print) 2,702; (digital) 844.
34.　ABC (June 2011–July 2012) average circulation per issue *The Grocer*: 30,730.
35.　ABC (Jan–Dec 2012) average circulation per issue *Farmer's Weekly*: 61,842.
36.　Braithewaite, 1995 p 134.
37.　Ibid: p 136.
38.　Ibid: p 140.
39.　Gill, 2003 p 51.
40.　Crewe, 2003 p 96.

REFERENCES

Altick, R. D. (1998) *The English Common Reader: A Social History of the Mass Reading Public, 1800–1900*. Ohio: Ohio State University Press.

Braithewaite, B. (1995) *Women's Magazines: The First 300 Years*. London: Peter Owen.

Braithewaite, B. (2009) *The Press Book: Adventures and Misadventures in Print Media*. London: Peter Owen Publishers.

Braithewaite, B. and Barrell, J. (1979) *The Business of Women's Magazines*. London: Associated Business Press.

Brimley, G. (1853) *Spectator*, 24 September, pp 923–5.

Crewe, B. (2003) 'Class, masculinity and editorial identity in the reformation of the UK men's press', in Benwell, B. (ed.), *Masculinity and Men's Lifestyle Magazines*. Oxford: Blackwell Publishing pp 91–111.

Drotner, K. (1988) *English Children and their Magazines, 1751–1945*. London: Yale University Press.

Gill, R. (2003) 'Power and the production of subjects: a genealogy of the New Man and the New Lad', in Benwell, B. (ed.), *Masculinity and Men's Lifestyle Magazines*. Oxford: Blackwell Publishing pp 34–56.

Kim, J. L. and Ward, L. M. (2004) 'Pleasure reading: associations between young women's sexual attitudes and their reading of contemporary women's magazines', *Psychology of Women Quarterly*, Volume 28, pp 48–58.

Reed, D. (1987) *The Popular Magazine in Britain and the United States of America 1880–1960*. Toronto: University of Toronto Press.

White, C. (1970) *Women's Magazines, 1693–1968*. London: Joseph.

Diana: magazines, her celebrity and its lasting impact on an industry

Leander Reeves

A Google search using the term 'Princess Diana' delivers up tens of millions of results in an instant, a fact which somewhat illustrates the daunting task of adding discussion to a cross platform landscape. This essay seeks to discuss a by-product of Diana's life and death: the commoditisation and use of her celebrity legacy. This angle of academic discourse regarding Diana is a less studied one and links many perspectives of scholarly research which appear in most studies regarding consumer magazines, such as celebrity, fame, class, gender and representation.

A quantitative measurement of consumer magazine circulation is readily available through the Audit Bureau of Circulation (ABC). Finding the more subjective measurement of assessing the lasting impact of Diana's legacy on these same magazines, however, is a more difficult task. This is because the burden of proof is both necessary and yet subjective, but also subject to a dichotomy of sorts. The magazine circulations benefit from the Diana legacy, namely via an increased 'use' and 'ownership' of celebrity, but the circulation trends for these same magazines are falling.

In the now infamous *Panorama* interview of 1995[1], Diana, utilising a repetitive superfluity of feminised body language, makes two very important statements: '[D]uring the years you see yourself as a good product that sits on a shelf and sells well, and people make a lot of money out of you.' Then later on in the interview: '[H]ere was a fairy story that everybody wanted to work.' Diana already had the 'honest fame' which Pope[2] and others[3] have mused on. Within the interview she appropriated the structure and discourse of the consumer magazines to weave her own feature.

Her interview is a collection of secrets shared with the audience and by extension, her readership. Diana attempted to control the confessional tone and exclusives given which still dominate mass market women's magazines to this day. Clearly, Diana understood the concept of a good product, coupled with the seductive appeal of the fairy story, complete with a genuine princess. Today, women's celebrity magazines such as *Now!* and *OK!* have adapted this recipe, with fabricated princesses of their own making.

Foucault and many other theorists cited by Yelin[4] have discussed at length these acts of confession, suggesting that the celebrity in question is seeking the forgiveness of those confessed to. The *Panorama* audience, and in the case of magazines the readership, have the power to grant absolution. This power represents a form of 'indulgence' and with it comes implied and expected ownership. Through Diana's celebrity rather than fame, she was owned by the masses and this was a fact which she essentially recognised in the interview.

Postle defines celebrity as a 'hybrid of fame driven by commerce and the cult of personality'[5]. The 'eternal truths' Diana sought to reveal to the viewers ranged from; motherhood, *her* bulimia, *her* marriage, *her* frailty, *her* depression, love, loss, desires, hopes etc. All of these helped herself evolve from her 'honest fame' into a celebrity. If Diana had hoped through the confessional content of the interview and close involvement with magazines such as *Vanity Fair* and *People* to own her celebrity, she was very mistaken. 'The curse of celebrity is that it finally cannot be controlled by those who achieve it.'[6]

Two years later in 1997 during the days that followed her death, this sense of Diana ownership by all became very apparent. Prime Minister Blair's 'The people's princess' tribute helped signify this. This idea of ownership was evidenced further by 'the people' in an unprecedented manner. The Queen, accused of isolation after the death, appeased the crowds outside the palace and on TV through her live address to a nation in mourning.

Her death in the late 1990s, coinciding with this evidenced power of ownership, came during an interesting period for women's consumer magazines. The increasingly competitive market environment for British women's glossies in the late 1990s in many ways encouraged those magazines to embrace the commercial appeal of celebrity journalism. The benefits to this editorial direction were clearly visible in the circulation figures of rival brands, such as *OK!* and *Hello!* which by 1996, were enjoying weekly circulation figures of just under 500,000[7].

An increasing taste for celebrity journalism coupled with the accelerated take-off of home internet use[8] created a growing market for mass celebrity access and consumption, which in turn led to an explosion in competing content for the magazines. Competition in the middle market sector, where certain editorial themes were shared the most, was particularly fierce.

Post Diana, magazines sought to create their own celebrities. 'The more important development ... is the scale upon which the media have begun to produce celebrity *on their own*.'[9] Celebrities from reality TV shows and those which practice 'augmented reality' such as *The Only Way is Essex* (*TOWIE*) and *Made in Chelsea*, have been created.

In some respects, one of the lasting legacies of a magazine landscape post Diana is the act of emotive emulation. The princess's signs and codes which the media continue to draw upon, have become appropriated by a raft of Disney-fuelled princesses. Jade Goody, Katie Price and others are born out of these 'augmented realities'. Many magazine exclusives have been given, acting as a behavioural homage to a real princess: Diana's approach to motherhood, *her* bulimia, *her* marriage, *her* frailty, *her* depression, love, loss, desires and always hoping for a fairy tale outcome. Since this celebrity is manufactured for commercial gain, it is owned by the magazines and they are the ones who control it.

... always hoping for a fairy tale outcome

This has allowed magazines to satisfy 'our culture's appetite for consuming celebrity'[10] but at the same time distance themselves from the relentless post Diana media guilt felt by both provider and consumer. Class also plays a part in this manufacture and guilt. The commoditised Disney princesses are often from working-class backgrounds, rather than nobility – their stolen holiday shots and invaded privacy are seen as deserved, a by-product of their willingness to gain employment from selling themselves as a product. Whereas Diana, and now by extension Kate, are not. Diana's sapphire ring ever present on Kate's hand, reminds us of her 'honest fame' rather than a manufactured celebrity. This idea of who deserves privacy and who does not has been widely evidenced in the UK media's moral outrage of 2012 French Magazine's *Closer's* long lens pictures of her sunbathing on holiday.

The learned reluctance of UK consumer magazines to absolutely consume 'the Royals' has been substituted with their guilt free practice of boosting circulation through celebrity manufacture. The consumption of Jade Goody's life and death by *OK!* magazine's *pre-death* 'Tribute' issue to her[11] and the resulting funeral – all carry Diana references. But this simulacrum princess from the dust of Bermondsey, with class origins that are all too obvious and pitilessly derided, had a death that was used by many for its commercial value and emotive editorial appeal – in a manner which magazines knew would provide circulation gains in an increasingly competitive, cross-platform, celebrity market.

... consumer magazines have evolved into a silent yet affable go-between in the celebrity gossip interchange

The Diana legacy for celebrity consumption is that no one is a victim – these manufactured celebrities are both complicit and culpable in the princess ruse; after all, they enjoy the monetary benefits. The consumer magazines have evolved into a silent yet affable go-between in the celebrity gossip interchange. The readers are now free from guilt to mock, judge and stalk the lives of these celebrities and the magazines are free from guilt to push boundaries and deliver more shocking exclusives in the wake of saturated markets.

However, with the spectre of post Leveson regulation hovering over these exclusives, have we reached the very limit of celebrity consumption?

NOTES

1.   BBC (1995).
2.   Pope, A. (1745).
3.   Postle, M. (2005).
4.   Yelin, H. (2013).
5.   Postle (2005) p 17.
6.   Anon (1997).
7.   Gough-Yates, A. (2003) p 137.
8.   Curran, J. and Seaton, J. (2010).
9.   Turner, G. (2010) p 15.
10. Ibid.
11. Plunkett, J. (2009).

REFERENCE SOURCES

Anon (1997) 'Princess Diana Her Death was Tragic, Her Life Often Inspiring', *The Memphis Commercial Appeal*, 3 September 1997 (Memphis, TN) [online archive]. Available at http://www.commercialappeal.com/archives/. (Accessed

26 April 2013) cited in Hindman, E. (2003) 'The Princess and the Paparazzi: Blame, Responsibility, and the Media's Role in the Death of Princess Diana', *Journalism and Mass Communication Quarterly* [e-journal] 80(3). (Accessed 7 April 2013.)

BBC (1995) *The Panorama Interview* [online]. Available at http://www.bbc.co.uk/ news/special/politics97/diana/panorama.html. (Accessed 10 March 2013.)

Curran, J. and Seaton, J. (2010) *Power Without Responsibility*, 7th ed., Oxford: Routledge.

Gough-Yates, A. (2003) *Understanding Women's Magazines: Publishing, Markets and Readerships in Late-Twentieth Century Britain*, Oxford: Routledge.

Plunkett, J. (2009) 'Magazine's Jade Goody tribute edition is not OK!', [online] *Guardian*. Available at http://www.guardian.co.uk/media/ organgrinder/2009/mar/17/jade-goody-ok-magazine. (Accessed 2 April 2013.)

Pope, A. (1745) *The Works of Alexander Pope*. Google Scanned Books [online]. Available at https://play.google.com/store/books/ details?id=QwwUAAAAQAAJ&hl=en. (Accessed 22 April 2013.)

Postle, M. (2005) 'The Modern Apelles: Joshua Reynolds and the Creation of Celebrity', in Postle, M., ed., *Joshua Reynolds, the Creation of Celebrity*, London: Tate Publishing.

Turner, G. (2010) *Ordinary People and the Media, the Demotic Turn*, London: Sage.

Yelin, H. (2013) *Gender, Class and 'White Trash' Celebrity*. April 25. [lecture] Oxford: Oxford Brookes University.

CHAPTER 2

Magazine publishing in the UK today

Andrew Scott

The idea behind this chapter is to look at the parameters of the magazine publishing model and describe the pressures on it. It will examine the three main sectors of the industry – consumer, business to business (B2B) and customer publications and how they are responding to challenges from largely digital media. The object is to highlight the opportunities as well as outline these threats. The magazine industry is a large one with a strong entrepreneurial element which is used to competition. This makes the various responses to its current difficulties an especially interesting area of study.

THE BOUNDARIES OF MAGAZINE PUBLISHING

The problem with the magazine industry – especially in the UK – is that it has been just too successful. People admire their favourite titles, they use them to filter the world and, crucially, they are willing to buy products advertised on their pages. Magazines are the cool kids who determine what other kids are wearing this year. Some people are very happy to be defined by the title they read – the *Private Eye* reader; *Cosmo*-woman; *Loaded's* new lad; or the gossip-hungry *Heat* addict. These expressions provide cultural shorthand for groups of people and we all know what they mean. Magazines work hard at telling their audiences that they can represent them and help them navigate the world. People love magazines.

This success resulted in other media looking at the magazine model and attempting to emulate it – the most sincere form of flattery. In fact it has been a two pronged attack – one from a media industry in terminal decline (traditional newspapers) and one from the great emerging world of technology.

The newspaper response

Analysis of ABC shows that newspaper sales in this country have been in decline since 1955. This often repeated fact masks the reality that newspaper circulations were actually very stable from the 1950s to the 1980s. The real decline began in the 1990s and the newspaper industry responded by looking across the fence at their glamorous publishing cousins in the magazine industry and began to copy them. Since the 1990s newspapers have become increasingly magazine-like. This

> The problem with the magazine industry – especially in the UK – is that it has been just too successful

is especially true of the weekend editions. In their own response to competitive 24 hour news reporting available on television and online, newspapers have become more interested in analysis, reviewing and lifestyle – the traditional preoccupations of magazines. These are now the core areas of activity for many of our daily and Sunday newspapers – as their primary function of bringing news to the populace has been rendered largely redundant. Who really needs yesterday's headlines which by the time they appear at the newsagent's door are already being dissected by Sky News, BBC Online or on Twitter? Of course newspapers can still break stories as a result of solid investigative journalism. Prominent recent examples include the *Daily Telegraph* exposing the MPs' expenses scandal in 2009 and the *Guardian* (and other news organisations worldwide) partnering with Wikileaks in 2010 to publish redacted emails from US foreign embassies.

Clearly newspapers can still print stories which can embarrass or topple government ministers and challenge authority. However, these instances where newspapers grab the news agenda are becoming less prevalent. In fact, it can feel like an echo of times past when they do take centre stage and become a must purchase for those looking to be informed on the major story of the day. The famous boast after the 1992 UK election win for the Conservative Party that it was 'the *Sun* Wot Won it', feels all of its 20 plus years of age.

In the face of their primary, defining purpose – delivering the news – being undermined by technological advance, one might naively assume that newspaper companies like News International, Trinity Mirror or Associated Newspapers may simply fade away. This would be incorrect, ignoring as it does two significant factors: the strength and size of these organisations built up over many decades and their shareholders who demand that profitable methods of delivering news are found, loss making operations discarded and dividends continue to flow. These structural facts have meant that newspapers were bound to reinvent themselves and their print reinvention has been largely to migrate to the form of (daily) magazines, be they tabloids or broadsheets. This shift in approach has been accompanied by even more explicit moves to compete with magazine publishers in the form of Saturday and Sunday magazine supplements. These can take the form of a TV listings magazine to rival IPC Media's *What's on TV* or Immediate Media's *Radio Times*; *You* magazine from the *Mail on Sunday*, which competes with women's interest titles across the board; or a general interest magazine from the *Guardian* or *The Times*. The latter is aimed right across its readership and provides another 'info-tainment' fix, thus reducing the need to purchase other titles. Simultaneously they have, of course, developed world-leading news websites.

If one agrees with the notion that magazines have come under attack from newspapers but that newspapers remain a distinct genre, are things as clear cut in the digital domain?

Digital magazines or page-turner?

Many magazines are now available in a digital format which mimics the look of the printed version and appears on screen with its own 'page turning' capability. Exact Editions market this format in the UK and offer a range of consumer titles available for purchase.

Although modest sales are currently associated with this medium, it has become an interesting option especially for specialist consumer publishers to create a low cost digital offer. It enables access to an international audience, without the effort of organising complicated logistics and handling the inherent cash flow difficulties of selling magazines worldwide. Such a literal representation of the traditional magazine reading experience will certainly not be the final word in digital magazine publishing; it is perhaps better understood as an initial attempt to grapple with the demands of digital by magazine publishers. Increasingly sophisticated and interactive digital editions appear weekly. The trick of the page-turning technology does provide a fun element, at least initially, but it remains a little perverse to so confine the digital delivery of editorial content. Why use a digital medium to re-create the functionality of paper? It is very obviously the digital manifestation of the printed magazine – not a stand-alone version.

Of course the page-turner is not the only response of magazine publishers to the digital revolution. The initial race to be online involved an ill-fated land grab, in which publishers rushed to build websites which essentially offered a large percentage of their editorial free of charge. The prevailing business logic was that advertising opportunities would more than offset the loss of print revenues and the low costs of production meant much higher profit margins. It is easy to sympathise with this thinking as the BBC was at the time building its vast web offering, as were national newspapers – this was still many years prior to the pay-wall introduced by News International. There was little or no prospect of the *Guardian* (or the BBC) ever going down the paid for digital model as they simply did not have the same pressure to deliver short-term profitability. So, many publishers launched free websites.

> The initial race to be online involved an ill-fated land grab

The result was an enormous amount of unsold advertisement inventory, as magazine publishers found that advertisers simply will not pay print equivalent amounts to advertise online. Even worse, the entire display advertising model began to look shaky as Google hoovered up a controlling percentage of web revenue via its search function. Users do not interact with banners on a web page in the same way as they do with display advertisements. Magazine publishers realised that it is very difficult for them to differentiate themselves from a plethora of websites on every possible subject, from other types of organisations, or even individuals via blogs. They slowly withdrew from committing significant new resources to the website model.

The Facebook problem

Not even the largest publishing houses have ever seen numbers such as Facebook can deliver. Despite passing the eye watering threshold of one billion users in 2012, the success of Facebook as an advertising model is yet to be definitively proven. Wobbles over its revenues and forecasting have caused share price dips. But who can compete with one billion users on a cost per thousand (CPT/M) basis? Facebook can reach more people in any demographic than any publisher in history has been able to do. At the heart of the online advertising issue is the fact that even this volume of eyeballs does not guarantee long-term stable advertising revenues. The obvious point is that if Facebook is vulnerable then what of everyone else?

Somewhere in between the page-turning copy of the printed magazine and the website offering free access to magazine content, came the digital only magazine. In 2006, Dennis Publishing who had had enormous international success with *Maxim* launched a weekly lads' magazine online called *Monkey*. Although it does feature a page turning element, this was much more a product tailored to a digital format. All the features had a digital element – such as embedded video or hyperlinks. This was not an online reading experience but a new media environment mimicking magazine format and frequency.

Others followed with varied success. The National Magazine Company (now Hearst Magazines UK) floundered with the launch of *Jellyfish* but Dennis continued to flourish in the sector with *imotor* and *Gizmo* launching in 2008. Many other online only titles followed and it is now a regular feature of the publishing scene that established titles are ceasing their print edition and going digital only. *Newsweek* announced the end of its print edition in October 2012 and *Auto Trader* in April 2013.

How established are digital magazines?

... in the last twelve months nearly one in five British adults has read a newspaper or magazine on a tablet, e-reader or app

The conclusions from a new, regular survey of American consumers carried out by the global market research firm Gfk MRI in November 2012 have cast some light on the extent to which people like reading digital magazines. The top line is that almost 90 per cent of people surveyed in the US still access printed magazines; the percentage of readers who have abandoned print altogether in favour of digital magazines is just 11 per cent[1]. Digital readership is clearly growing – in the last twelve months nearly one in five British adults has read a newspaper or magazine on a tablet, e-reader or app[2]. The combination of these two sets of statistics suggests that there is a considerable level of cross platform duplication.

If one is happy to define *Monkey* as a lads' magazine – which I am – or acknowledge that *Brand Republic* is a business to business (B2B) magazine delivered online by Haymarket Publishing (perhaps less clear cut but again no argument here) then are all websites with editorial content actually magazines?

An ex-magazine editor – now a prominent freelance journalist and columnist – was recently reviewing his latest commissions. Looming large among them was a request from Microsoft to review their editorial offer on their MSN home page. This is a widely accessed portal to a myriad of digital services such as Hotmail and Microsoft's search engine Bing. However, when one lands on this home page it is not at all dissimilar to that of a newspaper or a news-led magazine. It is without doubt a magazine format, as it offers access to a very wide range of stories – up to the minute news, TV gossip, sports, weather, finance, travel guides and motoring. The list is long and reflects an attempt to make the MSN home page the default online portal of choice for as many people as possible.

However, it is here that one draws the line between a digital magazine and other digital services. The former has at its core the desire to deliver editorial which draws in a readership, which can be offered up for advertisement revenue, the basis of the classic consumer magazine model pioneered by *The Ladies Home Journal* back in the 1880s, in the USA. It may also have a cost to access this editorial. A service like MSN, while displaying many of the same editorial attributes, is using its content to attract users to its core services of software provision or search. The editorial element does not constitute stand-alone product and it would contradict the business logic to impose a price barrier.

In the same way that it is known what is meant when one refers to newspapers despite their magazine like content, it is also equally clear that major internet service providers like Google, Microsoft, Facebook or Yahoo are not magazine publishers. While they are media owners in a general sense they provide us with another boundary for this inquiry.

SIZE OF THE MARKET

While the magazine market is under attack from some powerful commercial organisations, it is important to be clear that the UK magazine market remains a major media sector and industry in its own right.

Combined research for *Inside Magazine Publishing* estimates the annual value of the magazine industry in 2012 to be £3.55 billion. This is split as follows:

- Consumers spend £1.8 billion on magazines at retail or via subscriptions.
- Print magazine advertising totals a further £750 million.
- Content marketing agencies (the producers of customer magazines). contribute a further £1 billion.
- There are in excess of 2,400 consumer magazines.
- There are over 4,400 B2B magazines.

In addition, B2B publishers have a share of the wider UK business information market – itself worth £3.2 billion a year.

An important industry of this magnitude is not simply going to disappear in the face of increased competition and a higher than average dose of digital disruption. The core magazine business model – and print still remains at its heart in 2013 – is being questioned, and to some degree undermined, but it remains a behemoth with a close connection with its public.

> ... the UK magazine market remains a major media sector and industry in its own right

THE CONSUMER MAGAZINE SECTOR

Can you find 2,400 titles for sale on a newsstand near you? Well, not quite. As is explained in Chapter 6, the mechanics of magazine distribution mean that, in theory, every magazine is available in every newsagent. In reality this is not the case. In fact there are two companies at the heart of consumer publishing in the UK who account for over a third of the total consumer spend on magazines at retail – IPC Media and the combined Bauer interests. They have much in common including sales revenue, market share, overseas ownership, mass market women's and TV listings titles as their core offering as well as a healthy level of competitive spirit towards each other. This is demonstrated in Figure 2.1.

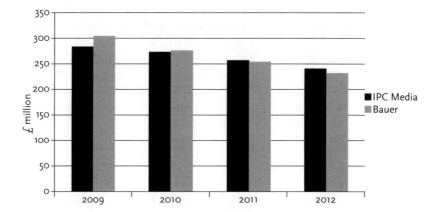

Figure 2.1 UK retail
sales value of IPC
Media and Bauer
(2009–12)

Source: ABC data
(Jan–Dec 2012) and
Marketforce (UK) Ltd

Figure 2.2 shows the market share of a number of principal companies in the UK. This chart includes all circulation sales as reported by ABC, home and overseas – print and digital. Again it reports IPC and Bauer to be the two giants of the business, significantly ahead of Immediate and Hearst UK.

Below IPC Media and Bauer there are many medium to smaller publishers – with 37 per cent of magazine publishers registering total turnover of less than £1 million[3]. Despite this the industry remains heavily centralised with 90 per cent of total circulation coming from within the ranks of the 200 plus members of the PPA.

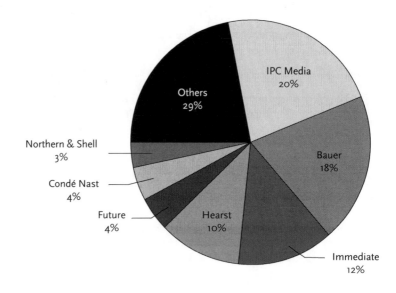

Figure 2.2 Market
share of UK
magazine publishers
(print and digital
sales)

Source: ABC data
(Jan–Dec 2012) and
Marketforce (UK) Ltd

Table 2.1 shows the top 25 selling titles published by UK companies as reported by ABC in their 'actively purchased category'.

Table 2.1 Top 25 UK magazines (actively purchased)

	Magazine	Publisher	Average issue sale
1	TV Choice	H Bauer Publishing	1,230,076
2	What's on TV	IPC Media	1,222,242
3	Radio Times	Immediate Media Company	893,512
4	Take a Break	H Bauer Publishing	749,526
5	Saga Magazine	Saga Publishing	591,223
6	Slimming World Magazine	Miles-Bramwell	447,456
7	Glamour	Condé Nast Publications	424,077
8	Good Housekeeping	Hearst Magazines UK	409,326
9	New!	Northern & Shell Magazines	403,425
10	Closer	Bauer Consumer Media	396,014
11	Chat	IPC Media	348,126
12	Woman & Home	IPC Media	352,586
13	OK! Magazine	Northern & Shell	342,495
14	Woman's Weekly	IPC Media	316,869
15	Cosmopolitan	Hearst Magazines UK	308,482
16	That's Life	H Bauer Publishing	294,467
17	Hello!	Hello!	305,567
18	National Geographic Magazine	National Geographic Society	285,515
19	TV Times	IPC Media	275,526
20	BBC Good Food	Immediate Media Company	274,297
21	Woman	IPC Media	261,170
22	Prima	Hearst Magazines UK	256,053
23	Heat	Bauer Consumer Media	261,715
24	Star	Northern & Shell	252,058
25	Yours	Bauer Consumer Media	272,040

Source: ABC report (Dec 2012)

Six leading consumer publishers

IPC is one of the largest consumer publishers in the UK with over 60 brands. The multinational media company, Bauer Media Group, operates in the UK with two divisions: H Bauer Publishing and Bauer Consumer Media. In addition please see a case study on Future plc in Chapter 3.

IPC Media
Key sectors:
> Women's weeklies, fashion, lifestyle, TV listings, home interest, sport and leisure, men's lifestyle and music, country and equestrian.

Key titles:
> *What's On TV, Now, Chat, Woman, Woman & Home, Marie Claire, Ideal Home, Country Life, Horse & Hound, Nuts, NME* and *nme.com.*
> Key brand extension with *NME Awards.*

Ownership:
> Acquired by Time Warner (US) in 2001.

IPC Media's portfolio will favour circulation over advertising as a revenue base. They have approximately 1,700 employees.

H. Bauer Publishing
Key sectors:
> Women's weeklies, TV listings, puzzle magazines.

Key titles:
> *TV Choice, Take a Break, That's Life, Bella.*
> Key brand extension with *TV Choice Awards.*

Ownership:
> Privately owned Bauer Media Group (Germany).

High circulation weeklies mean dependence upon circulation revenues. H. Bauer Publishing employs 270 staff (plus share of 240 support staff across Bauer companies).

Bauer Consumer Media
Key sectors:
> Women's interest, lifestyle, celebrity; music, film and entertainment; sport and outdoor pursuits.

Key titles:
> *Closer, Heat, Yours, Grazia, Empire, FHM, Q, Mojo, Angling Times.*
> Key brand extension with *Q Awards.*

Ownership:
Privately owned Bauer Media Group (Germany).

Bauer Consumer Media publish over 80 brands. They employ 1,043 staff (plus share of 240 support staff across Bauer companies).

Immediate Media Co

Key sectors:

TV listings, children's, food, motors and special interest.

Key titles:

Radio Times, Gardeners' World, Good Food, Top Gear, CBeebies, Olive, BBC History and *Homes and Antiques.* Specialist titles include *Focus, Perfect Wedding* and *Junior.*

Ownership:

Formed in 2011 by an amalgamation of BBC Magazines, Magicalia and Origin Publishing. With 850 staff Immediate Media publishes 36 websites and 56 magazines.

Hearst Magazines UK

Key sectors:

Women's weeklies, monthlies and lifestyle monthlies; health and fitness; men's lifestyle.

Key titles:

Good Housekeeping, Cosmopolitan, Harper's Bazaar, Best, Red, Elle, Men's Health.

Key digital expansion with *Netdoctor.com, Handbag.com.*

Ownership:

Formerly known as National Magazine Company. Hearst acquired the magazines of Hachette Fillipachi in 2011 and formed Hearst Magazines UK. Original founder was the legendary US publishing tycoon William Randolph Hearst in 1911 (Citizen Kane). Includes a joint venture partnership with US publisher Rodale.

Hearst Magazines UK publishes 20 magazines and 20 digital properties.

Condé Nast Publications UK

Key sectors:

Fashion and lifestyle served by predominantly up-market brands.

Key titles:

Vogue, House and Garden, Tatler, GQ, Vanity Fair, Glamour and *Wired.* Key brand extensions include *GQ Men of the Year, Glamour Women of the Year,* the *Vogue Festival* and the *Tatler Bystander Ball.*

Ownership:

The UK business launched in 1916, with British *Vogue.* Condé Nast Publications UK comes under the aegis of Condé Nast International, a private company, which is a division of Advance Publications Inc.

Condé Nast publishes 12 print titles with accompanying digital platforms.

THE SEEDS OF A PERFECT STORM FOR MAGAZINE PUBLISHING

UK publishing is a major industry that has a defined space in the media universe. It has established a very successful model and these islands have been at the centre of building brands which are the envy of the world. However, magazine publishing is in a state of considerable flux and what follows is an analysis of the factors that have caused this situation.

Technology hits retail sales

> The first visible impact of the birth of the digital age on consumer magazine publishing was ... felt by the technology sector

The first visible impact of the birth of the digital age on consumer magazine publishing was – in a curiously self-referential way – felt by the technology sector. Magazines aimed at young men with a highly developed interest in computers, software and games began to see sales dropping. Despite the rush to offer as many free gifts on the cover as gravity would allow, this market was moving online and the ride could not be halted. The success of these magazines had been key to the growth of innovative companies such as Future plc but the sector was now under pressure and this led to a race to push cover prices as high as possible to compensate for the decline in sales. The magazines also became increasingly expensively designed, with more pages and even better gifts to justify the rocketing cover prices.

Specialist magazines aimed at men are largely price inelastic and it is very rare that a cover price increase will not result in increased revenue for the publisher. Sales may fall a little but not so far as to offset the positive effect of the cover price increase. Thus other sectors watched enviously as technology publishers hit key price points and pushed on to the next one.

This ability to increase revenue from existing customers has kept this sector afloat but has had the effect of increasing the barrier to entry for a new young customer, who is now even more likely to head to the internet rather than pay £6 for a monthly computer magazine. The print readership is now ageing along with these technology titles.

The growth of bookazines since 2010 is another manifestation of this process (see Chapter 6 for more detail). Such products as *Ultimate Guide to Google* from Future retail at £9.99 or *The Cloud Computing Book* from Imagine Publishing selling for £12.99 have continued to boost technology publishers via the route of higher prices. Where the technology sector goes – other magazines will follow.

In 2003 the current publisher of *The Oldie*, James Pembroke, launched a new magazine called *Broadband World* to showcase the delights of faster internet access to an astonished audience. Is it coincidence that a year later retail magazine sales in the UK peaked and have been in decline since? As Chapter 6 shows, analysis reveals that publishers who are dependent upon sales at newsagents have had a difficult time in the last five years.

Other magazine sectors have been affected by new technology available on computer and tablet. However, the rise of the celebrity magazine and the march of the men's weekly lifestyle sector disguised this underlying decline for a long period, when looking at the overall market.

Technology wins the fight for kids' attention

In 2011 the UK computer games market was worth £3.26 billion[4]. The average time a child in the UK spends on computer games has risen to 8.5 hours per week, which includes a solid 12 days of screen time clocked up during school holidays[5]. The laptop has now replaced the TV as the UK's favourite piece of technology[6]. Meanwhile access to multi-channel TV is 93 per cent[7] and, as analogue transmission is switched off, will only expand to saturation point.

Just like the shelves of magazine retailers, leisure time is not infinitely flexible. As the hours devoted to digital activities increase, so other pastimes decrease, magazine reading being one. In addition readers are growing older. Research in the US, by Mediamark, shows that the median age of magazine readers rose by 3.1 years in the 2000s to 45.1 years.

The annual Pew Internet survey (2012), which charts the impact of the internet on young people, has very positive things to say about the effect this will have on society but also warns of the dangers of the 'always on' environment. It concludes that attention spans are shortening due to high levels of exposure to instant forms of information. This has implications for the longer article formats which feature heavily in magazines. Of course editors are highly sensitive to these changes and are adept at organising their content accordingly but the magazine format was not designed to offer only bite size chunks of information.

A triple technology effect is developing:

- growth of screen based entertainment – consoles, TV, internet
- always available information
- decline of attention span.

These factors are having a disproportionate effect on the young and a generational gap is forming, with magazines on the wrong side of a long-term trend. Context is required here before one turns out the lights on the industry. This analysis is of the current challenges to the industry and where it might be heading but in 2012 print magazines are still reaching 71 percent of the UK population. In addition to this, related websites and portals were used by a further 25 per cent, making combined unduplicated monthly reach of magazine media a high 77 per cent of the nation[8]. This is still a marginally higher percentage than adults in the UK who have access to broadband[9]. In addition, despite the threat of digital to the younger element of the magazine audience, according to the PPA the medium still delivers a younger, more upmarket audience than TV or newspapers.

The industry has successfully maintained its exclusion from value added tax and remains an attractive sector for retailers, as shoppers enjoy browsing the category. Perhaps the long-term trend will simply mean that magazines will change; people will interact a little less with them but they will continue to fight their corner versus any technology that comes along. But will magazines continue to attract the young audience they need?

Just like the shelves of magazine retailers, leisure time is not infinitely flexible

Free magazines – challenges yet opportunities

Perhaps the biggest threat to the traditional consumer publishers is not from technology per se but from free content, however it is delivered. Peter Preston outlined this in *The Observer* on 30 September 2012 when *Time Out* moved to free distribution.

> Here are 300,000 copies of an expensive old favourite turned free (*Time Out*). They sit alongside 431,000 free copies of *Stylist* magazine, 529,000 copies of *Shortlist* and 300,000 of *Sport*. That's 1.56 million of something or other each week that costs you nothing. Add them to 780,000 copies of *Metro* every weekday, plus 130,000 copies of burgeoning *City AM*. You're never alone – on a bus, tube or train – without anything to read. And you're never required to stump up a penny.

There is a strong argument here that magazine publishers themselves are in fact as big a challenge to the established consumer cover price model as any other. But is this trend simply just the next evolution of the consumer magazine – free – and therefore not a threat but an opportunity? Putting aside what the impact would be to retailers, wholesalers and distributors if all consumer magazines dropped their cover price – is the free model sustainable for IPC, Bauer et al?

This is a key question for the industry, made even more urgent by the growth of the customer magazines sector which again delivers high quality, glossy editorial to an apparitional audience free of charge. Perhaps the *Time Out* model of pared down pagination, massive increase in print order (and consequently readership) and the removal of cover price revenue will result in more advertisement revenue. According to their management, the changes have been financially neutral with increased paper and print numbers offset by reductions in pagination and editorial costs. Therefore any increase in ad revenue will be a positive change for a publication that had seen its newsstand sales slide to circa 10,000, this from over 90,000 at the start of the millennium[10]. The result of this change is awaited but the scale of sales decline *Time Out* suffered in the 2000s meant that the status quo was not an option for them. As newsstand sales fell through that 10,000 mark, this revenue stream became less something to protect and more something in need of replacement. Can we therefore conclude that *Time Out* was forced into the move to go free, despite the increase in annual subscriptions which partly offset the newsstand decline? It seems likely that this was an example of needs must; a calculated roll of the dice in tough circumstances rather than a strategic decision taken from a position of relative strength.

In fact, data from a Price Waterhouse Cooper's study (Figure 2.3) shows that revenue from circulation continues to dwarf that from advertising, making it by far the most important revenue stream for publishers.

It would be impossible for consumer magazine publishers to survive in their current incarnation if cover price revenues were to disappear. It is essential that publishers protect these revenues in an environment of falling volume sales. It means continued pressure on cover prices to increase, pressure on the retail supply chain to deliver increased margins and greater emphasis on subscription marketing. The *Time Out* solution – the nuclear option – will be a very difficult sell to the mainstream consumer publishers but it is clearly an innovative solution for some.

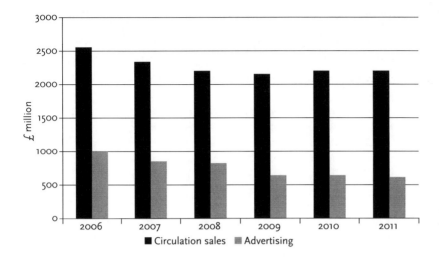

Figure 2.3 UK consumer magazines – revenue share split

Source: PWC

Case study 1

Street life

Free titles have transformed the reading habits of metropolitan areas since 2005, none more so than in London.

First up was *Sport* in 2005. Distributed on Friday before the sporting weekend, this launch was soon followed by men's interest *Shortlist* in the autumn of 2007, women's magazine *Stylist* two years later in 2009 and *Time Out* in 2012.

It was the launch of *Shortlist* that step changed the perceptions of readers and advertisers towards free mass media. Co-founded by Mike Soutar, already a highly experienced editor and publisher in men's publishing, *Shortlist* was created as a free title that men would be happy to be seen reading on the bus or tube with the emphasis on quality. Indeed at a PPA conference he coined the word *free-mium* to sum up his concept. He recalls:

> We were fascinated by the free business model. If you rule out circulation revenue then of course distribution becomes a cost – and a not inconsequential one. But we knew that marketing men's magazines carried high promotional costs, both consumer and trade marketing, so by taking out those expenses we could invest in quality of editorial. By developing the brand, by creating a magazine that the reader would seek out, we also believed that we could achieve a targeted distribution of a very high percentage of our print order, unlike competitors on the newsstand. Yes our print, paper and distribution costs are high but they are in our control and efficiently managed.

Talking to *The Times* when *Time Out* moved to free from a £3.25 cover price, Editor in Chief Tim Arthur also stressed the need for quality in the free market. 'People don't see free as meaning worthless any more, as long as we can produce a product that isn't dumbed down and still has distinctive editorial voice.'

For these metropolitan free titles, distribution numbers have to be measured in hundreds of thousands. Mike Soutar has no doubt:

> We did expect some advertisers to be somewhat sceptical about the ability to distribute all of our copies to the chosen target market – at least initially. So the decision to invest in scale persuaded even the most stubborn Doubting Thomas. You really have to generate numbers that put advertisers and their agencies in the position that they just cannot ignore you. Size matters.

Mass circulation free publishing is not for the risk adverse; probably a key factor is keeping the major consumer publishers from entering that market. Its model is clearly dependent upon the advertisement revenue stream and the incumbents research and work hard to extend their products into digital – *Time Out* already had an extensive new media presence before the switch to free.

Efficiency of distribution is a core competence within this business model. Distribution quantities to stations and other points are plotted with military efficiency and passenger flows examined to achieve minimum waste levels. The distribution model works because the publisher can hand out to hoards of people in a short time. Bulk distribution has to take place in the small hours to avoid traffic jams and every morning, rain or shine, a mini army of cheerful distributors have to be mobilised. All the titles are available for pick up in fixed display units in gyms, hotels and office receptions which are merchandised using the services of placement agencies. *Shortlist* and *Stylist* have significant distributions outside London which have to be coordinated. Litter and environmental considerations are paramount with ever watchful local authority environmental officers monitoring the process. Moreover, to give agencies the certainty they need when investing their client's advertising pounds, accurate auditing by ABC is an absolute must.

All four titles launched or changed their model in a recessionary advertisement climate and deserve credit for their entrepreneurship, boldness and job creation.

Therefore one sees a picture in which free magazines are challenging the position of paid-for titles and bringing a younger demographic of readers to the print market. Will they themselves survive and prosper? Probably yes. In the spring of 2013 *Stylist* mounted a successful launch in the French market. Perhaps the sector will deliver long-term profits and present itself as a major opportunity by bucking the downward trend of print advertising revenues?

It's not just the internet which is grabbing share

The penetration of multi-channel TV in UK households is significant – 93 per cent and rising – but it is not a just a quantitative fact that more TV channels are

Photo 2.1
Distribution of *Stylist* magazine in Paris

available. In a mirror image of newspapers, TV companies have many more hours of airtime to fill. They can, therefore, find a home for much more specialist content than was previously the case. A sports fan can watch football matches from all over Europe and beyond, often live, and so no longer has to rely on the excellent title *World Soccer* to analyse the Bundesliga in Germany or Serie A in Italy.

In a generation, TV channels have mushroomed from four to many hundreds on the Sky platform. Daytime TV covers similar ground to the women's weeklies; free TV listings are provided on the home screen pages of Sky and Virgin. Magazine brand extensions such as *National Geographic* and *Kerrang TV* are there to be watched.

All of these extra TV channels are funded by grabbing some of the advertisement revenue cake – they are not alone in this. Radio has undergone a major change to its own digital format with the accompanying growth of specialist commercial channels. When one adds the emergence of ambient media (ads on beer-mats, bus tickets and above gents' urinals to give a few glamorous examples) one sees a media landscape with a huge increase in the number of media owners.

Advertising

Figure 2.4 shows magazine advertising was less than half its 2001 value in 2012 at current prices. It also demonstrates a radical shift of share to digital, which now outperforms TV. The fragmentation of advertising revenues means that it has been impossible for the magazine sector to avoid decline. From 2007 to 2012 magazine ad revenue fell from £1,494 million to £736 million – a fall of 50 per

> The fragmentation of advertising revenues means that it has been impossible for the magazine sector to avoid decline

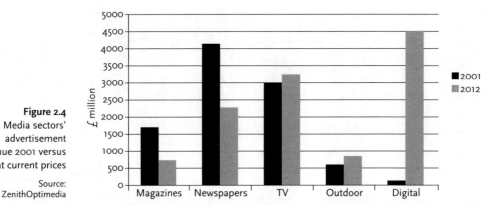

Figure 2.4
Media sectors'
advertisement
revenue 2001 versus
2012 at current prices

Source:
ZenithOptimedia

cent in six years[11]. However, the smaller positive movements in TV and outdoor bear out the argument that the proliferation of new media companies and marketing opportunities in these areas are all having a detrimental effect on print versions of both newspapers and magazines.

At the beginning of the 2000s print was the medium for classified advertisers. Recruitment advertising in particular was the backbone of certain newspaper and magazine revenues. B2B publishing thrived on the back of that revenue and was a key reason why a title was a must for industry insiders. Getting that first job, finding a promotion, comparing salaries – the recruitment section was essential reading. In 2002 online had less than two per cent of the total advertisement market (Figure 2.4).

As the decade progressed, the shift to internet job boards – and big employers simply using their own websites to advertise positions (BBC, government, local councils etc) – meant a new business model for B2B publishers (see below – the B2B story). Other key classified sections also moved online. Ebay became the place to buy and sell privately; *Auto Trader* has now moved the focus of its business completely online and become dominant in the motoring market, auction sites have appeared as have services like webuyanycar.com, backed by massive advertising campaigns. In addition, social media sites have become significant players in the recruitment market.

By 2012, print's share of classified revenue had fallen to only 25 per cent, according to industry estimates and is forecasted to fall further.

The extrapolation of the magazine market ad revenue tells a story of collapse within the B2B sector, particularly hastened by the post 2008 recession. This is shown in Figure 2.5. From a consumer perspective the peak of 2005 is identifiable, as is the impact of the banking crisis. Around this is a story of resilience in the face of massively increased competition.

Advertising is traditionally the first expenditure item to be cut when a recession hits a company and this was certainly felt immediately by magazines in 2008. The problem has been trying to ascertain how much of the fall is likely to come back as the UK economy begins to recover. It is tempting, though far from comforting, to conclude that the structural shifts identified throughout this chapter are the substance behind the enormous cloud of smoke, kicked up by the collapse of the banks. A long recession is likely to span a period of further decline

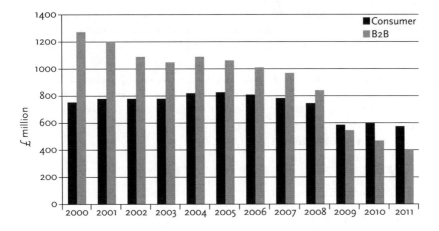

Figure 2.5
Consumer and
B2B advertisement
revenue (2000–11)

Source: PPA

in print, alongside digital expansion. Even if there is a return to economic growth, could it kick start a return to previous advertisement revenue levels? It is doubtful.

Launches – or lack of them

The shrinking of the industry is far from unique but the magazine market has traditionally been reliant on launches to rejuvenate itself. Lack of risks being taken by the large publishers, coupled with the decline of bank lending and venture capitalist activity, has led to a dearth of launches.

Figure 2.6 tracks the number of consumer launches and closures or 'births and deaths' from 2007 to 2012. The industry has always had a high birth rate with many specialist titles coming to market each year. The 'net' launch rate is the difference between the two columns – for the last two years under review it is a mere 50 and 18 titles per year. Moreover, the number of major launches, those with launch distribution of over 100,000 copies, has been running at much lower levels over this period. In fact, looking back to 2004, there have been only six mega-launches, those making available over one million copies for the first issue[12].

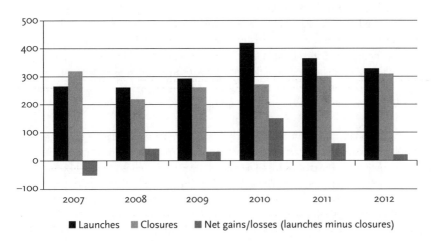

Figure 2.6 Number
of regular frequency
consumer magazine
launches and
closures (2007–12)

This presents a problem for the long term. If there are very few major launches then how does the industry generate any growth? All magazines are in the end victims of the sweep of social change as outlined in Chapter 1, so new titles are needed to come to the fore. They need the backing of major publishers but if mass market titles are not being launched, the structural decline of the consumer/newsstand model of magazine publishing will be accelerated.

Many traditional magazine publishers look back to the heady launch period of the 1990s with nostalgia – after all as we have seen in Chapter 1, 1994 saw the launch of the iconic *Loaded*.

Case study 2

The launch of *Loaded*

Loaded was the most important magazine launch since *Cosmopolitan* in the 1970s. It defined a generation and spawned a huge men's magazine sector.

During a job interview in 1993 to be the next editor of the *New Musical Express*, IPC Media's iconic music weekly, James Brown was asked if he wanted to launch a magazine. Unsurprisingly he said that he would and produced a template for men's lifestyle magazines worldwide. That the template was a one-pager which detailed James's youthful obsessions – football, nightclubs, music, travel – seems in keeping with the magazine that followed. *Loaded*.

Taking its name from a Primal Scream tune, *Loaded* was in development for a year. James recruited a staff of like minded individuals and tried to live up to mission statements to create 'generational tension' and to feature people who 'were knackered and past it with a great story to tell' or who were up and coming.

NME's editor, Alan Lewis, oversaw the project for IPC and is credited with having the foresight to see that the magazine would be a success and ensuring the IPC management would agree. This included downplaying some negative research, while accentuating the positive results, to ensure that the magazine got to the starting gate. Alan's reputation as a safe pair of hands gave IPC the confidence to back his hunch.

IPC felt that the title was low risk because the Music and Sport Division's advertisement sales team already existed and the launch was not heavily promoted. Substantial retail space however was purchased – again before the hike in such costs – and this was how IPC flexed their publishing muscle. Such was enough to push *Loaded* in front of its target audience of young men. It was on its way. Launching in January 1994, *Loaded* had a launch print order of 70,000 and sold 63,000 – a technical sell out (it is impossible, for distribution reasons, to sell all the copies of a magazine run). James Brown recalls:

> I landed at Heathrow on launch day and immediately headed in to the WH Smith store. Absolutely no sign of the mag anywhere. I had a sick feeling in my stomach as I searched the shelves and walked out of the shop in despair. Then I saw it. Right at the front of the store, a huge display of 12 *Loaded* covers and a neon logo ... IPC had bought the biggest unit in the shop.

for men who should know better

lOaded

MAY 1994

FIRST ISSUE! SPECIAL PRICE 95p NORMAL PRICE £2

withnail
you terrible cult

air strikers
sampdoria go to war

room servicing
why hotel sex is the best

aaaaaaaarrrrrgh!
skydiving for beginners

beavis and butt-head
they suck but they're cool

super lads !

gary oldman,
paul weller and eric cantona play to win

lee sharpe vic reeves chris donald elizabeth hurley dr mick

Photo 2.2 The launch issue of *Loaded* in January 1994 was a sell out

Famously the front cover of the launch issue featured Gary Oldman.

The combination of complete editorial freedom given to a team of people plugged into the zeitgeist and the deep pockets of IPC was the key to *Loaded*'s success. Despite the positive start, IPC remained relatively cautious about the magazine and kept a close eye on costs, including those of its largely youthful staff. The original business plan was to pay back the initial investment in three years but newsstand sales were so buoyant, this plan was revised upwards within a few months.

As the title became established, advertisement revenue began to make a real contribution and brands like Estée Lauder were able to target young men for the first time, in an environment in which they could prosper. Sales moved inexorably towards 500,000 per issue. The magazine ballooned to 400 pages.

After three years James Brown left the magazine, lured by a big salary to *GQ*. But *Loaded* had broken the mould and proved that men would read magazines if the product was good enough. Fuelled with an ambition to out-gonzo *Rolling Stone, Loaded* was a pioneer. The legacy of lads' magazines like *Nuts* and *Zoo*, featuring semi-naked D-list celebs and outrageous facts, do scant justice to the original *Loaded*, which under Brown's reign featured men on the cover of 27 of his 36 issues and eight page features on spaghetti westerns. And by accident created a hugely important new magazine genre.

Changes in the retail environment

Back in 2000 WH Smith was the big beast in the magazine retail jungle. The combined market share of its high street shops and travel outlets meant Smiths was the first port of call for publishers to discuss new launches and exclusive promotions. Publishers regarded Smiths as the destination for launch issues after which sales would often then migrate into other outlets. WH Smith was the magazine seller on Britain's high streets and a crucial element in the dominance of newsstand sales over subscriptions in the UK was their commitment to a wide range of titles on their shelves.

In 2004 and 2005 – in so many ways the tipping point for the magazine industry – another milestone occurred. Tesco became the single largest magazine retailer. The positive impact of the supermarkets on the supply chain is detailed in Chapter 6 but culturally this meant that more magazines were being purchased as part of a weekly shopping trip, not as part of a daily browse of the shelves at a newsagent.

There is no doubt that supermarkets have become essential to maintaining magazine sales volumes. Shoppers have changed the way they shop and so magazines have had to adapt – but that change has not led to increased sales overall as independent retailers close or convert to convenience stores and high streets stagnate.

The year 2011 saw 40 per cent of newsstand sales made in food retailers[13], a sector that does not see news products as core and has to manage range tightly in all but the largest of outlets. It also seeks to increase margins from publishers in the guise of increased promotional charges. While still being committed to an extensive range of magazines, WH Smith now also place financial hurdles upon publishers in the form of annual retail spend or promotional commitments.

Larger publishers will point to the overcrowded magazine market as part of the problem on the UK newsstands. With some 2,500 consumer titles competing for space, they believe that this pressure on shelf space simply inhibits the sales of larger and more popular titles. As such there are mixed opinions regarding retail consolidation between mass consumer and specialist businesses.

Smartphones … or more technology

Another unique selling point of the printed magazine is portability. The laptop gives you free access to information and entertainment but not readily on a crowded bus, tube (no signal) or commuter train. It may be a common sight to see people plugged in to their laptops in corporate coffee bars but they are yet to be seen stacked up next to the loo. The great advantage of the magazine is that it can be purchased and consumed on the move. Initial threats from mobile technology to this position looked doomed to failure as mobile operators struggled to convince consumers to access the internet on their phones. When Gordon Brown sold the 3G licences for £22.5 billion in 2000 to Vodafone and Orange (at the height of the technology bubble) it was seen as a great coup for the government as there appeared to be a very limited appetite for broadband mobile services. It was not helped by very patchy nationwide coverage. However, the arrival of the smartphones, from Blackberry and Apple in particular changed the game. With the number of devices capable of accessing the internet already outnumbering the entire human race, it is estimated that by 2015 the smartphone alone will reach 75 per cent penetration in the UK[14]. The smartphone is only outstripped by the iPad as the most wanted item when a house is burgled[15]. What could be a better measure of consumer desire? It is more coveted than cash or jewellery.

Unlike the tablet, the smartphone is not ideally conducive to magazine content. The format is too small to read for long periods and unable to showcase photographs at their best. Is it becoming a rival to magazines rather than a device which magazine publishers can take advantage of? These devices are time hungry. Smartphones can be used in transit so people are plugged into Facebook and Twitter when only three years ago that option was denied. Yet more possible magazine reading time is lost with another small win for technology.

Opportunity (finally) knocks

The first ten years of the new millennium felt like the beginning of the end for consumer publishing. It was going to be a matter of organising and surviving as well as one could but acknowledging that the key function will be managing decline. A long road, as the industry was well funded after some fantastic years, but decline nevertheless. That may well have turned out to be the case but in 2011 Apple launched Newsstand.

The Newsstand app gives consumer magazine publishers hope that finally a platform has arrived for which digital consumers will be willing to pay. The crucial element is that Apple is at the heart of it. They had proved themselves capable of selling music downloads in a world where 'free' has as big a hold on the market as it does in news. The Apple brand is coveted and trusted with products people want to use, even if they are more expensive than competitors. This coincided with the growth of tablets as the new exciting technology. Smartphones have not been particularly kind to magazine publishers but tablets promise a much fuller reader experience which can play to their strengths. As Chapter 8 shows, the rush to provide apps is on. Perhaps the cover price will be lower but there is a positive revenue stream and if tablet usage continues at its current pace of penetration then the circulation pricing model may have a major new lease of life.

> The first ten years of the new millennium felt like the beginning of the end for consumer publishing

THE BUSINESS TO BUSINESS STORY

If consumer publishers have spent the last decade preparing for and weathering this perfect storm, how have the major sectors of B2B fared?

B2B industry structure

Analysis of the current state of play in the B2B sector finds the industry split into two camps, although the large companies may straddle both. These are traditional brands and data information businesses.

Five leading B2B companies

Reed Business Information (RBI)

Part of Reed Elsevier stable since 1970s. Diversified from business magazines publisher to business information provider.

Employees: 1500 in the UK.

RBI trade in 13 sectors including aerospace, agriculture, chemicals, finance, HR, property, science and social care. Also owns *ICIS* petrochemical information provider and *Estates Gazette Interactive*: the leading commercial property website.

Key print titles *are Farmer's Weekly* and *New Scientist*.

Incisive Media

From the launch of its first title, *Investment Week*, in 1995, Incisive Media has been one of the fastest growing companies in the B2B sector. The company merged with Timothy Benn Publishing in 1998. In its first five years Incisive spent close to £90 million acquiring businesses. For a short period the company was owned by Apax Venture Capital before re-financing as a stand-alone business in 2009. It employs 600 employees worldwide.

Incisive Media publishes 100 brands in 16 markets with a focus on finance, insurance, technology and energy. Its 20 UK magazines include *Investment Week*, *Legal Week* and the *British Journal of Photography*.

Centaur Media

Centaur is a leading UK-based business media and events group. Its principal focus is on digital solutions, supported by print titles. Major brands include *Marketing Week, Creative Review, The Lawyer, Money Marketing, Homebuilding & Renovating, Employee Benefits* and *The Engineer*. *Perfect Information* is Centaur's principal move into business information, aimed at those monitoring globally quoted companies.

EMAP

Key sectors are retail, fashion retail, architecture, built environment, media, environment and public sectors. They operate in print, online and events.

Key brands are *Nursing Times, Retail Week, Construction News* and *Drapers*.

UBM

UBM is a global live media and B2B communications, marketing service and data provider. The company employs 5,500 staff. UBM operates in three main business segments: events, marketing services and *PR Newswire*. UBM has eleven businesses operating across these markets in different parts of the world. They are organised by region or function.

Traditional brands

On one side there are the traditional business media brands which have at their core a strong magazine. Even though it has long been a key aspect of the B2B business model that diverse sources of revenue are essential, this model is still predicated on a publishing venture. It has to deliver an audience with a level of brand loyalty which can be monetised by selling ads, organising events and allowing access to continuously updated databases of current industry professionals.

A good example is the weekly title *The Lawyer,* published in print by Centaur Media. In addition, a digest is published monthly at thelawyer.com. Registered users can sign up for email alerts to receive up-to-the-minute news, job advertisements, opinions and event information. A key revenue driver is to ensure the readership is regularly booking places on a myriad of training events run by Centaur. The nature of the target market means continual professional development is part of the job, so Centaur organises many short 'webinars' at a modest cost, which appeal across the range of legal services. It is also very important that this business is a truly global one with news, events and job opportunities across the continents. An annual subscription to the print edition costs £108 so sales revenue flows in, added to by recruitment advertising and regular events revenue.

Figure 2.7 shows revenue split within the B2B sector by source. It clearly demonstrates the growing importance of data services and live events.

Data information businesses

The main B2B publishers are aware that the traditional model is subject to all the prevailing factors of our age and growth is unlikely – with recruitment revenue migrating online, economic recession depressing sales and training revenue and online remaining difficult to monetise. The dramatic effect of the 2008 recession

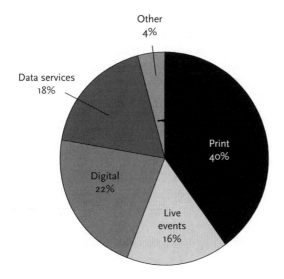

Figure 2.7
B2B revenue split by source

Source: Adapted from PPA Futures survey (2013)

... a concerted move to a new model, one which cuts the cord between publishing and advertising

as shown in Figure 2.5 accelerated an already negative trend. It is little surprise therefore that there is a concerted move to a new model, one which cuts the cord between publishing and advertising. This is the development of data businesses or directories. Below is RBI's description of its highly successful brand ICIS.

> ICIS is the world's largest petrochemical market information provider, with fast growing energy and fertilizer divisions. Their aim is to give companies in global commodities markets a competitive advantage by delivering trusted pricing data, high value news, analysis and independent consulting; enabling their customers to make better informed trading and planning decisions. With a global staff of more than 550, ICIS has experts based in London, Houston, Washington, New York, Milan, Montpelier, Dusseldorf, Mumbai, Singapore, Guangzhou, Beijing, Shanghai and Perth. The team covers over 120 commodity markets and has in depth knowledge across these markets in both upstream and downstream sectors worldwide.

ICIS is delivering information to business people on new media platforms. This is highly timely, online, business critical information to which any serious player in the petrochemical industry will have to subscribe. The key aim for RBI is to make their information a key part of the work flow of executives in the sector. This is aiming at a deeper level of connection with a business; the resources RBI are investing to deliver this information are worldwide and rely on specialists who are ahead of the sector they are serving, not merely reporting on it.

News is not a major part of this online model. The logical conclusion of the free to consumer delivery of news, which has become the norm online, is that news may no longer have a monetary value so why bother trying to sell it? Instead the focus of B2B publishers is to become the key data provider to an industry where customers will pay very high subscription rates for a service which provides absolutely essential information. ICIS was a strategically insightful acquisition made by RBI In 1994 and was synergistic to its successful chemical magazines division. They still publish, for subscription purchase, a legacy weekly print magazine in this sector with a clear focus on news. Rather quaint.

Figure 2.7 shows the PPA's estimate of B2B revenue split by its sources. At 40 per cent, print is still the largest contributor to the sector but digital is catching up and data services and live events are making a healthy contribution.

According to the PPA, the UK is now third in the world in this emerging business information market, behind the US and Germany, who have dominant shares driven by their vast domestic markets. This contrasts with fifth place in the traditional B2B sector. This business model is growing. It is considered the most robust response thus far to the challenges the industry face because it feeds on the weakness of search engines – the fact that they do not generate what is required by the customer with enough precision, often enough or quickly enough. Two factors are key for success. First, the brand must have established trust and therefore the ability to charge premium prices for data. Second, the companies themselves must also have sufficient investment funds. Sadly, this avenue for expansion may only be open to a highly specialised group of international businesses.

Micro publishing

As the large B2B publishers move away from the advertising model, they are selling magazine brands to new B2B start-ups. UBM has sold *Music Week* to Intent Media and *Farmers Guardian* to Briefing Media while rival RBI has sold its road transport division to Road Transport Media. These magazine brands may have been unable to make a sufficient contribution to the overheads of UBM or RBI but they are providing a profitable core to a smaller organisation and are breathing new life into traditional B2B publishing.

Print survival techniques

With over 4,000 printed B2B titles there is still a good business case for print editions. Stand-alone print titles are no longer in play and everyone acknowledges the need for a multi-platform strategy, but the details do vary. *Marketing Week*, from Centaur, is a long established title which, like many, was dependent on recruitment revenue. When this migrated online a new idea was required. Now the key revenue driver is *Marketing Week Live*, an annual event which attracts 13,000 plus marketers to visit 500 stands. The average ratecard cost for a stand at this exhibition is in excess of £10,000. This event is one of the main reasons for the continued existence of the printed version, which is used to drive attendance.

Cover prices

When faced with the dilemma of the declining profitability of the *British Journal of Photography (BJP)*, Incisive Media decided that they would focus on the high quality nature of the title's photography and invest in better paper stock to showcase it. At the same time the cover price was increased from £1.75 to £6.99. The BJP has a diverse readership of professional photographers and serious amateurs so will never be a business critical purchase, instead they have made the title more attractive to as wide an audience as possible. At the other end of the scale at Incisive, *Risk* magazine, covering the risk management sector of the finance industry, has moved to a series of annual subscription packages which begin at £1,000.

Transition

The B2B magazine market is very mature and even if the number of titles has fallen from a high of 5,000 plus to its current level of circa 4,400, there is a practical difficulty intrinsic in moving to an online or events model. Moving a title online is a time consuming, resource hungry activity. A large, multinational publisher with many brands could take many years before they all move to online only, even if they wanted to. It is also true that a digital title devoid of a print publication can be seen as just another website or app. It is still important for brands to differentiate themselves from the online competition by having print editions. This gives credibility and develops the legacy.

The main distribution model used by B2B is to send a free copy of a magazine to a specific list of employed individuals. (See controlled circulation in

Chapter 6.) This is expensive and depends heavily on postage, which is a rising cost. The obvious advantage of not having to send out a printed copy (or print a copy at all) is not lost on B2B businesses who have more opportunity to charge for specialist content than their consumer neighbours. It is an industry based on expert knowledge, specialist reporting, with respected industry figures editing trusted tiles – this package has translated better to a paywall model than has news and entertainment, the core of consumer publishing. Incisive Media cite *Legal Week*, simultaneously running a free print version and a paid for online version, as a model that has succeeded.

Haymarket traditionally published both *Campaign*, bible of the advertising industry, and *Marketing*. Both of these were dependent on recruitment advertising, a familiar story. In deciding on an online strategy they did not do the obvious and create a site for each title but instead created *Brand Republic* which was an amalgamation of both, thus offering a wider range of vacancies and giving Haymarket a better online platform to fight the new job boards. Similarly RBI decided to set up its own job board – *totaljobs.com* – not an offshoot of any magazine brand. With a wide range of recruitment ads from across its extensive portfolio it was able to launch a credible general job board of its own. They have since sold this business as they move away from advertising reliant models.

FROM CONTRACT PUBLISHING TO CONTENT MARKETING

The free model for business to consumer publishers is not a new phenomenon. British Airways *High Life* appears to carry the title of the first customer magazine launched in 1973 by Premier Magazines (now Cedar). Contract publishing boomed in the 1980s, with a vast array of companies providing printed marketing solutions (magazines) for corporate clients. By 2000 customer magazines were sitting atop the ABC rankings with *AA Magazine* reporting sales of 4.4 million, followed by *Sky*, *Boots* and *Safeway* before a traditional consumer title – IPC's *What's on TV* – made an appearance. As part of an annual membership fee *AA Magazine* and *Sky* sold themselves as paid for titles but were in reality sent free to subscribers of other services.

These magazines were high quality and often had editorial budgets which the mainstream consumer sectors could only envy. Their primary function was to enhance the brand and so they were not always tasked with making a profit. This meant they could deliver famous name contributors and high-end production values to the consumer in an effort to maximise interaction with the reader. The UK consumer became used to being given entertaining magazines free of charge.

In 2011 Sky closed their customer magazine amid cost-cutting measures, as they found the print and distribution costs prohibitive; in 2012 *AA Magazine* went digital only, under the same pressures. The largest magazines in the sector are now published on behalf of supermarkets who have the distribution channel to promote their message cost effectively in a print format.

Six leading content marketing companies

Cedar
Founded in 1992, it has 92 staff and a turnover of £19.2 million per year. Described as a creative and commercial content agency, Cedar's client list includes British Airways, Best Western, The Dorchester and Tesco. With British Airways *High Life* they have the honour of publishing one of the first and probably most famous customer publications.

John Brown
One of the largest content marketing companies working in the UK, with a turnover of £40 million per year. Founded in 1987 by the publishing entrepreneur of that name, the company now employs 220 staff. It boasts a varied client list including bookmaker Paddy Power, medical and charity foundations such as BUPA, Cancer Research and Great Ormond Street, and retailers John Lewis and Waitrose.

Publicis Blueprint
This branded content agency is part of the large, worldwide Publicis advertising and media agency network. Founded in 1999, the agency boasts a turnover in excess of £40 million per year and a staff of 110. It produces one of the UK's largest distributed magazines for supermarket giant Asda and also has retailer Cath Kidston and Heathrow Airport as clients.

Redactive Media Group
This group specialises in creating publishing and digital communications solutions for membership and professional services organisations. Founded in 1981 it has a turnover of £18 million per year and employs 130 staff.

Redwood
One of the oldest content marketing businesses in the UK, having been founded in 1983. Redwood's staff number 192 and turnover is £33 million per year. The client list has a strong representation from car marques and includes Fiat, Volvo and Mazda as well as Marks and Spencer, Barclays, Argos and Boots.

Seven
Founded in 2007, it has developed into a business employing 160 people with a turnover of £24 million. It produces *Sainsbury's Magazine*, a regular frequency publication with a first half 2012 ABC of 244,497, as well as undertaking work for the *Guardian*, the RAC, Lloyds Bank, Aviva, English Heritage and New Look.

Note: client portfolios as in 2013.

The withdrawal of these two titles from the market in print questions the long-term viability of the free printed publishing model, even as marketing vehicles. In the end, unless costs can be covered, then the client will decide that money is too tight to continue, business priorities will change and new ideas will replace old ones.

This is a sector constantly reinventing itself, redefining its service offer and trying to stay ahead of the curve. Perhaps because of its comparative youthfulness, it appears to have been more responsive to both the digital switch and the economic downturn than many consumer or B2B publishers. The culture of these companies is more closely allied to that of an advertising agency, rather than a publishing house, which means more entrepreneurial, more sales focussed and better at pitching and winning new business.

The name changes of the sector are instructive. Initially known as contract publishing, the focus was on producing a magazine for a major consumer brand. This evolved into customer publishing, the emphasis shifting away from the client relationship to reflect increased use of new sources of consumer data. Simultaneously (and adding to the confusion) the Association of Publishing Agencies (APA) was formed, strengthening the perception that the offer is more closely allied to that of an advertising agency with its connotation of a broad range of marketing services, not just a printed magazine. The latest move in 2012 is to rebrand again as content marketers, with the focus shifting away from (print) publishing to embrace digital in all its formats. The APA morphed into The Content Marketing Association (CMA).

Regardless of how one refers to it, this sector – let's agree on content marketing to be contemporary – has come through the 2008 recession intact and is independently forecasted to grow[16]. That in itself demands some analysis and a few hallelujahs.

> This is a sector constantly reinventing itself, redefining its service offer and trying to stay ahead of the curve

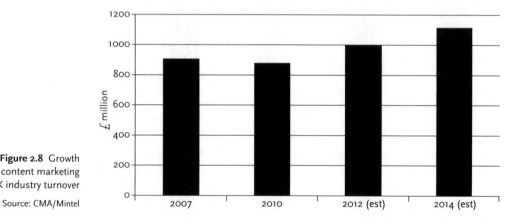

Figure 2.8 Growth of content marketing UK industry turnover

Source: CMA/Mintel

What do content marketers do?

The services on offer to a client (be they commercial, voluntary or public sector) are four-fold:

- increasing sales of products
- retaining customers and building relationships
- brand building or repositioning
- creative consistency across all marketing offerings.

The result is content is created and distributed via print, digital magazines, websites, microsites (allied to main commercial sites), e-newsletters, videos and social media interaction. The confidence of the sector is built on this variety of platforms and gives them an edge when pitching against social media agencies or digital agencies. Sean King, CEO of Seven, states:

> A digital agency doesn't have the editorial expertise to design and produce a glossy magazine for Sainsbury's and you won't find a social media agency creating engaging editorial while monetising an overall content marketing strategy.[17]

The business is a fusion between brand marketing and publishing, using the skills of the latter to promote the fortunes of the former. But is it journalism? Keith Grainger, CEO of Redwood, seems to think it is:

> We're not preventing our people from being journalists, as for many, that's their background and training. We're just asking them to adopt a different approach to content. Everything we do starts from an editorial position and, as journalists, we think in long-form, which differentiates us from agency copywriters who mainly think in short-form.[18]

The skills are journalistic and certainly present themselves to the world as journalism, but can such overtly commercial concerns allow for journalistic integrity? Unlike the B2B editor who may have to contend with a highly critical article about a key advertiser, this dilemma could not happen in this much more controlled environment. Similarly it is difficult to imagine a customer magazine thriving on a newsstand (though some, such as Waitrose's *Food Illustrated*, did try).

This is not to say that good quality journalism does not get into customer magazines, rather that there are commercial constraints which some may feel are too binding. An interesting example is *Colors* from Benetton which, freed from the normal parameters of publishing, has a licence to be provocative and campaigning which it does with aplomb. This title has survived because of its patronage, not been hindered by it.

The content marketing agencies have not so much blurred the line with commercial interests in publishing as dissolved it. For some they have been a catalyst that has created a new type of media owner. The arrival of major fast-moving consumer goods (FMCG) companies as yet another competitor for advertisement revenue has not been wholly welcomed by all traditional publishers.

Customer magazines have grown from being the patronised ugly duckling to the sexy new model which looks in better shape than its older sibling to develop the commercial tools to thrive. The ability to distance their revenue model from advertising enables these publishers to feel confident about the long term. Rather like the B2B publishers who are moving forward to business information provision, the content agencies can look to a future where they can move away from a revenue share deal with their client towards one based on fees. The CMA reports that this trend is already underway. Students will also be interested to know that this sector of publishing is recruiting new employees to fuel this growth and should be a prime target for those seeking to join the exciting world of magazines.

CONCLUSIONS

Looking across the whole spectrum of magazine publishing in the UK a pattern is developing. It suggests that the publishers and brands that will survive in the paid-for market are those which are able to continue to monetise their content but not by selling their readership to advertisers. The virtuous circle articulated by Cyrus Curtis, publisher of the *Ladies Home Journal* is in decline. The secret he shared with the public that publishing is 'to give you people who manufacture things that American women would want to buy a chance to tell them about your products'[19] is being seriously undermined. As a consumer publisher, unless there exists a particularly strong bond of trust with readers that others find very hard to replicate, then a future based on this classic model is going to be difficult to maintain at current levels. This underlines the importance of building and maintaining market leading brands.

As Chapter 7 shows, magazines take a bigger share of advertising revenue than they have of the audience. Publishers of strong, recognised titles such as *Private Eye, Grazia, Good Housekeeping, Vogue, GQ, The Economist, The Spectator, Woman and Home* or *Country Life* (to name but a few) must feel confident that they will continue to deliver a profitable magazine. Second tier brands will feel the pressure.

Specific markets within consumer magazines, not based on advertising, can also feel positive about the current situation. Children's publishers and partworks base their businesses on sales revenues from licensed products or highly researched and tested niches. These markets will have cyclical changes but are likely to remain buoyant in the long run. They join the B2B publisher selling information that feeds the daily work flow of industry professional and the content agency promoting FMCG brands as models with potential for growth. The impact of tablet sales is hard to assess definitively at this point but potentially it may enable many others to continue to play their part in the diverse UK publishing scene.

Media consumption is growing with one advertising agency forecasting that it will reach 90 hours per week by 2020. This underlying fact must give succour to all publishers and puts the industry in a potentially much better position than many others. Hours spent with printed media may be in decline but that does not mean magazine formats are similarly challenged. As many more types of companies become magazine publishers, and magazine publishers in turn become multi-platform media companies, the challenge for all involved is to tap into this growth.

Chapter 3 takes up this story as consumer publishers look for growth away from the traditional revenue streams of circulation and advertisement sales.

NOTES

1. GfK MRI Press Release 17 November 2011.
2. Carroll, J. (2013). Blog: Press Release re digital readership and Media Week Media citing latest NRS figures.
3. Wessenden (2012).
4. Author's estimate based on sales figures from various sources. Includes boxed software, peripherals and accessories, console hardware, online games etc.
5. Galt Toys: Summer screen time survey.
6. Deloitte State of the Media Democracy Survey 2012.
7. Ofcom research.
8. PPA News (2012).
9. Ofcom states that in Quarter 1 of 2012 76 per cent of UK adults had access to broadband.
10. ABC (Jan–June 2000) average circulation per issue *Time Out*: 90,476.
11. ZenithOptimedia (2013).
    The editors note that total advertising revenue sums may differ according to sources. This reflects the different methodologies employed by consulting companies and advertising agencies.
12. Anon. (2013) p 4.
13. Seymour (2012) p 14.
14. Williams-Grut, O. (2013).
15. ONS (2013).
16. Mintel (2011) p 4.
17. Fletcher, M. (2012).
18. Ibid.
19. Morrish, J. (2011) p 11.

REFERENCE SOURCES

Anon. (2013) *Wessenden Briefing*, March 2013, 165, Godalming: Wessenden Marketing.

Carroll, J. 'Tablets are plane sailing for publishers': Media Week blog 17 May 2013 available at http://mediablogged.mediaweek.co.uk/2013/05/17/tablets-are-plane-sailing-for-publishers/ (Accessed 11 June 2013.)

Deloitte 'State of the media democracy survey 2012' available at http://www.deloitte.com/view/en_GB/uk/industries/tmt/media-industry/media-democracy-survey/ (Accessed 14 June 2013.)

Fletcher, M. 'Sector analysis: customer publishing': Media Week, 4 April 2012 available at http://www.mediaweek.co.uk/news/1125670/Sector-analysis-Customer-publishing/?DCMP=ILC-SEARCH (Accessed 14 June 2013.)

Galt Toys Summer screen time survey available at http://blog.galttoys.com/tag/survey/ (Accessed 14 June 2013.)

GfK MRI Press release 17 November 2011 available at http://www.gfkmri.com/assets/PR/GfKMRI_111711PR_DigitalOnlyMagazineReading.htm (Accessed 11 June 2013.)

Mintel (2011) 'The customer publishing industry – 2011', Executive Summary prepared for APA, November 2011 available at http://www.the-cma.com/uploads/apa_documents/apa_report_2011_executive_summary.pdf (Accessed 14 June 2013.)

Morrish, J. (2011) *Magazine Editing in Print and Online*, Oxford: Routledge.

Ofcom research 'A nation addicted to smartphones' available at http://consumers.ofcom.org.uk/2011/08/a-nation-addicted-to-smartphones/ (Accessed 11 June 2013.)

ONS 'Release: crime statistics, focus on property crime, 2011/12', 9 May 2013 available at http://www.ons.gov.uk/ons/rel/crime-stats/crime-statistics/focus-on-property-crime--2011-12/index.html (Accessed 14 June 2013.)

PPA News 'NRS PADD shows continued appetite for magazine media', 12 September 2012 available at http://www.ppa.co.uk/about/activities/consumer-media-group/news/nrs-padd-shows-continued-appetite-for-magazine-media/ (Accessed 14 June 2013.)

Seymour (2012) *Wessenden Briefing*, July 2012, 161, Godalming: Wessenden Marketing.

Wessenden (2012) *PPA Publishing Futures 2012 Report* available at http://www.ppa.co.uk/events/news/publishing-futures-2012/ (Accessed 13 June 2013.)

Williams-Grut, O. 'Smartphones tipped to dominate UK by 2015', the *Independent*, 11 February 2013 available at http://www.independent.co.uk/news/business/news/smartphones-tipped-to-dominate-uk-by-2015-8490250.html# (Accessed 14 June 2013.)

ZenithOptimedia (2013) *Advertising Expenditure Forecasts June 2013*, London: ZenithOptimedia.

Changing business models in the magazine world

David Stam

This chapter explores a number of the key components of the modern magazine's business plan and how the industry is adapting to the media landscape as described in Chapter 2. In particular it will examine the challenges posed by a recessionary economic climate and the growth of tablet computers. Launches, research and development will be discussed in detail, as will the growing importance of international revenues. The chapter concludes with a brief look at how magazines are engaging profitably with their readers through live events. Case studies are widely used and there is comment from many industry experts.

Every single magazine has a bespoke business model with regard to its dependence upon different revenue and cost streams. This is akin to a DNA or financial footprint that, while being similar to a competitor, will be individual in its own right. Mass consumer magazines remain dependent upon retail sales revenues but the importance of subscriptions is growing. From a cost perspective this revenue will be offset by heavy marketing targeted at both retailers and consumers. Another factor affecting the financial model of a title will be its relevance and appeal to advertisers. Free titles of course have no circulation revenue; they rely totally upon advertisement sales. Their marketing costs are low but distribution costs high for delivery to and merchandising at distribution points.

B2B is even more diverse. For the last 30 years huge circulation free titles, driven by massive advertisement revenues, dominated this sector. As the previous chapter shows, these industry 'bibles' have come under financial pressure and have slimmed down, turned digital only or disappeared completely. The sector is reinventing itself with a keen focus on the need to secure reader revenues, be they print or digital subscriptions, data or business information sales or events and conferences.

Magazine publishing is a diverse matrix. One starts to make sense of this by looking at the key revenue and cost strands that may make up a typical business plan.

Magazine publishing is a diverse matrix

THE CHANGING FINANCIAL MODEL

Many magazine publishing companies are quite small. The PPA conducts an annual future expectations survey from its members and for a recent survey found that 37 per cent of respondents had a turnover of less than £1 million. Only nine per cent had turnovers in excess of £50 million[1]. However, large or small, Finance Directors will look to analyse a magazine's business performance as follows, with these headings being the key lines on an annual business plan.

Revenues

Circulation or copy sales

This key revenue stream is explored in detail in Chapter 6. The two key drivers are retail and subscription revenues. Consumer publishers can expect an average of 49 per cent of income to come from print circulation – for certain major weekly publishers the number will be even higher. B2B publishers can expect 12 per cent of turnover from this channel[2]. Print still dominates but digital is growing, principally from Apple Newsstand. Calculations should allow for all discounts and it is also important to note that in the UK, print revenues are exempt from VAT while digital are not.

Price Waterhouse Cooper (PWC) estimate that in 2012 only three per cent of consumer magazine revenues originated from digital but will increase to 14 per cent by 2016[3].

Most publishers will differentiate between UK and international sales. The growing importance of the latter will be explored later in this chapter.

Advertisement sales

Despite huge pressures on this revenue line since 2008, it remains the second most important source of income for publishers as a whole and the most important for certain companies, for example Condé Nast. It is articulated in full in Chapter 7. Revenues are spread across both print and digital platforms.

Reader events

In a 2012 magazine article[4] Jim Bilton of Wessenden Marketing compares the emerging business model for certain publishers to that of the music industry, a business which has seen revolutionary change in the face of paid for downloads and free streaming. Bilton cites an average of 20 per cent of record company revenue coming from live gigs and merchandising, with the label now taking on the role of impresario and music manager.

Few publishers will boast 20 per cent of turnover coming from live reader events but there is little doubt that this source is growing, particularly for the specialist press. This area is of significant importance to B2B publishers who can expect around 16 per cent of revenues to come from events. In 2011 PPA members responding to the Futures Survey staged 1,180 live events[5].

Sales of data and business information

Increasingly important for B2B publishers this revenue line will cover a multitude of opportunities. The most frequent will be sales of high value data, professional learning or tuition programmes, business conferences and exhibitions and specialist consultancy services, particularly in the recruitment sector.

Costs

Paper and printing

The largest cost item for any publisher remains the expense of paper and print. This is a complex world with the majority of publishers employing a specialist Production Department for paper and print procurement, the management of suppliers and the daily flow of editorial copy and advertisements. This topic is covered in Appendix 1.

Research, development and marketing budgets

Publishers participating in the Futures Survey estimated that they will be likely to spend on average five per cent of total turnover on marketing[6]. The level of spend is rising cautiously from a 2010 lower percentage of just 4.5 per cent. In particular, major consumer launches can represent huge one-off costs. Launches are covered in this chapter and consumer marketing in Chapter 6.

IT and digital costs

This cluster of cost items has increased exponentially in the last 20 years. For all publishers the creation and management of their editorial content is totally IT dependent. This dependency has seen a transfer of costs away from the printing budget. Typesetting and the need to produce colour separations have largely become processes of the past. Software and IT kit have to be paid for and depreciated together with the additional costs of support and maintenance.

In the early years of the millennium, significant sums were invested in website creation and development, the key digital focus now for publishers has moved to digital editions for tablet and mobile. Finance Directors know these significant costs of development are business critical but with digital in relative infancy it is more often the profitable revenue streams from print products funding the birth of the younger medium.

Human Resources

All publishers believe that to produce the best product, sold and marketed in the most creative way, they have to employ the most talented people. Even in recessionary times there is stiff competition for top performers in both the creative and commercial parts of the business. The centralisation of the industry in London and the South East of the UK intensifies these pressures; few people ever have to move house or disrupt children's education to take a new job.

For all mainstream publishers, staff costs remain a very significant item with the PPA, estimating that 48 people on average are employed in each member company[7].

... there is stiff competition for top performers in both the creative and commercial parts of the business

Overheads

Publishing companies are not virtual businesses; they need offices which have to be heated and lit and support staff such as HR and Finance. Like any business, publishing has to allow for a myriad of overhead costs. Pressures on profitability have led to general overheads being squeezed in recent years but that is no different to UK industry as a whole.

From the consumer goods revolution of the 1950s until the recessionary tides of 2008, magazine publishing in the UK has been a very profitable business sector. Entrepreneurial proprietors, shareholders and employees have all benefited. The PPA estimates that the profit margin of companies who report a profit to be 15 per cent of turnover. There is strong optimism for turnover growth during 2013[8].

> ... magazine publishing in the UK has been a very profitable business sector

The long walk to digital

Tim Brooks

> Anyone in media worth their salt has at some point woken up in a cold sweat and thought Holy shit! If I don't get my head around this, I'm history!
>
> Advertising Agency CEO

The migration to digital has been a long and painful road for the media and advertising industry – not that the journey will ever be completed. The shift in the competitive landscape has been seismic. Facebook, for example, now commands more UK consumer attention than the websites of all the UK's print media combined.

One key issue for businesses in transition is that – at least until the end of the first decade of this century – they were being led by people who proved themselves in the pre-digital world. Those in command of traditional mainstream media and advertising agencies can give you a ready, accurate account of how a newspaper is printed, a TV show is cast or a commercial is approved. Ask them how to decrease page-download times, or build a secure return channel for online competition entrants, and you're likely to be met with silence or bluster. The digital marketing manager of a major high street bank told me that 80 per cent of her time was spent explaining her department's work to colleagues.

These are two stories from my own experience. In the mid-1990s, the editor of a computing magazine bravely stood up at a management conference for his company to spread the word about this new thing called 'email'. Within years, he predicted, it would overtake franked post, and everyone on a magazine would be expected to publish their email address, so that readers could connect directly. His words were met with a mixture of amusement, bafflement, disbelief and condescension.

> The migration to digital has been a long and painful road ... not that the journey will ever be completed

Fast forward four years, and I am with colleagues from that same company, meeting some digital consultants. They bang on about the potential of 'Bluetooth' (then a novelty). After they have departed, one of us asks: 'So – does anyone have a clue what Bluetooth is?' To which we all confess that we neither did, nor had we the courage to admit it.

For those in power, the kinds of radical re-orientation demanded by digital were not congenial. Who, having spent 20 years scrambling up the corporate pole, would willingly suggest that their budgets or span of control be reduced in order to promote digital expansion? The failure of incumbent leadership to grasp the challenges of digital was underlined by the decision of ITV plc in 2010 to go outside television and hire Adam Crozier (Saatchi, Football Association and Royal Mail) to lead its reinvention for the digital era. Pre-tax profits for 2012 were triple the previous year. Similarly, Mark Wood, the CEO of Future plc, whilst having a strong media background at both Reuters and ITN, was new to consumer publishing when he took over the reins at Future, a business which is now making good progress in the multi-platform media world.

Figure 3.1, provided by Cilla Snowball, Group Chairman of advertising agency AMV BBDO, shows the five different structural approaches to going digital. She recalls the exasperated lobbying of younger AMV managers at the beginning of this century, wanting to set up a separate 'AMV Digital'. With hindsight – AMV's decision to opt for 'infusion' has been right: it remains now, as it was pre-web, London's largest creative agency.

Figure 3.1 illustrates the range of structures open to media businesses when considering corporate structures for the digital world. The spectrum ranges from a completely separate business (left) to complete integration or infusion (right). There is no correct answer but companies opting for separation have been prone to costly mistakes. As digital revenues increase companies are more likely to veer towards the right of the spectrum.

Other businesses tried several, or indeed all five, of the structural plays over a ten-year period, and there have been memorable failures. Under city pressure to 'do something', EMAP, the then powerful magazine and radio player, shifted abruptly in 2000 from 'Separate department' to 'Separate company' – EMAP Digital. It lasted two years, and cost EMAP a significant

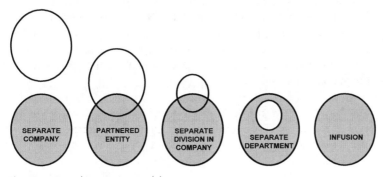

Figure 3.1 Digital integration models

eight figure sum. It wasn't only public companies that succumbed to these pressures. Telegraph Media Group set up its Euston Project – so called because it was deliberately based in Euston, away from head office in Victoria. Led by its Editor-in-chief Will Lewis, freshly returned from Harvard Business School, the Group was determined to take *The Telegraph* digital. That lasted an even shorter time, and again lost the company a multi-million sum – and Lewis.

Central to the challenge of digitising the media has been cost. As the strategy director of a major B2B publisher memorably put it, the dilemma is this: 'I either invest too little, and lose market share; or invest too much, and lose profit. And even if I spend just the right amount – I'm still making less money.'

The sums simply do not add up. Companies' long-term investment planning timeframes sit ill with digital development that tends to be continuously reiterative, and in a market which is changing with much greater rapidity than in the past. These investments must be funded from offline revenues that, especially in print media, are declining steeply.

In 2006 I was a director of IPC Media, one of the UK's largest magazine publishers, owned by Time Warner. The Time Warner CEO, Jeff Bewkes, flew in for a briefing. My boss had to explain why profits were not growing, due to intense competition on the newsstand, and flat-lining sales. My part was to explain that at the time we had very few viable digital assets, and needed to spend 10 per cent of profits on creating digital versions of our key brands, if we were not to be left behind. Jeff listened intently, and then asked: 'When I give a dollar to Warner Brothers or HBO, they give me back $1.20. Why would I give you a dollar when you're offering to give me back 90 cents?'

He then left the building; and so, shortly after, did I.

In his essay, Tim Brooks points to the difficulties in creating the business plan for the modern day magazine publisher. In the pre-digital age life was a lot simpler. Launches excepting, analysis of consumer spending and macro-economic trends made forecasting of circulation and advertisement revenues straightforward with inflation percentages applied to most cost lines.

Publishers, irrespective of size or genre, are now striving to turn their businesses into profitable deliverers of brands on both digital and conventional platforms. This is an incredibly exacting challenge given the relative size of the digital market, the uncertain shape of the emerging business model and the significant costs of innovation in new media. Case studies 3 and 4 clearly illustrate how different businesses are succeeding.

Case study 3

Trader Media changes gear from print to digital

The *Auto Trader* website is the number one UK marketplace for buying and selling cars. The publisher states that they serve over 11 million unique users per month. Back in 1996 this was the first classified magazine to launch a website and today stands as a striking example of a business that has largely left print behind to reincarnate itself solely as a digital provider. This they are doing very profitably.

The idea behind *Auto Trader* magazine was spotted by John Madejski (now Sir) whilst on holiday in Florida in the mid-1970s. He saw a magazine with photos of the cars for sale printed inside. Like so many good ideas based on a simple concept, Madejski returned home and launched the *Thames Valley Trader* as the first of a group of magazines that became branded as *Auto Trader*. I recall my wife successfully selling a car back in the early 1980s with the magazine's sales representative turning up with a camera to take the photo of the vehicle: quick, easy and effective.

Print editions developed to reach a combined circulation high of well over 300,000 copies per week at the turn of the millennium. The business became jointly owned by Guardian Media Group and Apax Partners Venture Capital.

More than 30 years since the original launch, *Auto Trader* has decisively left print behind to focus clearly on life as a digital business. The last print edition went to press on 28 June 2013. The likelihood of this event was there for all to foresee. For the year ending April 2012 the company posted digital revenues of £202 million, a significant 11 per cent increase year on year. Digital represented 83 per cent of group revenue. Total profit for the same year was £142.9 million[9]. Sales of print titles had fallen to 27,000 copies per week by the spring of 2013, significantly down on the previous year[10].

While supporting other digital brands, the success of the business has been the all-powerful *Auto Trader* website and digital app. Customers can buy or sell a car, estimate prices, check vehicle history and obtain quotes for insurance and other motoring services. The focus is on ease of use with clear signposting and functionality with a mix of trade and private sellers.

With clear strategic vision, purpose and significant investment Trader Media has successfully crossed the rivers of digital disruption and recession, made it to the other side and planted their flag. As the UK economy improves the business is well placed for further growth.

Case study 4

The Future's bright ...

Trader Media management have had real focus, for which they must be applauded. Their job was made easier, however, by having just one main market on which to concentrate – motoring. Bath-based magazine publisher Future plc is striving to regain lost profitability with an incredibly diverse portfolio – currently running to 80 magazines and 100 digital products. After a difficult period it shows encouraging signs of progress.

The early success of Future was stellar. Founded by journalist entrepreneur Chris Anderson in 1985, the business's first title was published from Chris's house in Somerton, a sleepy town in England's West Country. With computing and gaming at its heart, the business grew rapidly and diversified into new markets including cycling. Future floated on the London Stock Exchange at the height of internet share price excitement in 1999.

The print business model for Future was reliant upon high cover priced quality products aimed at an enthusiastic, young and largely male market. Magazines were often cover mounted with quality CDs and other gifts and surged through price point after price point to the jealous amazement of other publishers. Their international team were highly successful in developing overseas markets for both brand syndication and export sales. As recessionary times hit, however, hard pressed consumers started to find cover prices too high and their hobbies and interests widely reported on the internet for free. Future dropped sales and market share and in the financial year to September 2011 the company lost almost £20 million[11].

An energetic new management team is turning this performance around. The year to September 2012 has shown a pre-tax profit of just over £1 million. Chief Executive Officer Mark Wood reflected on this improved performance: '2012 has been a year of substantial progress for Future and the group is now well positioned to grow and diversify revenues as a global digital business.'[12]

A profit of a shade over £1 million on sales of £123.5 million is small but for Future an important step in the right direction. The company cut costs and restructured its US business. Putting those factors to one side, what has been the publishing strategy? These three factors are key:

- digital development
- a clear role for print
- focus on international sales.

First, there has been a clear emphasis on digital development which for Future cannot come quickly enough. The financial accounts for the year to end-September 2012 show an increase in digital revenues of 30 per cent and those revenues account for 18 per cent of all income. Trends for the first half of 2013 suggest that the move to digital revenues is growing. Future has made it clear that it is in the business of targeting its affluent, enthusiastic consumers be it in print, online or on the move. Across the portfolio of 100 digital products they boast some impressive statistics.

- Websites reach over 50 million unique users per month, up 70 per cent year on year.
- Over 2 million IPad editions sold with *T3* the UK's largest IPad monthly at 30,000. For the first half of 2013 the company reported digital subscribers to be up 75 per cent year on year.

As Tim Brooks has pointed out, this development will not have come easily. New skills will have been learnt and new editorial and content management systems put in place. Mistakes will have been made and hopefully lessons learnt – the growing base of developing knowledge and experience will stand the business in good stead in years to come. Wood states the business now has 'digital know-how in its DNA' and expects half of all revenue to come from digital sources within three to four years[13].

The company has invested in its own video production unit to enhance content on tablet editions. This facility is also offered to advertisers as a service to increase advertisement yields.

Second, Future differs from Trader Media by virtue of the fact that it still sees an important role for the traditional magazine format. High quality, no doubt relatively high cover price, print media is still very much part of the mix and will remain so. Over 80 per cent of 2012 revenues came from traditional media – the figure for the first half of 2013 was 75 per cent.

Third, Future sees itself increasingly as a global business. It sees its reach being affluent enthusiasts everywhere, be they cyclists in the US, Linux programmers in Korea or rock musicians in Japan. Targeting an international audience with multi-platforms of media will attract advertisers in increasing numbers. As will be discussed later in this chapter, technology is becoming a facilitator for publishers' worldwide ambitions. Note that 40 per cent of Future's digital sales go to countries outside of their core markets of the UK and US[14].

LAUNCHES – THE LIFEBLOOD OF THE INDUSTRY

All major consumer publishers need to budget annually for launch and development. Mass circulation print launches have traditionally stimulated the whole magazine market. As well as generating increased turnover for retailers, one new product has often spawned another as a whole sector has developed. The importance of new titles is clearly demonstrated by analysing the top 30 actively purchased magazines as reported by ABC. Sixteen of the top 30 titles were launched since 1980 and of these, twelve in a creative period between 1990 and 2005. Worryingly, no new title of scale since 2005 makes it into the top 30.

It would be wrong to give an impression of total launch stagnation. As this book is being written, selective markets are active. These include the children's market, craft titles, home cooking and baking and the rapidly growing number of bookazines (see Chapter 6) as well as recent entrants to the free distribution market such as *Stylist*. Whilst applauding such innovation, however, it is important to note that these do not make up for the lack of 'blockbuster' retail launches as seen in times past. Traditional print launch activity is at low ebb. Why is this case? Again, the two main reasons lie in the dual themes of recession and digital development which run through this chapter.

Any magazine launch represents a risk, albeit one that can be reduced by careful research. The budget must include the costs of a launch editorial and commercial team, research and development, TV advertising for the first issue and losses for the early years of a major new title. This financial commitment will easily exceed £5 million to introduce a new women's weekly successfully.

> This financial commitment will easily exceed £5 million to introduce a new women's weekly successfully

The quantitative data: the circulation and advertisement revenue estimates and forecasts will be made painstakingly but they are just that, forecasts and estimates. Major launches require both publishing vision and courage in equal doses. Difficult economic times significantly increase risk and lengthen payback periods. One cannot be too hard on publishing boards for coming up short of courage in the current environment.

The need to drive digital publishing has slowed development of new print brands in three ways. First, expansion onto new media platforms for existing titles has sapped the research and development funds of many publishing companies with the simple result – there is no money left for major print launches. Second, the speed to market for a purely digital launch is quicker as well as cheaper than for a print launch. Digital-only new titles are an emerging trend – Future plc now produces over 100 products for tablets[15]. Third, for any new print launch to secure publishing board approval it needs to incorporate a credible online strategy as an integral part of the proposed new brand. Again this increases overall launch costs and adds another layer of media complexity.

Be they print or digital, magazine publishing companies have to launch to ensure long-term survival in today's complex media world. What are the imperatives which drive publishers when pursuing new opportunities?

Launch imperatives

The history of magazine publishing is one of commercial opportunities taken when an entrepreneur spots a change in the society in which they live. This can be a step or incremental change or a technological development which affects people's lives. The following hierarchy categorises five different types of launches, be they print or digital, as:

- market defining
- market enhancing
- media inspired
- technology inspired
- for and by enthusiasts.

Market defining

The top tier of launch activity is called market defining. Examples of market defining launches are UK *Cosmopolitan* in 1972 and *Loaded* in 1994. Society is changing and there is a clear editorial vision for a publication to both reflect and further influence changing mores. The former brilliantly captured the emergence of female sexual empowerment in the 1970s and the latter became the collective noun for the laddish generation of the 1990s. For the readers of these fresh publications, 'the earth moved': they purchased in hundreds of thousands titles they had not seen the like of before.

Importantly, from an industry perspective, these pioneering titles inspired new genres. The publishers of *Cosmo* soon gave birth to sister magazine *Company* and IPC Media launched the UK edition of the highly successful French title *Marie Claire*. *Loaded* was the precursor to a line of magazines for lads, most notably the relaunched *FHM*, *Maxim* and the weeklies *Nuts* and *Zoo*.

Market enhancing

Publishers waiting for a market defining title to come about need patience, it may only be a once in a lifetime opportunity. They take great vision to spot and creative brilliance to execute. Most major consumer launches of the last thirty years fall into the second category: market enhancing.

Photo 3.1 The UK launch issue, March 1972, now a collectors' item

A market enhancing launch will build on an already apparent change in society or lifestyle. These launches are more likely to reflect gradual changes and develop markets in an incremental way. They may approach a topic with a different style, format or frequency than their competitors.

In 2001 Condé Nast launched *Glamour*, a highly successful monthly package of fashion, beauty, relationships and celebrities. The key to its huge launch circulation was its format: it was launched as an A5 or 'handbag' sized product, the antidote to large and chunky A4 competitors. Easy to buy and carry, especially when travelling, it was an overnight success and has consistently sold over 400,000 copies an issue since launch[16]. A visit to a WH Smith Travel store at a major station or airport will show today a range of similarly sized titles, many as an alternate purchase to the main A4 printed host magazine.

Three post-millennium launches into the women's sector, *Grazia*, *Look* and *Stylist* have enhanced this crowded space by producing high quality fashion and beauty editorial as weeklies. This was traditionally the preserve of the monthly sector, reflecting the faster pace required to succeed in a rapidly moving market driven by social media and chain and internet retailers.

Media inspired

The third category of launch activity consists of magazines inspired by other media. Examples of this in the US are titles founded by TV celebrities such as Martha Stewart or Oprah Winfrey. Individual celebrity magazines are rare in the UK and tend to focus on celebrity chefs.

There is, however, a large and vibrant sector of launch activity inspired by the media made up of online games, cinema and TV: children's magazines and comic publishing. This textbook notes in a number of places the success of this sector in the current business environment. Children's magazines account for 10 per cent of retail magazine turnover and grew by four per cent in 2012[17]. Particularly strong is launch activity for the pre-school and early school years age groups. Why is this?

Print, of course, remains the favoured medium and parents pay for the purchase. Despite seeing young children play with parent's tablets to keep them occupied on planes and trains, that technology belongs to Mum and Dad! Moreover, Mum and Dad want to inspire reading skills of traditional print products. The young reader is transient, growing through one title to an older one, providing an ever changing audience for publishers. From a retailing point of view, the growth of magazine sales in supermarkets has actively helped the pre-school sector, with display space available for a range of cover-mounted titles in child-friendly stores. A retailer from Yorkshire, Mike Brown, comments: 'We are seeing more titles, particularly in the pre-teen market, with an educational element and parents seem very happy to spend their money on them.'[18]

At 231,811 copies per issue, *Moshi Monsters* is the largest children's magazine in the UK today[19]. The title is based on the original online game whereby children can adopt a virtual pet monster and have fun playing a range of games and puzzles. Aimed at children from six to twelve years the magazine enhances digital by giving print readers secret codes to unlock unique online content as well as having old fashioned incentives such as free gifts, stickers and transfers.

In 2012, Immediate Media launched four new children's titles predicted to be worth over £7 million of retail sales value (RSV) with more to come[20]. Pre-teen titles such as *Girl Talk Art* and *Horrible Histories* sensibly focus on market opportunities offered by parents' educational aspirations. A relatively new company, founded largely by the acquisition of BBC magazine assets, Immediate Media have become an important contributor to the UK launch scene.

From the inspirations of Disney cartoons and the original American superheroes of *Spiderman* and *Superman*, through the heyday of BBC children's publishing with *Postman Pat* and *Doctor Who*, to the *Moshi Monsters* of today, children's publishers have been quick to launch quality titles based on ideas originated on screen or increasingly online.

Technology inspired

In the last fifty years, thousands of new magazine titles have fallen into this fourth category. If the role of a magazine is to inspire, entertain and inform – publishers are always quick on the draw to inform. The consumer's hunger for information about newly available gadgets and equipment has been a major contributor to the success of the industry. None more so than the volume market for IT publications.

Personal computing magazines have been a force in magazine publishing from the mid-1980s to the current day. As a market it has become a magnet for launches satisfying sheer thirst for knowledge. Initially magazines such as *Amstrad Action* were aimed at customers who owned the early Amstrad machines and who were desperately seeking information. Publications then grew into the telephone directory sized personal computing and gaming magazines of the 1990s such as *Personal Computer World*. In parallel with the physical growth of the titles, the market itself snowballed as a large number of PCs became available at affordable prices. One currently sees an array of regular frequency print, bookazines and digital titles focussed on smartphones and tablets.

Inside every magazine there is a new one waiting to emerge. Witness to this was the 1998 launch of *Computeractive*. At the height of the personal computing market and at the start of the internet boom, the innovative Dutch publisher VNU took an alternative editorial tack. Rather than delve into more complexity, with ever more similar looking pages of machine after machine, they stood back and produced a brilliant 'How To' title. Techniques, jargon, hardware and software were stripped back to basics and explained to readers in a user friendly, easy to follow format. In style the title owed much to the partwork format. Selling over 300,000 at launch, *Computeractive* has a current circulation of a creditable 98,560 copies per fortnight[21].

New technology is not only hard to understand but also changes lifestyles. There will always be a viable and fast moving magazine sector on hand to support desire for knowledge, as well as fulfil the needs of advertisers to reach early adopters and opinion formers.

Inside every magazine there is a new one waiting to emerge

For and by enthusiasts

The final tier of launch devotes itself to the many niche and specialist new titles from the marketplace devoted to hobbies, interests, sports and enthusiasms. The characteristics of this sector are:

- Relatively high cover prices and small circulations per title with a bias towards subscription sales. This is demonstrated by the fact that the hobby sector accounts for 13 per cent of titles in newsagents by number but only six per cent by turnover. The average cover price in the sector is 20 per cent higher than the industry norm[22].
- The enthusiast's magazine market is heavily clustered. There are significant numbers of titles within each niche with active publishers producing a portfolio. The Kelsey Publishing Group, by way of example, publishes 15 motoring magazines aimed at specialist car marques. The major wholesaler Smiths News handle 16 woodworking titles, 21 railways titles, 32 modelling titles and 56 craft titles. Enthusiasts are likely to buy more than one title of their passion.
- Launch budgets are relatively small and it is vital to cross promote in other titles within the publishers' portfolio.

Compared to the first four categories of launches, new magazines for enthusiasts tend to gain their new concept idea from internal rather than external influences. Reader involvement is absolutely key. A new idea may well come via a cluster of reader emails or Facebook posts, or meeting groups of readers at an exhibition or convention. The editorial team will have a deep rooted knowledge and passion for their subject – written 'by enthusiasts for enthusiasts' is often used to describe the genre.

Case study 5 by Carolyn Morgan examines how Future leveraged the resources of the internet to launch a print title for craft enthusiasts.

Case study 5

How *Mollie Makes* was made

Craft magazine *Mollie Makes* from Future was launched in an unusual way. The publisher spent several months online building up both following and content. This created great craft editorial which was then put into the printed magazine. Growth has been rapid, with subs of over 11,000 earning them a place on the 2012 Media Pioneers Awards shortlist.

Mollie Makes launched in May 2011 to cater to the growing online community of women who connect and share content. This audience shares a creative aesthetic which covers many aspects of their lives from interiors and styling to crafting and 'thrifting'.

With the ethos of 'living and loving handmade', *Mollie Makes* turns the usual magazine editorial model on its head by sourcing content online, then publishing it in print. By immortalising the best content from the blogging community, the title has become an unparalleled resource for craft project ideas and inspiration, and has quickly positioned itself as an aspirational centre piece for this community.

Future employed a Community Editor to engage with the online craft audience and build a buzz in the months leading up to the launch. This was achieved via a blog, Twitter account, Facebook page and YouTube channel. This meant that before the magazine even hit the shelves, *Mollie Makes* already had a strong internet following and an existing customer base.

The number of people engaging with online has continued to grow, and the title now has over 62,000 Facebook fans and 31,000 Twitter followers. *Mollie Makes* also broke Future's new subscription record; achieving 3,000 subscribers before issue two went on sale, with the majority of these subscriptions sold through online channels.

Collating the best content from blogs and websites, *Mollie Makes* offers inspirational and timeless editorial across a wide range of crafts including sewing, embroidery, crocheting, patchwork and knitting.

A typical project will follow a fashion or theme, showing readers how they can either enhance or embellish an item or create something new from scratch using fantastic fabrics and materials, both old and new. The essence of vintage charm alongside retro cool, combined with today's edgy fashions and designs make their take on crafting a world away from the average hobbyist title.

Photo 3.2 *Mollie Makes*, launched in 2011, has grown rapidly in sales by utilising the online community of craft enthusiasts

This difference is apparent in the readers *Mollie Makes* is attracting. Reader research reveals a significantly younger audience than traditional craft magazines – almost 50 per cent of readers are under 35[23] – very different from a traditional craft magazine. Key to the creative editorial is the beautiful environment in which it sits. The template includes line drawings, 'handwritten' fonts, original artwork, feminine, scalloped edges and simple, clean layouts. High quality paper showcases the design values throughout. The cover is matt paper making the magazine distinct in its market.

As the 'making-do and mending' sensibility of today's climate continues, so does *Mollie Makes'* success; the magazine has been a phenomenon so far, as its print circulation continues to grow with a 2012 ABC of 36,823 plus nearly 3,000 digital sales.

The unique launch experience

The launch hierarchy above has been structured to explain how new ideas originate. The five categories are not seen as mutually exclusive and there may be hot debate as to which of the levels a launch fits into, particularly between *market defining* and *market enhancing*. Those who work on major launches gain unique experience, it is a time for real creative teamwork with an adrenalin rush at the end as one waits for the first issue's sales figures.

In terms of cost, particularly research, development and marketing, there is a hierarchy to the template. New titles which are considered to be market defining or enhancing will have the highest cost. No sane publisher would embark upon such a launch without significant upfront investment in research; TV advertising will almost certainly be required to achieve circulation expectations. Range and listing agreements will have to be put in place with retailers (see chapter 6). New children's titles are also heavily dependent upon strong retail display and require innovative and responsible marketing to a young audience. As such, the publishing industry has costly hurdles for new publishers to clear before launching a volume consumer title.

At the other end of the spectrum, combined print and digital launches aimed at techno and hobby enthusiasts can reach their market for first year launch costs around the £200,000 mark. This low entry hurdle can and does encourage new market entries. Printers and distributors require assurances concerning creditworthiness but if the editorial vision is strong and the commercial case sound then a new publisher can get up and running.

Publishers stargazing the night skies of social or technological change do not do so in isolation

Magazine launches do not necessarily have to be spanking new or one off creative experiences. Publishers stargazing the night skies of social or technological change do not do so in isolation, every company is looking to innovate and expand. *Cosmopolitan* and *Loaded* were market defining one offs but in 2003 *Nuts* and *Zoo* were launched by competitive publishers within weeks of each other, chasing the same young men's weekly market.

Magazines are often purchased alongside each other and it is not uncommon for new titles to borrow the strengths of a successful existing brand. In time apparent similarities fade as titles pick their own distinctive look, feel and tone of voice.

Independent magazines – notes from the underground

There is an emerging – if small – genre of titles which prides itself on its creativity and eccentricity. Magazine publishing has traditionally attracted creative people who are more interested in new or alternative ideas than making money. As the industry has tightened its belt in the face of recession, and the main players have become inevitably more cautious, a small gap has appeared through which the independent magazine has squeezed. These titles are a diverse bunch but tend to focus on long form journalism, literary subjects, new artists or alternative lifestyles. They are essentially very well designed fanzines. Examples include *Huck, Delayed Gratification, The Ride Journal* and *The Chap.*

These magazines remain outside the mainstream, mainly because they do not use the established supply chain for consumer magazines – they are rarely sold in newsagents. This inevitably curtails their sales but means their business model has much less risk attached with lower start-up costs. Instead they are available by subscription/post only or available in a specific list of relevant outlets, often bookshops. They tend toward quarterly or bi-annual publishing schedules and cover prices can vary from £3 to over £10, albeit with the customer having to pay postage costs as well. *The Gourmand*, an off-beat and obsessive magazine about food launched in 2012, is priced at £12.

A standard bearer for this model is the title, *Little White Lies (LWL)*. The publishers, based in Shoreditch, London, state on the website that their 'biggest currency is our credibility. We don't answer to advertisers or film distributors; we answer firstly to our readers and secondly to ourselves. We believe in Truth & Movies.' It is unashamedly a film enthusiast's publication which champions its favourites and seems to effortlessly cloak itself in East London hipster values. An interesting aspect of the business model is that the flagship title has spawned a company (The Church of London) which not only publishes this magazine and *Huck* but has also established itself as a design agency. The business leverages the brand values of *LWL* to design film posters and work as content providers for (more) corporate brands. It is this level of business nous which sets *LWL* apart from many in this sector and may provide a new template for the creative editor or designer feeling the constraints of the corporate strait-jacket.

Freed from a strict publishing schedule imposed by the newsstand, major launch costs and the need to generate large profits to contribute to corporate overheads, these magazines are one of the more creative areas of the consumer industry. Launch activity is frenzied as specialist distribution organisations, like Stack Distribution, enable a new title to connect with its potential audience.

The issue is scalability. Can these publications gain a large audience? Probably not, but is that the point? These independents are making a virtue of being small in a similar way to that of the new entrants to the B2B market, who can make profits with traditional titles where the principal companies cannot.

> ... these magazines are one of the more creative areas of the consumer industry

THE INTERNATIONAL DIMENSION

International or cross border magazine publishing is not new. In 1910 American publisher Hearst founded The National Magazine Company in the UK from which it published the flagship *Good Housekeeping*. It took a further three quarters of a century before the magazine business started to become truly global, as it did in the 1990s, aided by the opening up of Eastern Europe and economic boom in Asia. Browsing the bookstalls of any major international airport today will demonstrate the international reach of European- and US-based publishers.

There are two main reasons why publishers look to expand their indigenous portfolios. First, to make more profits by driving syndication, licence or export circulation revenues. Second, to further the breadth and depth of their magazine brands. For many publishers, growth of international sales is becoming vital to the business plan.

There are essentially six ways to do this and most are relevant to both print and digital media.

The risk/reward ratio

Export copies

The easiest and most risk free method to increase international revenues is to sell the UK published copy to an international market. This requires appointing a local distributor in the designated region and shipping copies by air or sea. Freight costs and timings can be significant, as can percentages of unsold copies. Cover prices have to be converted to local currencies and many overseas markets do impose a VAT-type sales tax on magazines, unlike the UK. It can also take several weeks before sales levels are known.

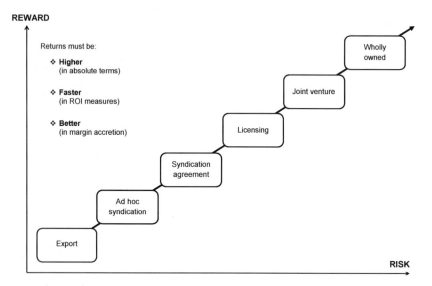

Figure 3.2
International
strategies – the
risk/reward ratio

Source:
FIPP – The Worldwide
Magazine Media
Association

Traditionally the main markets to which UK publishers export are Australia, New Zealand, South Africa, Spain, Scandinavia, Canada and the US. Overseas sales are claimed on ABC certificates. The market for printed export copies is being gradually eroded by sales through international digital stores such as Apple Newsstand or Google Play.

Photo 3.3 Magazine vendor in Delhi, India

Ad hoc syndication or syndication agreement

The term 'syndication' means the sale of editorial material, be it words or pictures, from one title to another. In this case the reference is a sale to an overseas publisher. The deal can be a one off for a particular article or image or (more likely) a formal agreement made with an international syndication agency or overseas publishing group. Financial arrangements will vary but the fee will be related to the uniqueness of the creative material offered and the number of times used. It is vital that the selling publisher secures the legal rights to offer words and pictures overseas from the original journalist, artist or photographer.

Licensing

This is an increasingly commonplace method for publishers to manage overseas business. This is explained by FIPP – the Worldwide Magazine Media Association – as the granting of rights to use a trademarked magazine or online brand in another country in (possibly) a different language for a specified period of time[24]. The licensor will receive royalty revenue, normally in the form of a percentage of turnover. For that he will have to provide a designated amount of editorial copy per issue. The licensee will have to maintain the host magazine's brand values. As well as taking on content from the licensor he will originate local material that reflects the magazine's brand ethos.

For example, Haymarket Publishing prides itself on having 130 licensed magazines and websites in 42 countries and 29 languages. FIPP states that there were 101 cross border launches in 2010 and 2011. The largest area of interest was Asia Pacific followed by Western Europe[25]. Case study 6 shows the development of a key Haymarket brand.

Case study 6

FourFourTwo

Haymarket Publishing's *FourFourTwo* (named after the classic field placing of ten of the eleven soccer team members) is an excellent working example of how a UK-based magazine has expanded internationally. Launched in 1994, the magazine is aimed at the intelligent male lover of soccer, probably in their mid to late twenties. Today, operating with 18 editions, the magazine claims over 2.3 million readers worldwide[26] – the UK edition boasts an ABC of over 84,000 print copies with over 14,000 of these sold overseas[27].

The English Premier Soccer League is the most commercially successful in the world with clubs such as Manchester United and Chelsea becoming international brands in their own right. *FourFourTwo* has capitalised on the success of the British export of soccer with rapid international success in recent years. In 2010 alone eight new editions were launched and a World Cup Guide was published in 33 markets.

The core brand values of *FourFourTwo* are: being insightful, having access to the top clubs and players and communicating with humour. The brand was launched in the UK just as the lads' mags boom of *Loaded* and *FHM* was getting under way and it was important for the soccer title to capture some of that spirit. Brand Director Hugh Sleight acknowledges that controlling the brand beyond the UK borders can at times be difficult. What may seem to be humorous in the UK may not be so overseas. Covers of the international editions are monitored and there is regular contact and training with the licensees. It is vital to understand the make-up of individual markets, for example the amount of English Premier League material which is required[28].

New media development is important. As well as a digital edition, *FourFourTwo* has an award-wining Stats Zone App for readers to follow during games as well as a Performance Site for players and coaching professionals. In Malaysia the publication has a significant TV show for soccer enthusiasts.

Joint venture or wholly owned companies

These two models for conducting international business are higher in risk and consequently less frequent. The latter may sometimes be difficult to structure around local media ownership legislation.

In this model the exporting publisher will take all or part of the local country's revenue depending whether joint or wholly owned. There are considerably higher set up costs than for licence agreements. This structure should only be entered into if one really understands the quirks and nuances of the overseas market in question and has total faith in the abilities of the other partner.

Since 2004, the highly successful *Men's Health* and *Runner's World* have been published as an equal joint venture between Hearst Magazines UK and the US publisher, Rodale International. Rodale, already knowledgeable of the UK market, brought titles to the table which Hearst had little experience of. Hearst brought its local leverage and existing cost base: a seemingly perfect match.

The importance of international brands

As the axes on Figure 3.2 show, the ladder represents both risk and reward with export copy sales on the bottom rung and joint ventures and wholly owned overseas magazines at the top. As publishers move up the scale from pure export through licensing to wholly owned, potential financial returns increase. FIPP argue that the return on investment from international business can be higher than from domestic publishing as well as faster.

Brand recognition and strength are at the heart of international success. Without that focal point of international recognition, local consumers and advertisers will buy indigenous titles rather than higher cost international titles. Kevin LaBonge, Rodale's International Development Director explains:

> In today's media environment, brands are the most important asset a publisher has. Advertisers and consumers have more choices than ever before, and a proven brand is the most immediate way to cut through the noise and connect with the right audience.[29]

A well-structured licensor–licensee agreement can be a genuine win–win arrangement with significant benefits for both parties. This is aptly demonstrated in the following role play between two publishers, one British and one Brazilian entitled 'James meets Maria'.

In today's media environment, brands are the most important asset a publisher has

Case study 7

James meets Maria

JAMES: I am flying down to San Paulo to meet a potential new licensee, Maria. I really want to tie up this deal. Brazil is one of the fastest growing magazine markets in the world and we need to establish our brands there. I have met Maria a couple of times before at conferences. She runs a good operation and is well respected locally – I think we can work together. They have got clout with local wholesalers and retailers and a good advertisement sales force. Once up and running I know this will make a good contribution to the bottom line.

The UK magazine market is pretty sluggish at the moment and our editorial costs are increasing faster than our revenues. Added to this are the huge costs of digital conversion, seemingly never ending. The more overseas revenue I can secure the more I can amortise these costs. Maria is also interested in licensing our websites and wants to launch digital editions in Portuguese.

We had a lunch for advertisers recently, all international luxury brands. To say that they are leaning on us to launch in Brazil is putting it a bit strongly but they left us in no doubt that if we did sign a licence deal they would support it with advertising. More and more they want to advertise in trusted international magazines.

Three hours to landing, I need to check my numbers one last time.

MARIA: In three hours I have to pick James up from the airport. I am making myself thoroughly unpopular with my team, double checking all is ready. My company really needs this license deal. James has a portfolio of truly international brands, as our economy expands and there is more disposable income I know they will sell. We can get higher cover prices than for local titles. Some consumers like to be seen reading international titles as a badge of success which says 'I'm cool'.

For us to start local magazines in these markets from scratch would take time and significant investment. We will secure quality editorial content as part of this deal. That would cost us a fortune to originate locally. We also do not really have the know-how, particularly in digital, though we are learning fast. Additionally I may be able to sell my locally produced material to other Portuguese-speaking markets through a content management system.

We have talked to the advertising managers of a number of international consumer brands here in Brazil. If the launch is good they will back it. That will also give my sales team contacts and inroads to sell the same advertiser into our local titles. The international brand will be a great door-opener for us.

This is a real opportunity for us to expand with little risk in a fast timeframe. Now is everything ready?

The importance of new technology

New technology has facilitated the global magazine business with benefits to the bottom lines of all publishers who engage.

It is important to understand that general technological enhancements in communication and print technology have significantly aided the overseas production or licensing of print products in their traditional form. Before the mid-1990s, if an edition was to be printed overseas then the original artwork and photographic transparencies had to be carefully packed up and sent via courier to the overseas printer or publisher. In particular, duplicate photo transparencies were expensive. Invariably items got lost in transit causing delay and further expense.

With the worldwide development of publishing software by Adobe and Quark, life got easier. All that needed to be couriered was a computer disk, much cheaper and quicker. Broadband technology then revolutionised international publishing; editorial copy and photographs could be transmitted across continents instantaneously.

Major international publishers have made significant investments in content management systems (CMS), highly secure digital electronic warehouses of editorial copy. Magazines in different countries can now be edited together in real time as opposed to the international edition being prepared when the domestic edition closed. Licensees have a complete picture of what copy the licensor is prepared to make available (if necessary for translation) and can adapt for local use. The licensee may also provide copy back to the host publication and to other partners, thus creating a global network.

Shipping printed magazines around the world has always been an expensive business and one made less attractive by rising fuel prices. The rush by publishers to create digital editions for tablet and the ease of download through sites such as Apple Newsstand or Google Play has put financial pressures on the traditional export of magazines. If an expatriate can download an issue immediately, why wait a week for the favourite magazine to turn up at an overseas newsagent?

Magazines viewed on tablet look good and are growing in number. Very importantly they are starting to provide sustainable business models for the publisher as both consumers and advertisers are prepared to pay for them. Publishers are in their comfort zones as they see digital businesses similar to their print models.

Given the volume of digital magazines 'whizzing' around the internet from country to country is there a threat of piracy hitherto unknown in the magazine industry? Chris Llewellyn, FIPP President and CEO, has concerns:

> Illegal downloads are definitely a threat. Hardly a week goes by without FIPP being alerted to a website selling (or in some cases giving away) pirated digital editions. Publishers and National Associations issue legal 'cease and desist' notices, which I guess the music industry used to do. We are probably getting pretty much the same reaction as they did. With every time you close one of these sites another springs up.
>
> It's not been a major issue up to now, but largely because we haven't had sufficient digital content circulating around to make it worthwhile for the pirates. Now we do, and we're starting to see piracy as an issue ratcheting up.

> We did a survey of National Publishing Associations from all around the
> world last year and piracy is now one of the top three concerns for the
> industry.

While many publishers of international brands will see their future as a digital
one, one must note that different geographical markets and publishing sectors
move at various speeds. The future for technological magazines in Asia may well
be digital only – but fashion and glamour magazines retain their cachet with
readers and advertisers by being glossy and in print.

There are significant benefits, however, to adopting digital as the
international platform of choice. Overseas start-up costs are lower and speed to
market quicker. The occasional failure can be closed down quietly. In certain
instances it may be possible to run some international digital editions from the
mother country with no need for international licence partnerships and
consequently no sharing of revenues.

Given digital technology, is the licensee relationship really necessary? Chris
Llewellyn of FIPP believes it is, and qualifies:

> We will see more titles produced from the brand HQ, but it's not totally
> straightforward. English language publications will have a massive footprint
> because of the ubiquity of English. However this will also depend on genre
> and content. Specialist titles may have interesting opportunities – playing
> guitars, keeping fish, or having an interest in tech gadgets. This is
> 'borderless' and so can largely work everywhere with minimal if any change
> to content matter. Lifestyle publications, however, will need to have local,
> quality content which argues against a centralised HQ produced title. So, for
> example, *FHM* will need to have local market glamour celebrities to go
> alongside the international names. Cultural references to music, TV and
> soccer also have to be local.
>
>   If you produce from HQ there is also the issue of advertisement sales
> relationships, though employing an international sales agency is a partial
> answer.

UK-based publishers are increasingly seeing international expansion as an
imperative for their businesses from both a brand and financial point of view.
The creative vibrancy of the UK industry, respected the world around, puts
forward-thinking British publishers in pole position to sell digital copies, award
international licences or form joint ventures overseas.

PUBLISHING LIVE

The two motivators for a publisher to interact with customers in live mode are the
same as for international development – make increased profits and enhance the
brand. A less strategic additional benefit is for editorial teams to meet with readers
face to face, gaining feedback and ideas for future issues.

There is a myriad of ways in which publishers meet readers outside the printed page or the digital swipe. Exhibitions are one of the most commonplace and profitable. The business model of an exhibition is akin to that of a magazine. Visiting customers make up the *circulation* and either pay for their tickets or enter free. The exhibition stands make up the *advertisements* and shows, lectures, demonstrations and talks constitute *editorial*.

Live events are profitable for magazines and vary in shape and size. The *BBC Good Food Show Summer* hosted 95,000 visitors for its 2012 event over five days at the National Exhibition Centre in Birmingham – with advance ticket prices for 2013 at £21.50. Stand space was sold to over 1,000 exhibitors. Capitalising on the current popularity of TV cookery programmes and celebrity chefs, the show offers demonstrations of culinary technique and an exciting retail environment. In January 2013 *The Spectator* hosted over 800 readers at a sell-out evening in London with Kofi Anan, former Secretary General of the United Nations.

To be successful the event must be in harmony with the magazine brand. In that way readers will feel comfortable in attending; they know that they will have a quality experience for which they are prepared to pay. In the case of *BBC Good Food* this will be high quality cookery demonstrations and a plethora of new products to sample; for *The Spectator* readers, an insightful evening's conversation with one of the worldwide statesmen of the age.

One of the most successful consumer magazine live events or brand extensions is the *GQ Men of the Year*. Now in its fifteenth year, this is a truly iconic occasion with 21 awards categories. Recent winners include Tinie Tempah, Sir Bradley Wiggins, Robbie Williams, Gary Barlow and Boris Johnson. Hugo Boss is the headline sponsor. The publicity generated by this event is enormous, estimated by the publisher to be worth over £3 million, principally in national newspapers – a key success criterion for both *GQ* and the sponsor. There is coverage of the event on the publisher's website – a key traffic driver. According to Publishing Director Jamie Bill this sizeable media take up illustrates the importance of the magazine's brand. He believes that such a highly prestigious awards night must reflect without compromise the core brand values of *GQ*[10].

If the reader live event is a 'nice to have' revenue item for the consumer publisher it has become a 'must have' line for many B2B publishers. The business model for that sector is fast changing from the traditional dominance of circulation and advertisement sales as has been demonstrated in Chapter 2. *Retail Week Live* is a highly successful forum for retail executives now in its twenty-second year. There is a cast list of key industry speakers and useful networking opportunities. With delegate ticket prices starting at £1,045, this makes for a profitable event for the publisher.

The Grosvenor House Hotel on London's Park Lane prides itself on having one of the largest reception rooms in the capital. It regularly hosts awards evenings for a whole spectrum of industries, more often than not organised by a key publication in that business sector. Awards evenings can richly enhance a magazine's bottom line. Advertisers will sponsor award categories and gain all that attendant publicity, shortlisted candidates will be encouraged to buy tables for colleagues. A good night is invariably had by all. *H&V News* (Heating and Ventilation) boasts one such event – the *H&V News Awards*. Table packages start at £2,900 per table of ten, over 1,000 guests are expected and 14 sponsors all make for a successful event.

> There is a myriad of ways in which publishers meet readers outside the printed page or the digital swipe

Live events can enhance brand profitability and stature. Before embarking upon such a programme, however, publishers must heed the following potential drawbacks:

- Conferences and exhibitions inevitably take time to build participation by both readers and advertisers. They rarely gel overnight with a potential for losses in the early years. Exhibitors have to cover staff costs and travelling expenses for the duration of the show. If the publisher fails to deliver visitors to the expected quantity and quality, exhibitors can get mighty angry and ask for rebates.
- Exhibitors would normally take stand costs from general marketing expenses and as such the exhibition idea will fight for funds alongside advertising and other publicity. To ensure a viable show and to book good venues, long lead times are required.
- Conferences and awards require umbrella sponsorship: they need a sponsor to pin his name to the event. Again this will have to take its chance in the marketing priority list and the benefits may not always be as quantifiable and tangible as other methods of promotion.
- Events which are in the open air or to which people have to make long journeys will be hostages of fortune to the British weather.
- Much as brand extensions are important, it is vital that the publisher does not side-track editorial and commercial teams from their main job of running the magazine. There must be enough staff to man these events, albeit on short-term contracts. Major events need a partner to help organise an exhibition or conference. Be sure to spend time managing these important relationships.
- The live event must be a physical endorsement of the core values at the heart of the magazine. It is important to remember that the ticket purchasers and attendees are likely to be readers and that the exhibitors and sponsors will almost certainly have an ongoing commercial relationship as advertisers. Respect those partnerships and do not cut the quality of the experience. All stakeholders want to leave with a warm feeling of trusting the brand and happy to repeat their custom.

> The live event must be a physical endorsement of the core values at the heart of the magazine

Publishing is a creative business driven by the innovation of entrepreneurs and their teams constantly coming up with new ideas. Finally here are the experiences of a small and genuinely innovative publishing company – Alfol Ltd. Their main title, *Creative HEAD* is a high quality, glossy read for hairdressers. Co-founder Catherine Handcock takes up the story of how brand extensions have grown in importance.

Hungry for an exciting new read, the UK hairdressing community devoured *Creative HEAD* with relish when we launched the title in September 2000. Innovative and stylish, *Creative HEAD* showcased hairdressing at the epicentre of a world of fashion, business, music, celebrity and international catwalks. Needless to say, it was an instant hit. Named Monthly Business Magazine of the Year at the 2009 PPA Awards, *Creative HEAD* is today read by over 100,000 hairdressing professionals.

Over the years, *Creative HEAD* has grown, not just in issue size, but also upwards and outwards to encompass a whole portfolio of exciting products and events. Brand extension has been a key part of our success, allowing our readers to experience the brand across a variety of different platforms. Today, *Creative HEAD* is not just a print magazine but also a fashionable website, a set of seasonal style bibles, an app, a members' club, and *two* awards events.

A business networking weekend, *Salon Smart,* is now a staple feature of the UK hairdressing calendar.

We launched *Salon Smart* in 2007 in order to give business advice and guidance to UK salon owners. Hairdressers tend to be visual, creative characters and terrible fidgets (they hate sitting down for long periods of time), so we knew that 'business' would have to be delivered in a creative way, and that the agenda would need to be action-packed – literally.

So every year some 300 salon owners and managers from all across the UK have descended upon *Salon Smart* for two days of non-stop networking and fresh thinking on business. Held in London, the event incorporates inspirational speakers, practical workshops such as 'How To Get Ahead with PR' and 'Social Media Masterclass', Q&A sessions and interviews. Live hair shows are served up with a four-course dinner and wine and – possibly the best bit – the 'Meet & Mix' session provides exciting opportunities to spend quality time with some of the biggest names in hairdressing. Delegates emerge at the end of it feeling inspired, exhilarated and with a notepad full of ideas they can implement in their own salon the following day.

Photo 3.4 At *Creative HEAD* magazine's business networking event, Salon Smart, salon owners from all over the UK learn how to shoot for success at a photographic masterclass

Sponsorship covers the actual cost of the event – our headline sponsors Goldwell and KMS California have backed us every year since launch, with other brands too many to mention.

What do we get out of it? First, the chance to meet our readers – always a pleasure and an important barometer of how much they love *Creative HEAD* or not! We derive important information about their salons and their teams via carefully structured questionnaires and feedback forms. Second, an opportunity to deliver important messages about our brand – *Salon Smart* provides a useful source of entrants to our awards events and subscriptions to the magazine. (A discounted subs price is incredibly successful.) Third: revenue. With the costs covered by sponsorship, every ticket sale takes us further into profit – and last year's event was a complete sell-out. *Salon Smart* Regional events are next on the agenda.

Magazine publishing is a fascinating and varied business. We have explained how new key revenue streams are developing to take up some of the shortfall of traditional circulation and advertisement turnover. The need to innovate and launch is paramount, not only in print but across other platforms both at home and abroad. International sales are growing in importance and live events becoming a firm part of the revenue mix.

Tim Brooks is CEO of BMJ, a global medical information business. He was Visiting Fellow in Strategy at London Business School, 2011–12, and prior to that was Managing Director of Guardian News & Media, whose website is one of the 20 most linked-to sites in the world. He sits on the Cabinet Office Digital Advisory Board.

Carolyn Morgan is Managing Director of the Specialist Media Show and SIIA UK Programme Director. She previously held senior publishing positions at Bauer and EMAP.

Catherine Handcock is Managing Director of Alfol Ltd, The Publisher of *Creative Head* Magazine.

The interview with Chris Llewellyn took place on 10 October 2012.

NOTES

1.   Wessenden (2012).
2.   Wessenden (2013) p 21.
3.   Anon. (2012) p 12.
4.   Bilton (2012) p 36.
5.   Wessenden (2012).
6.   Wessenden (2013) p 10.
7.   Wessenden (2012).
8.   Wessenden (2013) p 9.
9.   Trader Media Group Annual report and financial statements 2012, pp 1, 29.
10. Trader Media Group Press Release (2013).
11. Sweney (2012).
12. Ibid. See also Sweney (2013).

13. Future plc Annual Report and Accounts 2012, p 5.
14. Anon., p 12.
15. Future plc. Annual Report and Accounts 2012.
16. ABC analysis 2001–12.
17. Seymour (2012) p 18.
18. Chadwick (2013) p 8.
19. ABC (July–Dec 2012).
20. Chadwick (2013) p 8.
21. ABC (Jan–Dec 2012).
22. Based on analysis of Smith's News data by Comag.
23. Future (2013) p 10.
24. Cabell and Greehan (2012) p 15.
25. Ibid: p 128.
26. Sleight (2012) p 41.
27. ABC (July–Dec 2012).
28. Sleight (2012) p 41.
29. Cabell and Greehan p 25.
30. In interview with the author, 16 October 2012.

REFERENCE SOURCES

Anon. (2012) 'News update: direct + digital', *Wessenden Briefing*, December 2012, 164, pp 12–15.

Bilton, J. (2012) 'How do they make money from doing that?', *InPublishing* , May/June 2012 pp. 36, 38.

Cabell, J. T. and Greehan, M. (2012) *WWM Guide: licensing and syndication explained* (3rd edn). London: FIPP.

Chadwick, E. (2013) 'Immediate delight over its four hit 2012 launches', *Retail Newsagent*, 4 January 2013, p 8.

Future plc Annual Report and Accounts 2012, available at http://mos.futurenet.com/digital/futureplc/Future_Annual_Report2012.pdf (Accessed 13 June 2013.)

Future, *Women's lifestyle portfolio: media information*, 2013 available at http://issuu.com/futurepublishing/docs/lifestyle_media_pack (Accessed 13 June 2013.)

Seymour (2012) 'Magazine market retail sales pulse Q3 2012: trends + shares in magazine retails sales (2 of 2)', *Wessenden Briefing*, December 2012, 164, pp 17–18.

Sleight, H. (2012) 'Back of the net', *Magazine World*, Q1 2012, 72, pp 39, 41.

Sweney, M. (2012) 'Future returns to profitability', *Guardian*, 23 November 2012 available at http://www.guardian.co.uk/media/2012/nov/23/future-return-profitability (Accessed 13 June 2013.)

Sweney, M. (2013) 'Future's revenues slide as games titles await Xbox One and PlayStation 4', *Guardian*, 22 May 2013 available http://www.guardian.co.uk/media/2013/may/22/future-publishing-xbox-one-playstation-4 (Accessed 13 June 2013.)

Trader Media Group Annual report and financial statements 2012, available at http://www.tradermediagroup.com/media/38631/tmg%20ar%202012.pdf (Accessed 13 June 2013.)

Trader Media Group Press Release, 7 May 2013 available at http://www.tradermediagroup.com/media/59694/auto-trader-digital-transition-070513.pdf (Accessed 13 June 2013.)

Wessenden (2012) *PPA Publishing Futures 2012 Report* available at http://www.ppa.co.uk/events/news/publishing-futures-2012/ (Accessed 13 June 2013.)

Wessenden (2013) *PPA Publishing Futures 2013 Report*. Godalming: Wessenden.

CHAPTER 4

Editorial: originating and managing creative content

Richard Sharpe

The following two chapters of *Inside Magazine Publishing* will describe in detail how editorial content is produced. Chapter 5 is devoted to the importance of covers, key design principles and how to write for the magazine medium. The following is a brief description of the contents of this chapter which will focus principally upon editorial strategy and management.

We will examine the editorial department in its role as creator of quality content to serve readers. This content should inform and entertain the market at which it is aimed. Readers often have a specialist interest which the magazine serves. Publishers profile the reader and use a variety of sources to get closer to the reader – they also need a vision of how to serve the reader which is consistently implemented. Part of this vision is the attitude the magazine has to its readers and its subjects. There are four key questions to ask of a magazine: two about how they appeal to the head and two about how they appeal to the heart.

The content of the magazine now has a different path given the increasing use of digital media by titles. This new route allows the title to have more of a conversation with readers than in the past. There are different structures to the editorial department: from one person to a whole army. These structures have to be managed and the people within them have to be motivated. There are particular characteristics of editorial work which mean the standard methods of management are not always successful.

SERVING THE READER

The editorial team together with other contributors create the content of a magazine both on paper and online. They do so with a clear purpose which is more than just keeping the advertisements apart.

This purpose is to serve the readers on paper by creating content which will attract those in the market at which they are aiming and to keep them as readers for future issues. It is also important to keep them reading each issue for as long as possible. Their readers are also potential visitors to and creators of additional material on the different parts of the magazine which are online or digital. Editorial teams have now to think of their title as a whole publication in many different forms, rather than just as a paper magazine which happens to have a

... more than just keeping the advertisements apart

website. They need to consider what goes where: what material suits which media best? Much of the time of editors of magazines today is spent deciding where to publish. Should an article or feature be kept for next month's paper edition? Or should it be delivered to visitors to the various digital media the magazine offers so that the readers get the information faster? More and more the answer is the latter.

The editorial team also has to ask itself how it can involve the reader on paper and online. Magazines which engage and involve readers often have a greater chance of keeping them as customers. Increasingly people want information as fast as possible and on any device of their choosing. The world is becoming increasingly media agnostic: it does not care what the media is, only about getting all the content on all platforms.

Readers want information to help them in their everyday lives. It may be information about the specialism on which their chosen magazine focuses. For example, *Steam Railway* every month delivers news of restoration projects for steam engines and reviews of where steam is still used for railway locomotives. It does so in words and with high quality photography. This content is not everybody's choice but for the 31,805 people who buy *Steam Railway*, it is an important part of their lives. Moreover 14,000 of those people who buy the magazine subscribe rather than buy it at retail[1], such is their devotion to the subject and the title. A strong subscription base is a valuable financial asset for a magazine.

Photo 4.1
Steam Railway has a specialist and devoted community of readers

Magazines are a luxury

There was a late-Victorian magazine which summed up the appeal of magazines in its title: *The Leisure Hour*. It used a quotation from William Cowper's eighteenth-century poem, *Retirement*, to say what a magazine delivers to its readers: 'Behold in these what leisure hours demand / Amusement and true knowledge hand in hand'. Amusement and true knowledge are the keys to great editorial content. Editorial teams try to make the magazines they work on an important part of the lives of their readers: as sources of both amusement and true knowledge.

Magazines are a luxury – they are not like the journals of business or professions where practitioners have to read them in order to keep up with up-to-date information, skills and knowledge. However, there are some hybrid journals/magazines: *Nursing Standard* is one example which captures the Cowper quote well as it blends amusement and true knowledge. It is published by the Royal College of Nursing with a circulation of 50,885[2]. *Nursing Standard* is a magazine at the front, a journal in the middle and a section of careers advertising at the back. Most magazines do not have a 'professional information' section which makes them a hybrid: they are pure magazines. Yet they can still provide vital information about what their readers do or want to do, an example is *Farmers Weekly* published by Reed Business Information (RBI), with its circulation of 61,842[3]. Many elements of what *Farmers Weekly* delivers every week can be found elsewhere. So magazines are often the route, the condensed route, through which readers get their information. Magazines are like the shortcut on the desktop screen of the personal computer. They provide a package of information to their readers which, in this digital world, may be available somewhere else but only with a lot of effort. They serve as a collator of information. They are a store house of information; indeed, 'storehouse' in Arabic (*makhazan*) is the origin of the word 'magazine'.

> Magazines are like the shortcut on the desktop screen of the personal computer

Magazines are amusement

Magazines are also an indulgence, or an amusement to use Cowper's words, and editorial teams need to put together packages which deliver this. Returning to *Steam Railway*, the readers are treated to fine photography of steam engines, sometimes at night or after a rain shower or puffing up an incline pulling a row of carriages. The readers can feast their eyes on those gleaming engines and indulge themselves. They can almost smell the steam and oil and hear the clank of the engine parts. The readership has a passion for the subject and the editorial team and contributors are there to create content which serves this passion. The editorial must not only inform, it also has to delight and entertain. In this case it succeeds as readers keep coming back for more.

Many readers of *Steam Railway*, as with any other magazine, will think that it is *their* magazine; such is people's attachment to the medium. This says a lot about how important magazines are to readers' lives. Woe betides the editor who changes a magazine so much that its core readers no longer empathise with it. The editor's email box will be flooded with howls of anguish from buyers asking: 'What have you done to my magazine?' We shall look later at the emotional attachments readers have to magazines, but if the editorial team can evoke a feeling of ownership among readers, then it has done a good job.

Finding and profiling readers

Readers of *Steam Railway* and *Simply Knitting* are likely to be very different. As the publisher of *Steam Railway* states in the industry source, *Brad Insight*, the magazine has an 'almost exclusively male readership, average 56 years. Readership tends towards those with active involvement in preservation projects, and travel. Tendency towards high usage of camera film and purchase of books/ videos.' On the other hand, Future, the publisher of *Simply Knitting*, states that its readers are female and likely to be between 35 years and 64 years. The majority will be experienced knitters but one in ten will be a newcomer to the craft with less than one year's knitting experience. The title's media pack claims it is a knitter's 'best friend'[4]. *Simply Knitting* attracts over 43,869[5] purchasers, the majority of whom buy it at the newsagent rather than subscribe.

Interests, ages and gender are clearly different for both magazines. The same can be said of almost all magazines, whether focussing on a specialist subject or not – individual titles are unique.

Photo 4.2
Most readers of
Simply Knitting are
female and likely to
be between 35 years
and 64 years

Editorial teams have to know their readers: they have to have a clear profile of who the readers are and what they want. What is their age and demographic group? What other interests do they have away from the core subject matter of the magazine? These are some of the details content creators need to know and keep in mind as they produce the magazine.

Take *Red* magazine in the fiercely competitive women's magazine sector. Owned by Hearst Magazines UK, the publisher gathers as much information about its readers as possible. This helps not only to create the content along the lines *Red* readers demand but also to help advertisers understand the readership profile.

The profile of the *Red* reader:

She is likely to be a woman aged 30 plus and in the social category A,B or C1.

- *Red* readers spent a huge £599 million on clothes and accessories in the last twelve months. Two out of three *Red* readers agree that it is important to them to look well dressed. In addition, 52 per cent would say that they have a good sense of style.
- *Red* readers spent £41 million on watches and jewellery in the last 12 months.
- *Red* readers spent £22 million on handbags in the last 12 months.
- *Red* readers spend on average £9 million on beauty products per month. *Red* readers are almost twice as likely as the average woman to be brand champions of beauty products.
- Seventy-one per cent of *Red* readers agree they like to try out new food products.
- There are 316,000 *Red* readers who are always looking for ways to improve their home.
- *Red* readers spent £113 million on furniture in the last 12 months.
- *Red* readers spent £530 million on holidays and short breaks in the last 12 months, with an average of over £1,482 per person on their last holiday.
- There are 261,000 readers who are interested in reading about health and fitness.

Source: Hearst Magazines UK media pack for *Red*.[6]

Armed with this detailed information, the editorial team on *Red* can create a well-targeted package to maximise both circulation and advertisement revenues and delight the reader. *Red* is a highly successful monthly glossy title with key editorial 'pillars' packed with features on fashion and accessories, beauty, living, food and drink, health and escapes (travel and holidays).

Publishers obtain this depth of information from a number of sources. They research their own readers, often putting a survey into their magazine with a prize draw as an incentive to complete. They may also have detailed demographic profiles of their subscribers as they have a direct customer relationship with this group. They convene focus groups of readers to gather and analyse reactions to both new developments as well as the existing magazine. In addition, for larger magazines, the National Readership Survey (NRS) and Target Group Index (TGI) enables editorial teams to gain a more detailed statistical insight. Publishers clearly distinguish between those who buy the magazine and so make up the paid circulation and those who are 'pass-on readers'. See Chapter 7 for the differences between circulation and readership and how publishers use this data.

All of this information is grist for the mill of the content creators. Editorial teams often create pen portraits of readers, as individuals or groups. They include where and when they read the magazine, how they may holiday, what their income is and how they spend it. With this pen portrait they can angle the content they create, making contact with the reader as a result. For example, the editorial team of *Steam Railway* knows that the title appeals to keen photographers, so the quality of the photography in the magazine has to be high to delight these customers.

Editors take varying degrees of interest in the research into readers and potential readers. Some, foolishly, ignore research completely and then may find their readers have wandered away. Others let it inform them without being bound by the results. Crafting the content of magazines is not, after all, a science, but a skill.

> Some, foolishly, ignore research completely and then may find their readers have wandered away

> Crafting the content of magazines is not, after all, a science, but a skill

Is the time ripe for this magazine?

Please do not think that every magazine ever launched was carefully honed with masses of research and a clinical profile of its readers. Some very successful magazines of their era have been launched by publishers and editors who just believed that the time was ripe for such a publication. The UK launch of *Cosmopolitan*, as outlined by Christine Stam in Chapter 1, is a good example of this. Sometimes they captured the *zeitgeist*, the spirit of the times, for sufficient readers to make the new title a success.

When Tyler Brûlé and Alexander Geringer launched *Wallpaper* in 1996 they did so because they had a clear vision for a certain type of magazine. Brûlé, a journalist, had been badly injured as a war correspondent and when recovering decided to do what he wanted and that desire was to launch a new title. The magazine would be about all that which was around us, in other words, the wallpaper of our life, hence the title. Brûlé and Geringer expressed their own interests in their magazine; it soon caught on and was later successfully sold to Time Inc. They had a vision of their magazine which had attracted a solid following.

The same was true for *Private Eye* which was launched in 1961. Peter Usborne, a co-founder of *Private Eye* later wrote: 'The idea was to find out whether we were any good. And whether anybody else thought we were any good, and then whether anybody would actually buy it'. The first issue sold quite well, they decided to do a second, then a third before Christmas 1961.Editor Christopher

Booker, continues: 'And they'd all gone so well that the feeling was that in the new year we should start the thing on a regular basis'[7]. *The Face* was a similar projection of values, as the following brief case study shows.

Case study 8

The Face: catching the moment and losing it

The Face was launched by Nick Logan in 1980 and caught the spirit of the emerging decade. Logan had previously worked on music titles *Smash Hits* and *New Musical Express*.

The Face was aimed at young men and covered fashion, popular music and style and did so with a degree of extravagance and excess. It popularised the style of the New Romantics and other 1980s' trends. There had been nothing like this package before and it soon became a 'must have' magazine within youth culture.

It was a projection of values to its young readers and an expression of a lifestyle by its writers.

The Face attracted writers with style including Julie Burchill and Tony Parsons. It was also famed for its iconic design and typography. However, other magazines caught up with it and focussed on the same subjects. Its approach was imitated and spread so far that *The Face* was no longer unique. Circulation peaked in the mid-1990s. As Britpop became the popular music culture of the 1990s, 'lads mags' such as *Loaded* and *FHM* came to the fore after 1994. *The Face* was closed in 2004 having lost both its edge and much of its readership.

CREATING THE VISION

All successful magazines must have a clear vision for creative content. Within the editorial team there are two people, the editor and the art editor, who are crucial to creating this. With words and illustrations, on paper and online, this duo has to craft an overall feel of the magazine and its appeal to readers. This vision has to be consistent with the expectations, needs and standards of the target readership. For example, Bauer Consumer Magazines publishes the top-selling title magazine *Yours*. *Yours* 'entertains, informs and advises the 50 years plus market with advice on topics that matter to life today plus memories of the way we used to live' – according to its self-description in *Brad Insight*. For £1.40 a fortnight *Yours* delivers a generous package of advice, nostalgia and friendship for its largely female readership with a circulation of over 270,000[8]. Its layout has a slightly retro feel to it and its cover may feature an older celebrity to whom the readership can respond. Imagine your Gran, she could be the reader. Indeed one feature at the time of writing was headed 'Gran's my best friend'. In the same issue is an article on the day the UK went decimal, health advice, and a piece headed 'At last I'm free of pain'. Its tone is chatty and intimate, a friend of the reader who may be living alone.

> All successful magazines must have a clear vision for creative content

Photo 4.3
The top-selling title
magazine *Yours* is
aimed at a target
audience aged over
50 years

This is, of course, a far different vision from other Bauer titles such as *Steam Railway* or *Motor Cycle News (MCN)*, the motorcycle news and reviews weekly. *MCN* feeds the passion of its readers for motorcycling, giving them the first and best reviews from the biking world. Page format and paper quality also differentiate the titles and heighten relevance to their chosen markets – *Steam Railway* has a traditional magazine format: glossy cover and is A4 in size. *MCN* is tabloid and printed on newsprint quality paper – it has a clear feel of immediacy and of being led by news.

In all of these cases, editors and art editors have worked together closely to create and project the vision of the magazine.

To be a commercial success this vision has to attract enough readers to provide both copy sales income and enough eyeballs to entice advertisers to invest in advertising space. Some magazines have caught the imagination of the reading public and become soar away successes because they envisioned a hugely innovative way of looking at the world. This is discussed in more detail by David Stam in Chapter 3 when referring to launches that defined markets such as UK *Cosmopolitan* or *Loaded*. This vision has to be continuously attuned to the shifts in attitudes of readers. As we have seen with *The Face*, if the magazine does not adapt to these shifts in attitudes its circulation will decline. This is also illustrated with the following case study of *Hello!*

Case study 9

The rise and slide of *Hello!*

Hello! was launched in the UK in 1988 as a UK version of the highly successful Spanish magazine *¡Hola*, itself launched back in 1944. 'Things of human interest would have a particular place in the magazine, and people more than things' its founder said. It focussed on celebrities and was respectful towards them. A classic double page spread was typically a visit to the home of a celebrity such as a football star or a minor royal. The largest circulations were achieved for its coverage of the weddings of its subjects. It offered this weekly coverage in full colour with a format slightly larger than the average women's magazine which provided a point of difference. Newspapers were not yet printing in full colour which also gave *Hello!* a unique advantage. Readers were let into the homes and lives of these celebrity subjects but the magazine was never critical or mocking of their lifestyles.

Hello! caught the imagination of readers with gusto. In 1990 it was named as the Professional Publishers Association's (PPA) Consumer Magazine of the year and rose to have a circulation over half a million – for the period July to December 2000 the posted ABC was 502,679.

This successful UK launch prompted its owners to expand globally and there are currently 24 international editions. From 1993 *Hello!* faced tough competition in the UK from rival *OK!* published by Northern and Shell. Initially monthly, this title subsequently turned weekly.

As we entered the new millennium the attitude of many readers towards celebrities changed. It became less respectful. *Heat,* initially launched as an entertainment and listings title, radically repositioned under editor Mark Frith. It caught the mood of the times and was quite happy to poke fun at and mock well known people and include gossip. In the same year as *Heat* was relaunched the *Big Brother* reality television programme showed celebrities in a 24/7 environment making fools of themselves. Fast forward ten more years – Facebook, Twitter and dedicated websites allow fans to talk to the famous in a direct and instantaneous way.

Hello! became increasingly squeezed between changing attitude and technologies and the fierce competition from *OK!* The title's circulation for the second half of 2012 was 305,567 compared with 342,495 for *OK!* The latter magazine is £1 per copy compared with *Hello!* priced at £2. *Heat* has sales of 261,715[9].

Hello! has kept to its vision and still maintains a respectful regard for the famous people it covers. Did the title make the right decision by resisting the chase after sales at the more populist end of the market? Circulation may be close to half the number sold at its zenith but the ABC is still healthy in the current circulation environment and it has not dropped the cover price.

Elements of the vision

There are several different elements to the overall vision created by the editor and art editor. Three are key:

- size
- look
- attitude.

Size and look

Magazines can use size or format as a factor to differentiate themselves. Publications have traditionally been printed to standard sizes, normally American letter or A4. (American letter is 279.4mm x 215.9mm and A4 the longer but slightly narrower 297mm x 210mm.) A visit to a well-stocked newsstand today reveals a greater variety of page sizes.

Tyler Brûlé's next venture after leaving *Wallpaper* was *Monocle*, a briefing on global affairs, travel, business, culture and design. With *Monocle*, he went for a compact shape: 265mm x 200mm – smaller than *Wallpaper*. This makes it easy to slip into your briefcase or handbag and convenient to open when on an aeroplane. The smaller format also gives the publication bulk. Is it possible to say which is best? No, but it is important for the editorial and publishing team to opt for a format which both suits the needs of the target market and which reflects the overall vision for the magazine brand. Some women's magazines publish now in both full and compact format.

Having settled on the size of the magazine the editor and art editor will work on the look. This is a key part of executing the editorial vision. The key determinants will be the choice of type fonts, the design grid and the structure of covers and layouts. We will look at these main principles of design in the next chapter.

Attitude

Two aspects of attitude need to be considered – the attitude of the magazine to the subject matter and its attitude to readers. As we have seen in the case study, when *Hello!* was first launched in the UK it opened up the lives and homes of stars and royals and delivered full colour pictures to its readers. It was a great success, setting the trend for gazing at celebrities. Its gaze was steady and its attitude to its subject was almost reverential. When *Heat* was first launched in 1999 as a listings and entertainment magazine it was not a success. Only when the editorial team started to take an ironic look at celebrities and gave the title a radical relaunch did it hit the dizzy circulation heights. Its attitude to its subjects became tongue in cheek.

The second attitude is to the readers: how far are they to be let into the secret world of the magazine and how are they to be addressed? *The Economist* addresses its readers in a sober, detached way. It informs them with top quality analysis without letting the reader into the magazine apart from its letters pages. The editorial team does not reveal itself: there are no by lines, only *noms de plumes* for some columns such as Bagehot and Charlemagne. It carries this anonymity on to its web pages but here readers can post comments.

On the other hand, in a very different market *Essentials,* the women's magazine, has taken celebrities off its covers and now only puts on real readers. It even invites a group of readers to edit the readers' special edition every year. In 2013, *Essentials* won the PPA diversity award for 'clearing its front covers for unique portraits of real women'. *Essentials* is one of the few magazines in the fiercely competitive women's sector to increase circulation or to hold onto its existing buyers. It is the same with *Elle* Magazine: 'Behind the Scenes at Elle' was the cover line of the October 2012 issue with a whole section edited by 10 interns. What works for *The Economist* will not work for *Essentials* or *Elle*.

Another approach increasingly used is to have a celebrity or guest editor. This makes the magazine, or that issue, a personal statement by the celebrity and can drive tremendous publicity for that issue. No less than Prince Charles was the guest editor of *Country Life* in November 2013. This one off issue focus will work for *Country Life* but not for *Take a Break*. The latter title has a formula-based editorial approach which a guest editor could not greatly influence. *New Statesman* uses occasional guest editors to great effect.

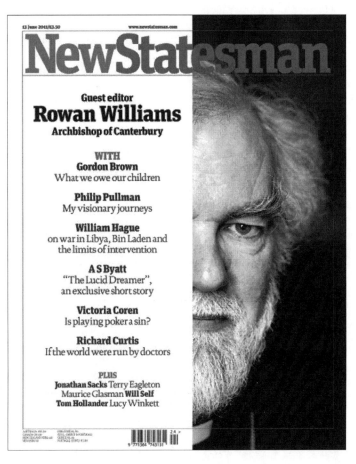

Photo 4.4 In 2011 the guest editor for one issue was the then Archbishop of Canterbury, Dr Rowan Williams. Cover lines are printed on a wraparound flap for added impact

Notice that word 'work'. In making these crucial decisions about the vision of the magazine right down to the most trivial matters the editorial team needs to find out what works. Very often, in meetings about covers for example, people say 'I like that'. We should ban the word 'like'. See the boxed text for why.

> **Very often, in meetings about covers for example, people say 'I like that'. We should ban the word 'like'**

> **The magazine is not created for the editorial team ...**

Ban the word 'like'; use the word 'works'

When making any judgements about editorial content always try to establish what works and what does not. The magazine is not created for the editorial team; it is created for the readers of the paper edition and the visitors and users of the digital editions. The various team members spend their working lives putting the content together. The reader, visitor or user may spend seconds on a tweet, minutes on a website and any time upwards of 45 minutes reading the paper edition.

The editorial team of *Yours*, for example, is not made up of 50 years plus women. It will be staffed by professional journalists young and old, male and female. Remember the magazine is not aimed at the team. Many specialist magazines are staffed by enthusiasts for their subjects. However, even these enthusiasts, who may have been avid readers before they were lucky enough to get a job on the title, need to realise that they are now in a privileged position. They are on the inside, the magazine does not have to satisfy them; it has to satisfy the readers.

FOUR KEY QUESTIONS

There are four key questions we can ask when analysing any magazine and creating its vision. Two appeal to the head, and two to the heart.

Appeals to the head

The first and most commonly asked question of a magazine is what is its content and what does it deliver or give to the reader? Is it a news and features-based magazine which tells its readers about their specialist subject such as *Steam Railway*? Is it a business magazine which tells the readers about their business such as *Farmers Weekly*? Is it a mixture of cartoons, jokes and investigative journalism such as *Private Eye*? This all appeals to the head of the reader: what do they want to know?

The second question follows on logically: what can the reader do now that they have this content that they could not do previously? Many magazines focus on hobbies and pastimes such as walking, collecting or model making. *Country Walking* is a good example. With each issue its readers can follow the paths mapped out for them and explore new parts of the country that they may not have experienced before. With *Simply Knitting* the reader can tackle increasingly complex patterns and develop their knitting techniques. *Private Eye* enables the reader to gain a deeper understanding of politics, finance, the media, the armed forces and the medical profession – as well as having a laugh.

Appeals to the heart

Titles which make a successful appeal to the hearts of readers turn any old magazine into the magazine which the readers think they own. Our third question is: what does it make the reader feel? If a magazine can make people feel empowered, part of a community and supported then it has touched their hearts and they are more likely to be repeat purchasers. They are also more likely to think of the title as *their* magazine. Take *Farmers Weekly*: farming is unfortunately regarded as a high risk occupation when looking at rates of suicide. Farmers often feel isolated, working hard as both nature and government regulations batter them. Every week *Farmers Weekly* tells them that they are doing a good job, they are not alone and there are answers to their problems. Some of the headlines may threaten: 'Regulations forcing small flock owners out of business' runs one. Others offer opportunity: 'Good soil health could be the key to poor livestock fertility' and 'Program helps farmers make the most of pig data' and again 'Struggling Scots to get financial aid'. The magazine is providing clear purpose to its readers' lives.

The magazine *Bizarre* from Dennis Publishing lives out its title to the letter. The publishers says of it that it is a 'men's lifestyle magazine with a difference'. The magazine is outrageous yet informative ... everything for the British male'. It includes *Your Bizarre* 'The next 19 pages are dedicated to you, you, you!' and features news and events from the *Bizarre* scene. For its male 18 to 30-year-old readers *Bizarre* gives them a sense of community in their interest in some of the weirder things of life. They feel as if they belong: individual readers can consume their magazine but feel part of a web of readers.

The real-life story magazines, such as *Take a Break* and *Chat*, give the readers another feeling: glad it did not happen to me. They read the cover lines such as 'She would not leave the man who killed her' and shiver, but in the knowledge that it is not their experience they are observing. They peer into the lives of others and can take some satisfaction that, to them it is fiction, but centred in life.

The fourth important question which also addresses the hearts of the readers concerns that vital part of modern life: identity. What does it say about the reader that they read this magazine? What would the world think of that reader if they were reading it in public? What identity does it give them in the world?

Most often magazines are read in public and they can make positive statements about the reader. The 50-year-old male reading *Private Eye* wants to look well informed but with a keen sense of humour; the 20-year-old woman reading *Vogue* is saying she is strongly fashion conscious. *Country Life* on a coffee table shows the owner has an understanding of the finer things in life. The owner may in fact live in a town but he or she has aspirations towards a rural lifestyle. All of these are public statements about who we are because we are showing the world what we consume by way of magazine media.

Case study 10

Yours: appeals to the head and heart – putting the four vision questions to the test

Jack Harvey, University of East London

Yours is published by Bauer Consumer Media fortnightly and priced at a pension-affordable £1.40 per issue. It is aimed at the 50 years plus market. Circulation for the ABC period July to December 2012 was 272,040 per issue; its readership is 472,000. In terms of social class, with readers split almost equally – 221,000 are Adults ABC1 while 251,000 are Adults C2DE. It is clearly read more by women, only 14 per cent of its readers are male. (NRS Jan–Dec 2012.)

A focus group of eight women readers was convened to gain their reaction to *Yours* and to get them to answer the four key questions. One was a subscriber, six were regular readers and one classed herself as an occasional reader. They were aged between 57 years and 68 years. Only one was still working.

The group consider the covers of *Yours* to work hard. They feature the magic words 'Win', 'Free' and 'Healthy'. The focus group said they want to be healthy, they want interviews with female TV celebrities and they love spending evenings with a Sudoku puzzle. They are presented with all of that on the cover.

The focus group was asked the following four key questions and the results support the success of *Yours* as a magazine well targeted at its readers with a strong vision.

What does *Yours* give the reader?

Yours is a package of real life stories, chats with stars, fashion and beauty tips, health and diet items, leisure time activities, problems solved, offers of prizes and products, puzzles, fiction, horoscopes, offers of friendships and nostalgia. It gives the readers not only an opportunity to consume but an opportunity to interact.

What can the reader do as a result of reading *Yours*?

The reader of *Yours* can retain their health as they get older, cook on a budget, find new friends, relax with puzzles and connect to their past. They can also get the latest news and interviews on their favourite TV shows – such as Strictly Come Dancing – in addition it gives them something to talk about. In relation to the puzzle pages, helping to keep the brain active is important for those who are retired.

What does *Yours* make the reader feel?

The reader of *Yours* feels comfortable, informed and entertained. They feel connected to a wider community they otherwise could not attach themselves to. One of the most interesting responses was that they felt occupied. As the majority of the focus group was retired, reading *Yours* was something to do, a part of their routine. One of the focus group said using some of the health tips made her feel younger.

What does *Yours* say about the reader?

The reader of *Yours* is looking to take part in a wider community of mature people who are still active. The magazine addresses this by looking at health and keeping fit related topics. The title also says that, despite their age, readers are still seeking to learn new things and meet new people. They want to find out new tips on cooking, travelling, finances, health, relationships. This shows that they're not set in their ways and they still look to improve certain aspects of their life. In short, *Yours* works well for its target readers, answering the four key vision questions and reaching both the heads and hearts of its readers.

THE CONTENT

Once the overall title's vision has been debated and agreed, editorial content has to be originated to match that vision. This content is now spread across different media platforms, not just print on paper magazines. It has to be different for each media because each form has its different mode of consumption by readers and viewers. Increasingly the consumers of magazines see themselves as viewers using tablets and smartphones to view images on screen.

Magazine brands are both now print on paper and digital and they play differing roles in the way they interact with readers. The style of a tweeted reply to an article or a blog is very different from the more leisurely read of a magazine on paper, just as the visual domination of Facebook is far different from the text-based nature of Linkedin. When publishers first toyed with magazine websites at the turn of the millennium, they saw this as an extension of their paper presence. They 'shovelled' the content from paper magazines online. The more innovative publishers soon realised that the paper presence and the website were different media; they needed a variety of approaches because they were consumed in different ways.

The paper publication was a leisurely read during its lifespan, be it weekly, fortnightly or monthly: whereas the website could provide an immediate and continuing link to the reader. Publishers stopped seeing information on the website as an extension of the paper edition, and saw this presence as a publication in its own right. Online immediacy taught publishers that magazines can last longer in the lives of readers than the relatively short time span that many readers of the paper edition consume the print magazine. They could lengthen the time spent with the reader and have a larger impact on their lives: bringing them more amusement and true knowledge.

> Magazine brands are both now print on paper and digital and they play differing roles in the way they interact with readers

Starting a conversation with readers

Publishers also learned that the digital presence of the magazine allowed them to start a conversation with the reader. The reader no longer had to consume or reject what was published in their title; they could comment, contribute and even craft their own magazine from the snippets of products they followed online. Editors then realised, in their role as the creators of content, the story now had a different path as a result of this conversation with readers. The article could take different directions; it was no longer a single piece but a series of interactions with readers.

When the magazine only existed on paper the direction of the story was that it was researched, written, illustrated, subedited, laid out and printed for the reader to consume. Now, in the new world of conversations with readers and the proliferation of digital platforms, the story takes a new path, engaging the reader at each point. For example, take an interview piece. The writer can tweet that they are to interview somebody and ask for questions. They can repeat this on Facebook or Linkedin, depending on whether the title is a consumer publication or a B2B publication and even video the interview. The 'killer quote' can be tweeted from the interview as the journalist writes for the paper edition and streams the video online.

With investigative features, through the various digital channels, the writer can ask if the wider world has contacts which would aid the investigation or instances of the events under the microscope. In each step on this new path readers are more involved in a conversation rather than being spoken to by the publication on paper. The hope is that they will then identify with the publication in more depth than simply just buying or subscribing to the magazine.

Juggling the content

Many magazine editors are now running multimedia content generation rooms. They are juggling the regular frequency of their paper edition with the immediate media of the digital world. As we have seen in Chapter 2, some publishers, particularly in B2B markets, have taken the bold step of ceasing the paper edition altogether – with all the commensurate print and distribution costs – and only publishing a digital issue.

The new path of the story on paper and on digital raises a central question for all editors – where does this story go? Must it be tweeted and put on our blog immediately because it is perishable? Or do we have material which we can hold for the paper edition and splash over digital media once it is at the newsagents and on its way to subscribers. If a story can be held over for the paper edition, then so much the better because its impact will likely be bigger. However, a magazine, even a monthly, does not want to be beaten to an online story by its competition. Therefore all the different platforms of the magazine have to work together. The paper issue feeds interest in and points to the digital offering which in turn builds anticipation for the next paper edition.

> Many magazine editors are now running multimedia content generation rooms

Correct content for the market

Similar content can be repackaged and edited into magazines which – while seemingly performing similar roles in serving the reader – will have differing visions as to how they go about their task. A good example of this attribute of magazine publishing is seen in the highly competitive TV listings market. The seven established titles have a combined unduplicated readership of over ten million, the largest of which offer the highest weekly readerships of all paid for magazines. TV listings are readily available in daily and weekly newspapers, online or on the TV screen itself. Yet *What's on TV, Radio Times, TV Choice, TV Times, Total TV Guide, TV Easy* and *TV & Satellite Week* still thrive.

Each may be carrying listings but has carved for itself a niche in the market with its different approach. *Radio Times*, for example, still carries radio programming: the others do not, and it has regular columns from its broadcasters. It is considered to be an up-market publication. *TV Times* is an 'old hand' and was launched along with ITV in the 1950s, retaining a loyal readership. Table 4.1 clearly shows the respective social demographic positions of these titles. *TV Choice* and *What's On TV* are in the middle or 'budget' market and have a focus on soap operas. *TV Easy* differentiates itself with a compact format, while *Total TV Guide* and *TV & Satellite Week* offer details of a large range of satellite and cable channels.

The typical contract or customer magazine is necessarily constrained: it has to fit the brand values of the company for whom the magazine is being produced. You will not find a plug for Sainsbury's in the *Tesco Magazine*. Readers do not seem to mind this: they are sophisticated and used to differentiating between brand messages. Readers respond to supermarket magazines so favourably that *Tesco Magazine* was the most read of all print publications at the end of 2012, according to the NRS. It even topped the *Sun*. This proves three things:

- Magazines do work as a means of communication, despite some dire tales from publishers about falling circulations, and a squeeze on advertising budgets.
- Free content is increasingly becoming the norm.
- In terms of growth, branded content in the form of customer publishing is the bright spot of magazine publishing.

Table 4.1 UK TV Listings magazines

	Publisher	Price	Average Weekly Circulation	Profile ABC1 %	Profile C2DE %
TV Choice	Bauer	45p	1,230,076	40	60
What's on TV	IPC	52p	1,222,242	38	62
Radio Times	Immediate	£1.60	893,512	76	24
TV Times	IPC	£1.25	275,526	47	53
TV and Satellite Weekly	IPC	£1.40	165,735	40	60
TV Easy	IPC	52p	148,759	31	69
Total TV Guide	Bauer	£1.00	121,169	39	61

Source: ABC (July–Dec 2012); NRS (Jan–Dec 2012)

STRUCTURE – THE DIFFERENT PARTS OF EDITORIAL

The structure of the editorial department varies greatly depending on the type of publication and the roles needed to generate the content. Post the 2008 recession, staff budgets have undoubtedly been under pressure across the whole industry. Therefore the structure is determined not only by what needs to be done but also how much the publication can afford to spend on the creation of content.

The key role is that of the editor or editor-in-chief. It is at this level that the principal decisions about content are made. All editors are legally responsible for the whole magazine. Editors need to influence the production process at an early stage in order to mould their title. Some break this rule and only become involved at the latter phases, often necessitating members of the team to rework layouts and copy, consequently wasting time.

> ... the editor needs to have an eye on commercial aspects in order to understand the magazine as a business

The editor is also often the external voice of the magazine: used by other media as an expert in their field. The editor of *The Spectator*, Fraser Nelson, is often invited by other media to comment on politics.

As a key member of the publishing team, the editor needs to have an eye on commercial aspects in order to understand the magazine as a business. Some smaller monthly magazines may have an editor who mainly writes and commissions freelance and specialist contributors. The production work of laying out and subediting can be done by freelance staff used only when needed and paid by the day. Small, three-person teams are also commonplace with an editor and two writers.

Another possible structure is a three-person team supported by a hub for layout and production. In this structure there is an editor, an editorial assistant, and an online news editor. These are supported by a group of sub editors and art editors who will work across a number of different magazines. Sub editors work on the copy, checking it for factual accuracy and making sure it fits the style of the magazine. They also craft captions, headlines, and standfirsts and select pull quotes – see Chapter 5.

The classic structure of a weekly news magazine, for example *Farmers Weekly*, is to have an editor, a news editor, a chief reporter, and then specialist editors: in this case business, livestock, poultry, arable, community and farmlife and machinery. They are supported by an art editor, a content editor and staff writers. In addition there is an online team of three.

Large, glossy, fashion monthlies are at the top of the scale of staff numbers. They will have an editor or editor-in-chief, a fashion and beauty department of up to nine possibly with interns, a features editor with supporting staff, a photography section of two or more, four or five in the art department and four or more in the copy section for subediting. In all, the list of staff, called the flannel panel, of *Elle* has 53 in the editorial team across all disciplines and including contributing editors, interns and a dedicated resource on elleuk.com.

MANAGING THE OPERATION

Editorial departments are teams of individuals creating content. They need to be managed and to be able to manage themselves. Quality content is created by people working well together: sometimes with conflict but with common purposes. They have to manage time, manage upwards, manage downwards, manage their own motivation and manage external contributors.

Managing time – ten time-saving tips

Editorial departments have one non-renewable resource vital to creating content – time. Creativity takes time and is not always best fostered under pressure. The editorial department has a press deadline for the print version and all timings work back from that. The department also has set slots at which it has to refresh its digital content. It will want to beat its competition to the punch and give fresh content to visitors to sites just before the peaks of viewing. For many sites such occasions are during coffee breaks and at lunch. So, time is the key.

Yet many editorial departments can be very inefficient. They produce the magazine in its different forms but often under pressure. For monthly magazines this is sometimes called the 'monthly miracle', it's a miracle that the product gets out at all.

Ten ways to save time

1. Every member of the department can identify somebody inside or outside the department who is a time bandit: a person who is stealing their precious time. For example, are people constantly asking the production editor what goes where in this issue of the magazine? If so, the flat-plan should be readily available to all staff.

2. Keep to the cycle of meetings where all the important decisions are made. Use them to discuss processes. For example, ask if the sub editors have to work over copy again and again: if so maybe the briefings are not accurate enough before writers start their tasks of creating content.

3. Look for the times in the cycle of production where much the same decisions are being made. For example, in discussions with the display advertising department over every issue: are there rules of thumb that can be settled once and then only adjusted when required?

4. Make sure people report on what they have got instead of what they've done. News editors should report to editors about the progress of stories, how close they are to getting what is needed for quality coverage, not on what each person in their news team has done.

5. Lurking in every feature article there is a news article. It will save time for the news section if every feature is also rewritten as a short news story. For example, assign a sub editor on a news-fronted magazine to write a short news story for the news section.

6. Complete a piece of work once it has been started. There is a lot of time wasted as people come back to a piece of work and have to remember where they were. The 'start up' time for a piece of work should be expended only once. This means keeping distractions and interruptions to a minimum.

7. Keep to the purpose of the meeting. Make sure that each meeting is chaired appropriately.

8. Some departments get into a poor habit of not starting meetings on time. Start promptly and there is a saving for all.

9. Review processes and cut out those which are just repeats: try to apply the rule of touching work only once. For example, are the proofs going to the right people and at the right time?

10. There are some processes which take a long time and some shorter. It may take a long time to get permission for an interview: in which case seek the permission as early as possible and get on with background research in the meantime.

OK, there is actually an eleventh point – make all trivial decisions as soon as possible and keep all vital decisions as late as possible. The magazine, on paper and on digital, is now 'plastic' until it is fixed. If it is not vital which case study is in a box beside a feature, then write it soon. In this manner that intermediate task is competed and the focus can be on critical matters at the end of production.

Managing upwards

Editors of magazines manage upwards in two directions: to a publisher or managing director, and to an editorial director. Some magazine publishing companies do not have an editorial director – most do. This role is a senior editorial executive who may also be an editor in the group. Conversations between editors and editorial directors are often easier than those with the managing director or publisher. The editorial director and the editor come to the magazine with much the same skills and focus on the quality of the content. Quality means 'fit for purpose', which in its turn means 'how far does this magazine meet the demands of the readers?'.

Managing directors and publishers are more interested in issues of circulation, advertisement sales and budget. More often than not, they are from a commercial rather than an editorial background. Here the discussions can be more tense: the editor talking about the quality of the content and the managing director or publisher talking about how much it costs to create.

Editors need to acknowledge that, if the publication regularly makes a loss, they will not have a job. If their content does not attract sufficient readers and advertisers, then, however good it may appear, there is no future. In the past some managing directors and publishers may have seen the editorial department as a cost centre: it did not generate any revenue but only spent money. Fortunately in the changed multi-media world, a new generation of managers have seen the value of investing in high quality content but recessionary times mean that budgets and staff numbers are in general lower than prior to 2008. However, workloads are up due to the pressures of generating new digital media.

In order to successfully advocate for the resources the editorial department needs, the editor needs to listen carefully to their managing director or publisher and understand their priorities. What are the key phrases and management tools this person uses? Editors, when reporting on their operations and pushing for resources, need to use the same expressions and tools as the person to whom they report. In this way, they can enter a real dialogue, rather than having a strained conversation which, unfortunately, is still too frequently the nature of communication between editorial and commercial management.

Imagine the scenario whereby an editor wants to open up a new section on a developing subject area. Instead of just requesting extra budget or a reallocation of existing funds it is important to do some research into the types of readers that will be attracted. They may be new customers or in a target market which the magazine does not yet reach in large numbers. Will they be an attractive group for advertisers? Will we be able to sell more copies? The proposal to the publisher should be positioned as an investment, not merely as an increase in costs. This line of argument has a far greater chance of success than just outlining the section and making the budget request.

This approach also means that editors have to deal with numbers. There is a perception in the business that editors are innumerate! That is clearly unfair but many do need to work on the skill of understanding and presenting financial information. A starting point is to set out a set of guidelines for costs: how much does each photo cost on average and how much each 1,000 words? These can then be used in discussions about future editorial investment.

This is, however, not all a one-way street. Editors, who report to management who do not have an editorial background and who have not yet understood the central place of content generation in the life of magazines, need to start educating their bosses. They can pick out instances and show what makes a good spread, a good feature and a good opinion piece so that the boss gets an idea of what makes up quality editorial. Encourage them into the editorial office; introduce even the youngest member of staff. Many commercial executives are in the business because they love media and will respond accordingly.

Managing sideways

Publishing companies are not managed by rote. They are flexible organisations in which the individual character and style of the manager is given a lot of leeway. That is part of their strength: it can also be part of their weakness. The editor now has to manage sideways as well as up and down and this management of the relationships with the commercial departments is an important part of the editor's life. The editor and the display advertising department need to build a strong professional partnership. The editor needs to brief the department on the editorial direction, highlighting any issues which may concern advertisers and identifying to the sales team where there may be commercial opportunities. They need to discuss and set copy deadlines and have guidelines agreed about the placement of advertising. Key advertisers often like to talk to and, more importantly, listen to editors to understand the internal thinking in the magazine. Editors should allocate some of their time for this, in select groups or one-to-one.

One group with whom the editor has to manage relations in today's world is the set of technical teams who support and service the online and digital aspects of publication. In the late 1990s, when publishers started to become interested in the worldwide web, they had to employ technical specialists. However, they often did not spread them through the organisation by appointing a specialist onto each publication. They frequently grouped the web experts in a technical department or centre of excellence.

When a magazine was solely on paper the editorial team could place the content where they liked, within the design grid. The layout was in their hands. With the advent of content on the web, editorial departments had to work inside the content management systems used by the overall company: this largely determined where articles and features were placed. The technical departments which set up the content management systems were often in a different area of the business. In management speak; the content generation went from a functional specialisation structure, where the content was generated within one department with a vertical flow to the final pages, to a matrix structure, where the placing of the content was determined by both the editorial and the technical departments. Any matrix structure is difficult to operate and needs sophisticated management. There is one thing that magazine publishing companies do not tend to have: sophisticated management. They have good management, but it is normally straightforward and direct.

Time and again in magazine businesses the matrix has thrown up difficulties. The main problem is over prioritising the work of the technical department. Take two magazines in the same company, each with a web presence. One is the flagship magazine, the other less financially important to the publisher. Both face online competition. The flagship web presence will get the priority. However, the less important magazine may find that it cannot achieve the changes needed to its web pages fast enough, or at all, in order to compete with its own rival. This leads to frustration within the editorial department of the secondary title and to a weaker web presence for the reader. This cuts into its appeal and, ultimately, damages its circulation. This sad tale is told too often in the industry.

The complexity of the matrix structure has been added to in many magazine publishing companies by the introduction of production hubs. Instead of the magazine having its own production editor, sub editors and even art editor these functions are put into a centralised hub which serves several publications. Again the issue of prioritisation arises. More important for the impact on the quality of the editorial content, the hub will be working on different magazines, although they may be on the same generic subject. As this chapter has shown, each magazine has its own tone, its own language and its own readers to satisfy. The danger, and it is a real one, is that the hub team will not be able to switch from one tone to another as members of the hub work on the different magazines served. What comes out of the hub is generalised, rather than the specific tone which each magazine was able to attain previously.

> The complexity of the matrix structure has been added to ... by the introduction of production hubs

There is one good reason to adopt the hub approach: it can be cheaper. Studies of production editors, sub editors and art editors allocated to individual magazines show that each of these functions has slack time when they are waiting for content further down the creative process. Management therefore propose that this slack time is eliminated by creating the hub and having fewer people in total than there were on each magazine.

There is no easy solution to the management of matrix structures in companies that have been used to simpler linear structures. The editorial department cannot order the technical department to do its work to suit its timetable. The editor must negotiate for the services the department needs and seek help from management.

Managing downwards

Editors need to manage their editorial department, yes, *manage*. They are part of that oxymoron: editorial management. Many editors are appointed because they are good journalists. They suddenly find they are involved in managing others and are unprepared for the task. You cannot run an editorial department by being one of the team: that will create a void at the top. I met one editor who said he had a brilliant method of management: 'I let them get on with it,' he said. I knew the team well and knew that they were dissatisfied: they felt there was a vacuum at the top, a lack of guidance, advocacy and decision making.

Much of the management role which the editor performs is done through the regular round of reviews and meetings on content. These regular meetings bring the editorial department together as a unit. Editors need to emphasise the team nature of the work in creating content and should use that term 'team' as many times as possible, to show that everyone is working together.

Editors have to decide how much company information to reveal to their departments. Some of the discussions held by the editor upwards are, by their nature, confidential: others less so. How much of this sensitive material should they share? There are two extremes and many positions in the middle. Some think it best to shield their team from wider issues so that the members can concentrate on their own work and not be distracted or concerned about matters beyond their control. Others prefer to let the team members know as much as possible, so that they have realistic aspirations and expectations. That was my style and it often worked. But, I acknowledge, it could at times burden team members with concerns.

The editor will have several people reporting in. There will be a person who has the role of production editor, in name or in function. Their role is to manage the flow of the creative process as the magazine is assembled: to keep a track of where articles are and to make sure deadlines are adhered to. Many titles run with a news department and news editor and features area with a features editor. There may be section heads: on women's magazines there are likely to be fashion editors and health and beauty editors. The key role of art editor has been discussed and larger magazines operate with a separate pictures editor. It is the role of the leader to orchestrate these parts into a whole: to conduct this large orchestra. No conductor can play all the instruments just as few editors can perform all of the above roles. They have to manage people whose skills and knowledge they may not possess themselves and achieve this through voicing and refining the overall vision of the magazine for each of the sections that create its content.

With many people reporting to the editor it is essential that the leader does not get bogged down in the detail of their work. A good rule is to insist that people brief the editor with what they have achieved, not what they have done. Consider a writer who is working on the main cover feature for a particular issue. They will be guided in tandem by the features editor as well as the editor. The writer could report what they have done to get the feature completed: 'I've researched this, I've requested that interview, I've asked for that information.' This involves those the writer is reporting to in the detailed narrative of the actions of the writer. Instead the writer should be encouraged to report on what they have got. If they have very little prepared then we can delve into the details and help them to the next steps. 'I've got an interview on the 7th with ... ,' is the best way to report.

> A good rule is to insist that people brief the editor with what they have achieved, not what they have done

Creating motivation

Producing editorial content is, by its nature, a creative process. It is not possible to make people more creative by shouting at them or demanding more imaginative work. It has to come from inside themselves and they have to be motivated. There is a body of literature and research on motivation but much of it seems to be trying to solve the problems of low morale of workers in repetitive jobs. The creative process is different.

Advertisement sales teams can be incentivised by money: they earn commission or a bonus for the space sold. Editorial staff are rarely financially motivated. Of course they wish to be paid as much as they can earn, but riches do not produce better quality work in the long run. I have conducted tests on the motivation of editorial staff and only very seldom has pay been on the top or close to the top of the list. When it was, it was because of particular circumstances such as a new house or the arrival of a baby. If anybody goes into the editorial side of

> It is not possible to make people more creative by shouting at them or demanding more imaginative work

magazines for the money, they are making a mistake. Their motivation comes from the creative process itself, from the exercise of performing their craft to a high standard. Editorial staff need to have some prospects for promotion. They should be hungry to get on but there is a downside to this: they may have to leave the craft they love and become part of the management to get promotion. Does the great senior reporter really want to be news editor? Perhaps not.

It is not possible to look into the head of the editorial staff member as they create, nor is it easy to see how they arrive at the solutions they deliver. They may spend a long time pondering the best way to lay out the page or write the copy and then be able to do it very quickly. It may seem that they are just looking out of the window but in fact they are thinking about the next step. Therefore, there has to be a certain amount of trust with editorial staff: in return they have to bring their talents into play and deliver.

Some editors can inspire others: what in fact they are doing, by example and encouragement, is creating a motivational atmosphere. They praise, openly, those who produce good work and guide those whose work needs improvement. There is nothing more uplifting than being openly applauded when you think you have done a good job of work and the editor also thinks so. This is particularly true for those who are not the departmental stars: public praise for a sub editor who crafts a good headline or a junior writer who puts in their first long piece will enthuse them and encourage others. Beware of editors who can destroy motivation by their moods – they need to realise that they are public figures to the editorial department and their attitude is a key part of the atmosphere.

> ... what in fact they are doing, by example and encouragement, is creating a motivational atmosphere

Managing external contributors

External contributors are an essential part of any magazine. They may be freelance journalists or specialists in the areas covered by the title. They work outside the office but still need to be made part of the editorial team with constant communication from the editor and section heads. When I was a freelance journalist I recall one editor who was brilliant at this: she had a clear vision of her magazine and who it was addressing. She would remind her contributors that she did not want a generic piece which could go into any magazine on that general subject but she wanted writing which fitted her detailed vision. This was made clear in the commissioning email and in her response to the copy delivered. Again this demonstrates that the vision the editor has created for the magazine is a key tool of management. Freelancers must be briefed clearly and accurately and with deadlines.

Managing the cycle

Magazines have a cycle of creation and production: on paper this is determined by the frequency of the publication and online by daily events. The cycle goes from the original idea to the completion of the content. There are three phases in the cycle of producing quality editorial content: planning, executing and reviewing. Many editorial departments only focus on the execution and do not plan or review sufficiently. Meetings should have two key purposes – to plan and to review.

Planning needs to be done in advance of execution and its output should be widely distributed with the department. The process is best done in meetings of the key members of staff. Editorial departments often think that meetings are pointless: they want to get on with the job and generate the content. In the case of some sessions this may be the case – they may be chaired poorly or fail to focus on the task in hand. Well conducted planning meetings are essential for all titles – the floor should be open to all: good ideas can come from anywhere. Make and circulate key action points to review at the next session.

Many editorial departments do not review at all; and if they do, they review the content of their publication against competitors. By failing to review their processes a serious mistake is made. After all, it is the processes which generate the content.

Meetings are held in the cycle of the publication: weekly, fortnightly or monthly. The cycle should be regarded as a spiral for planning future issues well in advance of that issue's execution. With ever smaller teams, editorial departments are hard squeezed to find time for planning and reviewing. However, they will actually save time in the long run if they are disciplined and have these conferences. There will be less confusion in the execution phase and they will be able to identify where they can speed up their processes.

The review of content can be led by members of staff other than the editor. This ensures that the whole team is both aware of and judging the content of the publication according to the vision. Finally, remember that the criteria should be what works to implement that vision and not just what people like.

Having discussed in detail editorial targeting, strategy and management, Chapter 5 will look at the detailed techniques of creating quality content in design and words.

Thanks to Jack Harvey, a graduate of the University of East London.

NOTES

1.   ABC (Jan–Dec 2012).
2.   Ibid.
3.   Ibid.
4.   Future, Yarn craft portfolio: media information, 2013, p 4.
5.   ABC (Jan–Dec 2012).
6.   *Red* Media Pack 2013 from Hearst UK. Data source for media pack NRS (Oct 2011–Sept 2012), TGI (Oct 2010–Sept 2011) and Premier TGI (2011).
7.   MacQueen (2011) p 96.
8.   ABC (July–Dec 2012) is 272,040.
9.   ABC (July–Dec 2012).

REFERENCE SOURCE

MacQueen, A. (2011) *Private Eye: the first 50 years*. London: Private Eye Productions.

What is a magazine?

Andrew Calcutt

Trust an academic to ask the obvious. Magazines are periodically published, professionally produced, commercially viable, primarily printed packages covering the specific interests of particular readers at an appropriate cover price, OK? Unless your interests lie on the publishing side, if you reach your office via a lift labelled 'Sales and Marketing' rather than 'Editorial', in which case you may well define magazines as vehicles for delivering readers' eyeballs to advertisers. Either way, the question answers itself in a single sentence, right?

Wrong.

Much of what we knew about magazines or thought we did, has recently come undone. While academics habitually question their 'objects of study', today, unusually, the questioning of magazines is not confined to the academy. All kinds of people are interrogating magazines and the magazine business, raising key questions such as: what are magazines for, and who will continue to buy them when much of what they offer can now be obtained online without payment? Besides magazine readers – or should that be 'users' – the queue of questioners includes almost everyone involved in the business: publishers, editors, reporters, designers, advertisers, distributors and retailers. The smartest of these know how much they don't know; the few who aren't worried are the ones with most to worry about.

Facing a host of questions, the industry's answers have been mostly piecemeal, for example employing a tactical use of social media in an effort to hold onto readers; or perfunctory, hoping that the end of recession will bring back business as usual. Clearly, the fundamental nature of the questions raised is not matched by the superficial character of the answers given.

Yet for all the interrogation of magazines, inside and outside publishing, there is one question which has hardly been raised because the answer to it is taken as given: it's the technology, stupid; digital technology has been the disruptive element, obviously. But it really would be silly not to ask whether digital technology is indeed the message or only the messenger of magazines' current predicament. The fact that in some developing countries not only journalism but even print journalism is expanding at the same time as internet usage should make it immediately obvious that technology per se is neither the problem, nor the solution to the problems pressing down on magazine publishing, especially in the West.

> Much of what we knew about magazines or thought we did, has recently come undone

THE ESSENTIAL QUESTION

This brings us back to the essential question: what is a magazine? One way to address this question is to make a very brief excursion into the history of magazines – not at this stage in order to trace their historical development (this is laid out clearly in Chapter 1) but rather to establish their essential character: what magazines have to be; or else, even if they remain, they will remain magazines in name only.

Founded in 1731, *The Gentleman's Magazine* was one of the earliest English publications to be referred to as a magazine, and the first to title itself as such. Just as the magazine of a gun is the compartment where ammunition is stored, so this printed periodical was a magazine of essential information for the eighteenth-century gentleman, including information on how the best people were behaving and what they were talking about. This enabled the reader to join in the conversation of polite society and affirm his status as a gentleman.

Already the essential role of the magazine is becoming apparent. The reader reads it, and is prepared to pay for the privilege, because it serves as his stepping stone into society. Without it, he risks saying the wrong thing, or, worse still, coming across as a country bumpkin who lacks conversation. Having read *The Gentleman's Magazine*, however, he will have something to say to Jane Austen's ladies, his successful appearance on the social scene being dependent on the entrée afforded not so much by aristocratic title as by this magazine title.

As an early example of modern media, **mediation** was the core business of *The Gentleman's Magazine*.

Accordingly, when the division between town and country was the burning question of the age, the editor/publisher of *The Gentleman's Magazine*, Edward Cave, took as his pseudonym the Latin tag, Sylvanus Urban. 'Urban' to indicate a man of the city, whereas 'Sylvanus', after the Roman god of fields and flocks, suggests a countryman. Thus the person behind the first magazine identified himself with a *persona* connecting town and country.

Similarly, Cave's offices in St John's Gate, Clerkenwell, frequently featured on the front page (more like a masthead than a cover photo), suggesting that the magazine itself was a gateway or a mediating link between individual readers and civil society inside the gates. In both these aspects, mediation was the role that readers paid *The Gentleman's Magazine* to perform on their behalf; reading magazines came to serve as a kind of rite of passage between isolation on the one hand and society on the other.

MEDIATION BETWEEN PRIVATE AND PUBLIC

The subject matter featured in Cave's *The Gentleman's Magazine* was no more wide-ranging than the array of topics appearing in near-contemporary publications such as Joseph Addison's *The Spectator* and Richard Steele's *Tatler*. But these periodicals were not generally referred to as magazines; conversely, the particular designation of Cave's title as a 'magazine' cannot be accounted for by the miscellaneous character of its content. The application of the term 'magazine' might have been connected to the editor/publisher's willingness to sample and re-package material published elsewhere, in the manner of a present-day DJ. On the other hand, eighteenth-century usage of the term 'magazine' may itself have been somewhat miscellaneous.

In the nineteenth century, however, a clear distinction emerged between newspaper journalism published primarily in pursuit of political interests, and magazines published in response to individual concerns, especially those of a domestic nature.

Whether described as newspapers or magazines, both sets of printed matter addressed the public domain in which they themselves appeared. Moreover, their continued appearance helped to constitute that public domain by building the necessary bridge between individual existence and social life. All publications, in other words, continued to play a mediating role between the individual and society. But the subdivision of periodicals into newspapers and magazines also initiated a division between different aspects of mediation.

If we imagine 'private' and 'public' as polarities linked by an axis comprised of different publications, then magazines have tended to cluster around the private end of this axis, whereas newspapers – though delivered to individuals at the privacy of their own breakfast table – normally concentrate on matters of public concern, primarily political in character.

In the context of nineteenth-century confidence in 'progress', this meant that newspapers were to inform their readership of the political world and the part they were called upon to play in society's progressive development. In contrast, magazines mainly enabled their readers to cultivate themselves: to perform the part expected of them in the progressive development of the individual.

Alongside rest and recuperation, the Victorian home was a place for self-cultivation. All three aspects, with the emphasis on the latter, were epitomised in that manual of home improvement, *Household Words* – the mid-nineteenth century magazine edited by Charles Dickens himself. Thus in the separation of magazines from newspapers, magazines defined themselves as normally beginning (but not necessarily ending) at home.

MAGAZINES IN THE MODERN WORLD

If the mediating role of magazines is really essential to our existence, surely the magazine cannot simply cease to exist? That earlier bout of questioning, all those doubts we previously expressed about the future of magazines – what was all the fuss about?

The point is that both sides of the contradiction are equally true: professionally produced, commercially viable magazines, as conventionally understood, have been crucial to our existence in the modern world. On the other hand, the world we are accustomed to call modern, may now have moved on. If so, it's not given that there will be quite the same need for the magazine; or precisely the same requirement for it to play a mediating role.

Even if individual titles were often dispensable as well as disposable items, until now the existence of magazines as such has been essential. Without magazines, billions of people would never have known how to be modern. Yet today it seems that growing numbers of thoroughly modern individuals regard the

Without magazines, billions of people would never have known how to be modern magazine – not just specific issues of particular titles – as optional, contingent, inessential. It transpires that the functions which magazines have hitherto been called upon to carry out may not be as crucial as they were before. Or, even if they are, they might no longer be the sole preserve of magazines. Hence the questioning of professionally produced magazines, and the question mark hanging over the commercial future of the magazine.

In order to understand this contradiction, let's continue to set aside both digital technology and the disruption of traditional business models on the grounds that, though important, neither of these is the independent variable or determining factor. Instead, let's look again at what we have identified as core activities of the magazine – what magazines have had to be and do so as to remain magazines in more than name. We said that mediation has been the core business of magazines. From this it follows that the more the-people-formerly-known-as-readers can undertake mediating activity for themselves, the less they require other people, the professional journalists and commercial publishers, to perform such activity on their behalf. The wholesale questioning of magazines, we suggest, is derived from this social development, rather than narrowly technical or economic issues.

LIFELONG LOYALTY

We also said that readers traditionally looked to magazines in order to cultivate themselves; in the attempt to be a fuller, better version of the person they saw themselves becoming. In Victorian times, self-development was seen as the individual counterpart of social development enshrined in the concept of 'progress'. This expectation was further predicated on the idea of adulthood, which, once reached, comprised a state or way of being that lasted for life. In recent decades, however, the Victorian ideal of progress has been widely criticised, along with the traditional idea of adulthood; and these developments have threatened the position of magazines as well as offering new business opportunities for magazine publishers.

In today's context, while there is no shortage of individuals wanting a short-term fix for their make-up or their mind-set, fewer consumers are in it for the long haul. Less likely to see their adult lives as an unfolding pattern of progressive self-cultivation, they are also less likely to take out a lifelong subscription to a suitably self-improving magazine.

This is not to say that there has been absolute decline in magazine subscriptions. What has gone into abeyance is the prospect of cultivated readers who previously *took* a particular title – *Punch*, perhaps, or *The Strand* – until they themselves were taken out in a box. Neither does the general demise of the lifelong subscriber preclude consumer loyalty to particular titles. But such loyalties tend to be comparatively short-lived: this is loyalty that cannot last any longer than the age-bracket the magazine is aimed at, if that.

Predicated on the erosion of adulthood and the corrosion of Victorian ideals, market segmentation has allowed publishers to access whole new cohorts of 'adultescent' readers. Restless consumers, always questing for something different to define themselves by, have served as the launch pad for thousands of new magazine titles. Equally, readers who never grow up are not the stuff of stable markets. Thus since the 1960s the UK magazines business has expanded and destabilised at the same time.

BLURRING PUBLIC AND PRIVATE

What, then, of the magazine's further role in mediating between public and private? It turns out that the continued performance of this role depends not only on the co-existence of public and private realms; it also depends on their separation. To be joined up by a combination of magazines and newspapers, public and private must first be sufficiently separate. Conversely, if the distinction between public and private is lost or diminished, it follows that the character of magazines will tend to become equally indistinct. Surely this is just what has happened recently. As public life has gone into sharp decline, to the point where even the national political stage has come to be seen – rightly or wrongly – as a Westminster village some of whose residents are only out for private gain, so the distinction between newspapers and magazines has become blurred. Newspapers now resemble a succession of different daily 'magazines', while traditional magazine titles have lost much of their distinctiveness as a result.

Of course the trend for newspapers to become more like magazines might be taken to represent the supremacy of the magazine, now coming out from the shadow of its senior sibling. On the other hand, there's nothing written on the stone which says that magazine publishers will always be the best people to undertake the duties associated with magazines. Some newspapers have turned out to be unexpectedly good at being a magazine; often to the detriment of magazines themselves.

EVERY ONE A MEDIATOR?

Surely there is always mediation. As no man is an island, there must always be something which mediates between human beings, connecting them with each other, or else being human becomes impossible. Quite so. But as we have already seen with regard to the subdivision of periodicals into magazines as distinct from newspapers, the specific kind of mediation that society requires is subject to historical development. Similarly, the way in which mediation is performed – who performs it and how – is likely to change over time.

When the authors of this textbook were trainee journalists and publishers, mediation was an almost exclusively professional activity, just as media were the sole preserve of the trained professionals we were keen to be. We came to be recognised as professionals by demonstrating superior knowledge – knowledge of our magazines' subject matter and knowledge of the media marketing and production process – far in advance of what we would expect our readers to know.

Back in the 1970s, the authors of Punk fanzine *Sideburns* were among the first to dismiss the idea of the professional musician, famously declaring: 'This is a Chord, This is Another, This is a Third – Now Form A Band'[1]. Mark Perry, editor of *Sniffin' Glue*, applied the same attitude to music journalism: 'all you kids out

'This is a Chord, This is Another, This is a Third – Now Form A Band.'

there who read *SG*, don't be satisfied with what we write. Go out and start your own fanzines.'[2] (Perry 1976). At the time, *Sideburns* and *Sniffin' Glue* represented only a tiny minority: their DIY ethos was discernible, but also marginal. Since the days of *Sniffin' Glue*, however, widening distrust of professionalism has been matched by the increased capacity for non-professionals to communicate with each other using digital technology. Digitisation helped to disseminate existing distrust of professional authority, catalysing its move to the foreground and cranking up the user-generator fairground. Hence the recent prospect of 'here comes everybody', in which 'everybody' – not just media professionals – is a mediator now.

Responding to such developments, many publishers have chosen to invest their remaining resources in a range of devices for creating 'community' and building seemingly egalitarian relationships with the-people-formerly-known-as-readers. Indeed this emphasis has become the hallmark of a new kind of professionalism which is pleased to avoid the allegedly authoritarian pitfalls of its predecessors. Those who refuse to compromise their authority, such as Anna Wintour at *Vogue* and successive editors of *The Economist,* are now something of a rarity. They are also some of the most successful magazine editors of the recent period. This suggests that regaining editorial authority, rather than following the fashion for renouncing the claim to superior knowledge, may be what readers really want from their magazines. At least, that's what they continue to expect from the ones for which they're actually prepared to pay.

The chapters and essays in this textbook analyse what is and is not working inside magazine publishing. In this the book is diagnostic; but it also offers a positive prognosis. *Inside Magazine Publishing* shows how magazines can renew their mediating role, not by subtracting from the authority of their content but by adding to it.

NOTES

1. *Sideburns,* December 1976, quoted in Jon Savage (2005) *England's Dreaming: Sex Pistols and punk rock.* London: Faber & Faber, p 281.
2. Perry, M. (1976) *Sniffin' Glue* No 5, quoted in Jon Savage (2005) *England's Dreaming: Sex Pistols and punk rock.* London: Faber & Faber, p 279.

CHAPTER 5

Designing and writing for magazines

Richard Sharpe

The second of the two editorial chapters will look at pictures and words – the design of magazines and the writing styles which make up content. We will discuss what makes the cover the most important part of the print on paper title. It is the point of recognition for regular readers and the 'come and buy me' attraction for occasional purchasers. Key elements include cover lines which sell the magazine to the reader, enticing them in. The typography of the cover and the whole magazine is part of its vision: a statement of authority, friendliness or modernity.

Design principles on paper are not the same as online: digital is a different media and has to be handled accordingly.

The pace and flow of the magazine is part of its appeal: get readers hooked with the cover then keep them involved with a lively flow. Readers want variety within a magazine, both in design and content. This includes the front section, with its different components, the body or middle of the edition and the back.

Design for either platform is often to a grid structure: regular ways to lay out content. In particular, online design needs to be crafted so that whatever is on the screen is clear: the reader does not have a full page on paper in front of them.

Writers need a discipline to create good written content. Later in this chapter we will look at 'POWER', a useful tool or method for separating two key elements of the writing process – structure and language. The different elements of news, features and opinion columns will also be examined.

DESIGN – COVERS, COVERS AND COVERS

The cover is the most important part of the print on paper magazine. It serves to attract new readers, to persuade occasional purchasers to buy more frequently and to entice regular readers to buy every issue. It is also the starting point for the postal subscriber. It is the key selling point of the magazine. There is a general consensus that around three quarters of impulse sales on the newsstands are determined by the effectiveness of the cover.

The key elements of the cover are largely the same for magazines with differing types of content.

> ... around three quarters of impulse sales on the newsstands are determined by the effectiveness of the cover

Masthead or logo

From the point of view of both the designer and of the consumer already familiar with the magazine – the starting point of the cover is the masthead. This is also known as the logo. This should be distinctive and in keeping with the vision of the title: it should be cut by a typographer so that the typeface is unique. Magazines can use one of the many standard fonts available, but a bespoke logo gives the magazine a point of distinction. Maybe only a handful of readers will notice that it is a special font – at least consciously; but there will be recognition of a difference. A unique logo typeface can also defend the magazine from imitations. Mastheads can be bounded, such as *The Economist* logo with its distinctive red background. Ensure the masthead is distinctive and in line with the vision and it can be repeatedly used inside the magazine, on web pages and in other formats.

The news magazine, often in the B2B market, such as *Campaign*, will have a front cover which features the relevant masthead, the main news story and samples of the content inside. In these cases, it is the quality of the lead story which sells the topical magazine.

Above the masthead on a consumer magazine may be the 'skyline', this is the space where an extra message can be communicated to the potential buyer, often concerning promotions or competitions that the title may be running. The skyline is likely to be highlighted in a bold colour, frequently red.

Cover image

For magazines which do not feature news-related covers the selection of image or images is key. The visual appearance of this key front page should be consistent. If there is one large image on one issue then there should be one large photo on all issues. If the cover is broken up with multiple photographs then this should also be consistent on a weekly or monthly basis. However, all rules are there to be broken. If the cover is normally made up of multiple images then a single image can create impact and drama, as long as it is the right image. For example, when a key celebrity or statesman/woman dies, the single image of that person and their dates makes for drama.

Very often magazines will use the image of a person, a model or celebrity, looking out of the cover. This makes eye contact with the potential buyer, drawing them in. The eyeline of this photo is normally towards the top of the cover, often beside or intersecting the masthead. This becomes the eyeline of the cover. It also, if it is in front of the logo, creates a 3D effect on the 2D surface of the cover.

Figure 5.1 shows the basic components of a typical magazine front cover and a suggested template for layout.

Cover lines

Once the main image has been selected, the team will focus on the cover lines, sometimes referred to as sell lines or strap lines. Here the magazine announces its content to the buyer. They act as a contents page in poster form. These lines need to have key words in them for the potential buyer. For example, **'chocolate'** is

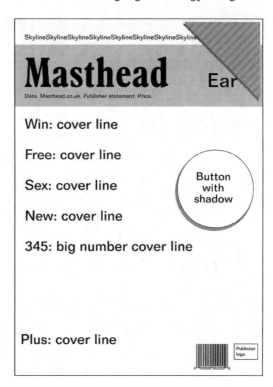

Figure 5.1 Make-up of a cover

a key choice for titles which feature cookery and baking. The three cover words, or their equivalent, which attract many readers of consumer magazines are '**win**', '**free**' and '**sex**'. 'Win' feeds the pleasure and gratification of the buyer. 'Free' gives the consumer something extra above the magazine itself. As for that little word 'sex', it may appear on a men's magazine or on *Cosmopolitan* and refer to enjoyment or a new technique. However, taking that word in a less literal sense, there is invariably some equivalent for readers of most magazines.

Believe it or not, a sewing magazine is no exception – it needs to design covers in the knowledge of what will drive purchase. Take *Sew*, published by Aceville. The top cover line on an issue of *Sew* was 'Quick Home Styling Tricks to Stitch and Share!' For the buyer interested in sewing this can have a similar effect as a sex-related line on a young women's title – it will persuade the buyer to pick it off the shelf. Two other cover lines are 'Win £2,200 of prizes in our bumper birthday giveaway!' and 'Make with your free pattern' on a label pointing to a photo of a model in a dress. The cover in question ticks all the right boxes in terms of grabbing reader attention in a retail environment.

Covers can be beautiful and inspire the emotions of love and desire even when their subject matter is not people. The property and garden photographs which are frequently portrayed on the cover of *Country Life* are often mouth-watering and hugely aspirational; the readers want to walk into and sense the beauty of those surroundings. The cover of the 10 April 2013 issue of *Country Life* had all of the elements of a great cover: the image of a beautiful cottage; the innuendo in 'somewhere for the weekend', and the announcement that Prince Charles will be a guest editor. Add in chocolate and love and you have a winner.

The three cover words ... which attract many readers of consumer magazines are '**win**', '**free**' and '**sex**'

Add in chocolate and love and you have a winner

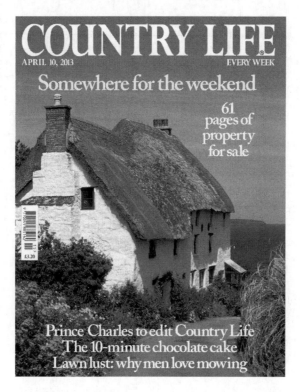

Different specialist titles inspire different emotions. *Dogs Today* has a small dog looking wistfully out of its April 2013 cover – a breed of Basset called a Fauve. The job of the designer is to make the reader want to reach out and pat the dog. Fishing magazines regularly have an enormous catch photographed – the patient angler and consumer is saying 'I wish that were me'.

'New' is another hard-working word. The same issue of *Sew* runs the interesting line 'New Vintage Section'. For a craft magazine the word 'easy' is important as in 'Log Cabin Quilt in Easy Steps'. Easy is implied in another cover line: 'Instant Weekend Makeovers'. But maybe this implies sex again! Some of the finest examples of cover lines are crafted for the real life magazines. These are battling in a crowded market and have to trumpet their content. One of the best I ever saw was 'My Dave was Stuffing another Bird at Christmas', a must read for reality devotees.

There is a trend for large and unusual (not rounded) numbers in cover lines to show the potential buyer that they are getting a packed feature. *Elle* says it has '436 Pages of Fashion'; *Tesco Real Food* says it has '42 gorgeous spring dishes' and *BBC Music* says it has '113 Reviews of CDS, DVDs and Books'.

Framing the cover

It is possible to introduce another element into the design of the cover. For example, *National Geographic* is instantly recognisable to the buyer not only because of its size and logo but because of its yellow border. These yellow borders are then used inside the magazine and with related titles to emphasise the brand identity.

Photo 5.2 The cover of *Angler's Mail* frequently pictures a 'big catch'

The following three items also have to be included – date, price and barcode. In order to ensure accurate scanning by retailers the PPA issues guidelines for the design and printing of the barcode[1]. It is vital that these three items are checked on an issue-by-issue basis and it should be a designated responsibility to sign off. Major retailers can surcharge publishers who make mistakes on barcodes.

All of these design elements have to be arranged on the cover so that it is easy for the potential buyer to see the message and be able to quickly decode the content. This positioning includes the sometimes contentious decision whether or not to partly obscure the masthead.

Three dimensions in two

Magazines confident of their appeal and established in the market can run the risk of partially covering their masthead with the main image on the cover. *Vogue*, for example, may cover part of its logo by the head of the model on the cover. This creates a 3D effect on what is a 2D surface. It allows the person portrayed to come out from the cover towards the reader as they seem to be standing in front of the masthead. Other fashion and celebrity titles also do this. But there is an important question about this approach: does it obscure the appeal of the magazine's brand on the newsstand and lessen visibility? For this reason circulation executives rarely like mastheads covered up.

Other devices are used to create this important 3D effect: these include shading on type used for cover lines or on boxes or buttons carrying cover lines.

Grazia uses this approach frequently to create the impression that the cover is coming to the buyer. This makes it stand out from competitors who may not use this effect.

This 3D effect can be further enhanced by using an 'ear' over the right top of the cover: a triangle holding information which is seemingly above the cover. As with circular 'buttons', it can be enhanced by shading.

Sweet spot

The most important part of the cover is the top left quarter. Whichever way the magazine is racked and displayed at the point of sale, either overlapping with the full masthead visible (waterfall racking), or with the right hand side obscured, this top left quarter of the cover is always visible. It is, therefore, called the 'sweet spot' of the cover. It needs to be packed with information. I recall when one cover designer forgot this and put the barcode there so that when the title was racked overlapping in a newsagent only the barcode was visible.

> The most important part of the cover is the top left quarter

Get the cover, the contents and the copy in line

Imagine this: you are browsing the newsstand for a magazine to read on your flight or train journey. You are attracted to a cover and a particular line interests you. You want to see more about it before purchasing, so you turn to the contents pages with that particular cover line in mind. But it is not clear from the contents page which article you should turn to. You have to hunt for this page and look for wording similar to the cover line. Now you are getting frustrated. You may persevere and find it but you have not been helped by the fact that the cover line and the description in the contents pages are not the same. You finally turn to the relevant page and see a headline which might be what you are looking for but your journey as a reader has been less than easy.

This often happens because different people are working on the different parts. The section editor may write the headline for the copy; the production editor may assemble the content pages. The editor and art editor will work on the cover.

A 2013 issue of *Grazia* had a cover line 'Oscar Pistorius Latest', referring to the South African athlete accused of murdering his girlfriend. That is a good cover line for a weekly: a topical talking point. You turn to the contents page and there is no reference to Pistorius. You hunt the list. Above several items in the contents list there are the words 'Cover Story'. You hunt through them looking for an article that fits. One says 'She adored him. He adored her. It's crazy.' It could be that one. You turn to the page and find it is, indeed, the story you want. But you have had to solve a puzzle to get there and the only puzzles the reader should have to solve in a magazine should be on the puzzle pages.

> ... the only puzzles the reader should have to solve in a magazine should be on the puzzle pages

All the great work done on covers can be undone when the magazine is in a bag with a free gift inside. To ensure that bagged magazines generate maximum impact, it is vital that the marketing team and the cover designer have clear lines of communication and ensure that the packaging uses both opaque and clear polythene, to drive home commercial and editorial selling points.

Colours: using a palette

An important part of the vision of the magazine is the palette of colours used both on the cover and throughout the contents. Women's craft magazines tend to go for a muted palette of pastel shades. Real life and other women's titles use a riot of colour to get their message across in that competitive market. Look at any newsstand and you will see a principal selling colour of red. *What Car?* from Haymarket always uses a strong red for its masthead, making it leap out of the shelf. On the other hand, *FourFourTwo* from the same publishing company cleverly changes its masthead colour, depending on the colours of the soccer club it is focussing on in that issue.

GRIDS, TEMPLATES AND STYLE SHEETS

All magazines are designed to a grid, a template for that magazine which shows the positioning of the words and images. This will be set up on the chosen desk top publishing (DTP) software package. The grid includes the width of the margins and columns of text and the options for the placement of headlines. As with all the elements of design, the grid is an important part of the vision of the magazine. The more sober and formal the grid, so the tone of the magazine; the busier the grid, the more lively the title. An important part of this template on paper is 'white space', the areas left unprinted. They let the content of the page breathe – they can also be called simply 'air'. Cramming content onto pages confuses the eye of the reader and makes them work too hard to distinguish one part of editorial from another.

Readers should be able to navigate the design quickly and know whereabouts on the spread in front of them they want to go. But beware that too much white space makes the magazine look like an art catalogue or a scholarly journal. After all, readers want to see that they are getting a full magazine and value for money. Page designers should also use the symmetry of the alternating horizontal and vertical blocks of content on the page. This is clearly demonstrated by comic designers who use strong verticals and horizontals to create drama and pace.

Grids, for layouts on paper or online, provide the 'buckets' into which the content is poured. Although stated earlier that all magazines are designed to a grid, there is the occasional exception. Some designers dislike and avoid these fixed templates because they see them as a constraint on their ability to lay out content: they believe that the make-up of that particular content should determine the layout. For example, the design variety for the pages of *i-D* magazine means that the uniqueness of the editorial shapes the look of the title. However, this can be at odds with creating the vision of a magazine and projecting it consistently. As

... readers want to see that they are getting a full magazine and value for money

Christine Stam has shown in Chapter 1, in the 1980s two highly successful German publishers introduced magazines into the UK. Part of their success was driven by a clear and fixed visual layout and formula for the new titles.

The content of an article which has to be put into the grid is:

- the headline
- the standfirst, if there is one: the copy under the headline before the article proper starts. This will give a very brief outline of what the reader should expect
- the run of copy
- the pull quotes, if there are some: these are the fragments of sentences in a larger typeface which are used to break up the run of copy and to give entry points into the article
- the illustrations and captions
- box outs, also known as side bars. These are used for information which is relevant to the article but may be tangential, for example a brief biography of the celebrity if the piece is an interview.

A trend in magazine journalism in the past 20 years has been towards shorter articles to create the impression of value for money and to grab readers' attention. Designers are increasingly cutting up the run of copy and taking parts of longer articles and making them box outs with their own headings to achieve this.

Readers can 'enter' a longer feature article today at a number of places. They will not all read the headline first and move seamlessly on to the copy. The eye is often drawn to the illustration: a picture or a diagram. Each illustration should have a caption, as many readers read the caption before the headline. Captions should be close to, superimposed upon or under the illustration. Some magazines, including *Monocle*, make the reader hunt for the caption: two or three pictures on a page will be numbered on the bottom left and the captions grouped together. The reader then has to find the number, go to the block of captions and read it, then back to the picture to link the caption and picture together. Why make the reader work so hard?

The grid chosen for the magazine on paper can be formatted in page production software such as InDesign: then the page layout can be chosen from a select sample of grids and the discipline of grid-based design implemented through the desk top publishing software.

Style sheets are also defined and set within DTP packages. These define the detail of what the article will look like and for regular frequency magazines should not be tinkered with from issue to issue. A style sheet will cover a range of visual layout formulae such as typeface (font) style and size, colour variations for type, column width and graduation of heading levels. Good quality style sheets allow the designer to create pages with speed – and if enough options are included – with creativity.

TYPOGRAPHY

The typefaces used to deliver the words to the readers are all part of the vision of the magazine. Magazine designers have to be particularly selective about their choice of typefaces because that very choice conveys a tone to the copy. Set the article in a typeface such as Times Roman and it speaks with authority. The Times Roman font was developed in the 1930s, based on the Roman typeface used in classical inscriptions. Times Roman is a serif typeface: it has vertical and horizontal lines which guide the eye along the page. Here is an example:

> This is Times New Roman, used since the 1940s for *The Times*. Notice how the serifs guide the eye along the line.

Set the copy in a sans serif face, without the serifs, and that speaks of a modern approach. The most frequently used today is Arial.

> This is Arial, known as a sans serif typeface. It is more 'modern looking' than Times Roman.

Sans serif typefaces are hard to read when in a long line of text: the reader's eye can lose its place and jump lines. *FourFourTwo* sets its copy in sans serif typefaces therefore the columns have to be narrow to maintain reader concentration. It is common to use a sans serif bold typeface for headlines.

Another aspect of typography is the use of drop caps: a single letter starting a section printed in a large point with lines of copy indented. This is a good device for breaking up longer stories into sections and gives more white space on the page. The *New Statesman*, for example, often uses drop capitals within its articles and prints them in a soft grey, again lightening the page. Its pull quotes are often in red: so one sees a colour combination on the page of black for the copy, grey for the drop caps and red for the pull quote.

ONLINE DESIGN

When magazines started to develop websites, designers often just transferred the on page design to the site. They had not appreciated that the web and the printed page are different media and read by consumers in different ways. This differentiation was accentuated when magazines branched out from the standard website and started putting their content onto mobile devices, from an iPad down to the size of a mobile phone screen.

The grids used for digital content tend to be even more rigid than the grids used on paper. They are hard wired into the magazine's content management system and can appear to the design team as a series of very rigid content templates into which the content is fitted. However that content may not always fit. To overcome this problem one of two successful approaches for designing digital grids should be adopted.

The first is to audit the content generated and create the grid from the content types. The second looks at the advertisements: what shapes are required

> ... the web and the printed page are different media and read by consumers in different ways

and where will they best be positioned? The digital grid for the editorial content can then be moulded accordingly. In my view the best way to create the grid for online content is to start with the content and work from there. But often designers start with the shapes of advertisements: this makes the editorial content work around the advertising, de-emphasising the content.

The eyes of the reader move faster over digital content than over content on paper. Such is the nature of how we consume digital products. Research shows that the digital reader shows more interest in what is on the left hand side of the screen than the reader of a magazine on paper. (Interestingly enough for print on paper readers the right hand side of a spread is often first looked at – hence advertisers request to site advertisements on right hand pages.) The masthead should head the online page, but some publishers want to sell the space over the masthead for a banner advertisement. This is understandable but regrettable as it can create a slight moment of confusion for the viewer: 'where am I?' they ask: 'is this the magazine website or the website of the advertiser'?

The more interesting and arresting editorial items should be down the left side of the digital grid. The consultancy, Neilson Norman Group, has found by utilising eye tracking technology that the eyes of the readers move at amazing speeds across websites, picking out the information. The dominant pattern of eye movement is an F shape. Usually readers start by scanning horizontally across the top part of the page (the F's top bar). Then their eyes move slightly down the page and, again read horizontally, often on a shorter path than their first reading (the F's lower bar). Finally they read the page's left side vertically, thus forming the F's stem. The research has shown that this last scan can vary in speed. 'Sometimes this is a fairly slow and systematic scan that appears as a solid stripe on an eye tracking heatmap. Other times users move faster, creating a spottier heatmap.'[2]

There needs to be greater use of cross headings for digital content than on paper so that the visitor can see multiple entry points to the content. A cross heading (sometimes called a cross head) is where the title or heading fills the full width of the column it sits in. Viewers do not have a double-page spread in front of them; they have a scrollable screen. Traditional ratios of vertical to horizontal used on the page no longer work as the designer cannot determine the view the reader has of the digital content – they have the ability to scroll and will not see a full spread, merely an emerging snapshot of the page.

THE STRUCTURE: WHAT GOES WHERE IN PRINT

Magazines have a structure on paper or online: they present their content in a series of sequential page spreads or screens.

Contents

From the front cover onwards the magazine on paper presents the reader with a variety of different content delivered within conventions. By far and away the most common is to run contents pages early in the magazine but there can be exceptions. *Country Life* has its contents page after the high profile property and antiques advertisements. Contents pages are often accompanied by an editor's letter which gives personality to the title. For glossy monthlies these sections are most likely to be interleaved with ads.

In *Red,* the first editorial content presented to readers after the cover is an editor's letter. More advertising follows, and then there is a two-page contents spread. Then more advertising, the staff list (called the flannel panel) and details of special contributors. Then *Red* allows the readers' voices in quickly with a page of letters, tweets etc. In contrast, *Farmers Weekly*, as a topical weekly, opens with the staff list and the editor's letter on one page and goes straight to the contents double spread and swiftly into news.

Contents and numbers

An important detail: where do the page numbers go on contents pages? Most magazines have got into what I consider to be a bad habit on their contents pages: they put the number of the page containing the content before its description. Is that the most important information? Do people regularly read what is on page 43 and are looking for '43'? Of course not. They are looking for the key words and images which describe or stand for the content. In this way the reader's eye does not have to travel back to the start of the item to read the page number. It is a small detail but demonstrates whether the designer was thinking of the readers and how to make their lives a little easier – or whether they are just focussing on the design.

From the contents page and editor's letter the magazine can open out into a number of directions. Some magazines provide 'eye candy 'for the readers, some strong visuals with captions to gladden the eye. This is the practice of Haymarket's *F1 Racing* magazine which has large dramatic pictures of F1 racing cars in action. Other magazines follow up the content page(s) with newsy items or short items about new trends. *Tesco Magazine*, for example, follows its two-page content spread with, on the left, an editor's letter and on the right 'This month I'm loving … ', the top product picks of the editor.

The front section

This front section of the magazine, however it is structured, is a vital tool in selling the title to the occasional reader and satisfying the demands of the regular reader. The potential buyer looks at the cover and flips through the magazine. The more enticing the front section – as long as the cover works – the higher the likelihood that the reader will buy the title. Therefore the early pages have to reflect the vision of the brand. In the case of *Tesco Magazine* it is bright and personal with the editor's letter and the pages are focussed on products. Much the same opening is used by *Fabulous*, the supplement magazine for the *Sun on Sunday*. A single page is used for the editor's letter, content and a plug for an online competition and then it is straight into a two-page spread of new products called 'Lust List'.

In the case of *The Spectator* the first editorial contents after the cover are the leaders, the opinion of the editorial team. These are unsigned and will have no picture of the editor: this anonymity gives the magazine gravitas; it says: 'this is our view and where we stand'. Only after that do we move into features which are by-lined. It is much the same at *The Economist* with contents pages, followed by a review of events in the week and then the leader articles. Again, this clearly communicates authority. *Monocle* spreads its content summary over two pages, separated by advertisements, lists the staff, gives pen pictures of the special contributors, and then, on a two-page spread, creatively presents a map of the world showing where the stories originate from. It also shows contents for other *Monocle* platforms such as online and radio.

Whatever structure is chosen to present the vision of the magazine to the reader in the front section, it should be consistently adhered to. The flow should only be changed in a major redesign and then only with an eye to projecting the existing or new vision in a stronger fashion. There is nothing more annoying for the regular reader than for the pieces of the front section to be in a different order issue after issue. It is like having the furniture in your favourite room rearranged every time you enter. Editors may juggle with the front section but they must realise that their readers lead busy lives. Because the editor is bored with the structure, it does not mean the readers are. As I discussed in Chapter 4, it comes down to that little word 'like': the question needs to be 'does it work?'

Magazines of course need to 'refresh' their design from time to time, a word beloved of art editors. There is a need to bring in new readers or keep up with the competition. Design styles change and are influenced by the wider world of popular culture, as I have shown with the 1980s title *The Face* in Chapter 4. *The Lady* became stuck in a time warp for many years, neither refreshing its design nor its content. Circulation dipped, despite the fact that demographics were on its side and it could have been of appeal to a growing population of affluent women over 35 years of age. The redesign and relaunch in 2009 helped to stabilise copy sales.

The back section

A significant proportion of existing and potential readers flip from back to front of the title and not the other way around. It is something of a convention now among consumer magazines to have a personality column facing the inside back cover. This can be a regular contributor or a profile, a day in the life of, or question and answers to an interesting celebrity. *FourFourTwo* has a football star picking his perfect team. *Essentials,* focussing on ordinary readers, uses its back inside cover to interview a celebrity under the banner 'She's so one of us'. Women's magazines which carry horoscopes also often place them at the back and final pages are a traditional location for prizes and puzzles.

In times gone by, many B2B magazines ran hefty recruitment or classified sections at the back – this is still their practice but as we have seen elsewhere in this book this revenue is rapidly migrating online. Of note is *Farmers Weekly*, still with a healthy advertisement section of properties, tractors, machinery and jobs which carries a coverline. That title also places the essential 'Prices and Trends' section at the rear to drive reader traffic.

Photo 5.3
Farmers Weekly has
a healthy classified
advertisements
section of properties,
tractors, machinery
and jobs

Titles influenced by American design often use the last pages of the magazine for the run-on pages from articles in the body of the magazine. This can make them a graveyard of text and gives the impression of a magazine petering out.

The body of the magazine

The object of the body of the magazine is to keep the reader entertained and interested. This middle section needs what I call Velcro: lots of little hooks to keep the attention of the reader. We want people to spend as much time as possible reading our title. If the pace of the magazine slackens then the consumer will lose attention and even put the publication down.

Feature material is likely to be placed in the centre of the magazine – this will be covered in detail towards the end of this chapter.

Use the centre fold

Magazines which are saddle stitched and not perfect bound (see Appendix 1 for explanation of these printing terms) have a great opportunity with their centre fold: the two pages where the magazine opens flat at the centre. This can be used for a two-page editorial spread to lift the pace at the centre. It should be designed accordingly. In my view not enough saddle-stitched magazines exploit this position

> This middle section needs what I call Velcro: lots of little hooks to keep the attention of the reader

– lessons should be learned from teenage girls' or music magazines which traditionally used this centre fold for posters to adorn bedroom walls.

We can judge the pace and flow of the magazine by using a pace/flow chart with any focus group.

Sectioned or rippled?

There are two main options for the flow of the content in the magazine: sectioned or rippled. With a sectioned flow the different subjects are gathered into a section, it is labelled and may be colour coded with a tab at the top of the page. For example in a

The pace/flow chart

Turn a sheet of graph paper landscape. Mark it half way up the left side. That creates the start point of the cover. Open any magazine and present the first double-page spread to the focus group. Does their interest go up, remain the same or go down? Mark up, down or level on the graph. Keep going through the magazine, getting the interest of the focus group for each spread. That will create a simple pace/flow chart.

Figure 5.2 shows a basic pace/flow chart for a fictional weekly business title. There is a high degree of interest in news, finance, general statistics and classified advertisements. The lowest degree of interest is shown in the special report – although this will obviously vary due to subject matter. The editor ends with a celebrity end-piece to hold attention levels to the very last page.

Just because a feature scores lower ratings does not justify its removal. In the case of a business special report it is highly likely that it will be devoured by a smaller group of highly interested readers and the stock of the magazine will rise as a result. I recall one editor in the consumer market relating to me an occasion when he tried to remove tough brainteaser puzzles from the back of the magazine. 'They were completed by a minority of readers but when I tried to drop them there were howls of anguish. They provided one of the main reasons why certain readers bought us. I reinstated them shortly afterwards'.

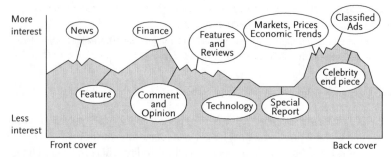

Figure 5.2 The pace/flow of a weekly business title

women's magazine, cookery placed in one part, fashion in another and beauty in a third. Designers use a mechanic called signposting – with themed sections signposted or flagged to the reader by using different tabs at the top and different colour borders.

Another option is to order the content in what I call the ripple: think of it as a kebab with has alternately meat, onion, pimento and tomato. Instead of all the tomatoes being in one place they are in different places, blending in the different tastes. *Yours* magazine often adopts this approach: there is a bit of nostalgia, a health tip, a feature, another bit of nostalgia and so it goes on. This means that the different elements are deliberately scattered through the magazine to enhance its flow and keep the reader interested.

The flat-plan

The flat-plan is the layout of an issue of a magazine, in effect the route map from the front cover to the back. It is often the product of a series of compromises and negotiations internally within editorial and externally with other departments – in particular the display advertisement sales team. Right hand pages are sought for their clients, as over many years advertising research has demonstrated that an advertisement on a right hand page is more likely to be read and noted by the reader. Also, advertisers believe that the earlier in the title their ad appears, the better. Similarly, news and features writers want right hand pages for content. I recall one experienced production manager saying: if only we could have a magazine made up of all right hand pages.

It is important to have ground rules worked out in advance so that the flat-plan of each issue does not have to be negotiated or become a battle ground. The publisher may have to adjudicate and agree the formula for both to follow. It is important to remember that the title has to serve both readers and advertisers. One creative solution is to run very popular single page contributors on a right hand page and sell the facing left hand page to the advertiser as a benefit.

Editorial teams must be open-minded: readers value advertisements and enjoy seeing products and services offered to them. Advertising agencies go to enormous time, trouble and expense to ensure their advertisements are creative. Long runs of editorial pages without a break of advertising can demand too much attention from the reader and should be used sparingly.

As with many of the guidelines I have laid down in this chapter, it is sometimes necessary to bend them – in this case to use a long run of editorial, perhaps as much as 16 pages or 24 pages. This is known as an editorial 'well'. If the cover price rises or a competitive launch emerges, the publisher may wish to demonstrate real value for money to the reader and a 'well' should be part of the flat-plan.

Figure 5.3 gives an example of a basic flat-plan. In this case we have illustrated the first 16 pages and the last 8 pages of this title.

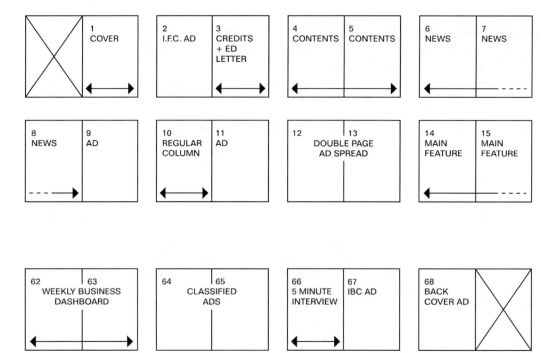

Figure 5.3 Basic
example of a
magazine flat-plan:
the first 16 and final
8 pages

THE ROLE OF PRODUCTION AND SUB EDITORS

In Chapter 4 I underlined the importance of the relationship between the editor and senior designer in creating and maintaining that all-important editorial vision. On a day-to-day basis there is another key duo within the editorial team – the production editor and sub editor (sub). Their role is akin to the rhythm section of a great rock band – the bassist and drummer maintaining tempo and structure to a song, keeping the egos of the lead singer and guitarist from straying too far.

> Their role is akin to the rhythm section of a great rock band ...

At the start of the magazine's working cycle, the production editor will produce a flat-plan, having first consulted the advertisement department. The sales team will have forecast what they expect to sell and any special requests for positioning. By their nature, commercial teams are optimistic and they may reserve more slots in a flat-plan than orders eventually received. In that instance, the production editor will have back up or 'filler' pages that can be dropped in at the last minute.

The key role of the production editor is to ensure that all copy flows through the content generation process on time. Modern DTP systems will track this and indicate what stage of readiness any piece is at one time. In a large publication, the production editor will be a dedicated role, in smaller titles the duties may be taken on by an existing member of the editorial team. Figure 5.4 gives a simplified chart of editorial workflow.

It is vital to have a good relationship with the printer. The production editor will be sharing layouts and flat-plans to ensure that machinery and paper is available to

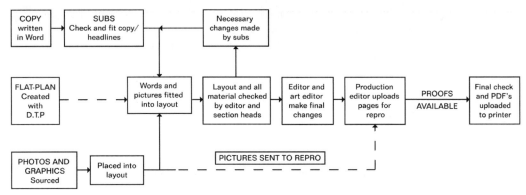

Figure 5.4 Simplified example of editorial workflow

produce the appropriate pagination. They will also be responsible for up-loading copy to the printer to an agreed schedule.

All magazines set great store by accuracy – the sub editors are the guardians of this. Copy is checked for spelling and grammar as well as facts verified. They will ensure that the writing is clear and consistent with house style and fits the proposed layout. Subs must also have a good working knowledge of legal issues affecting magazines and a sixth sense in spotting them. They will also be responsible for writing headlines, pull quotes, standfirsts and captions.

WRITING FOR MAGAZINES – CONTENT IS KING

The remainder of this chapter focuses on the written word and tried and tested writing techniques – both for print and online.

Words are serial

The chief characteristic of verbal and written communication is very simple – one thing comes after another. Words are in strings: determined by syntax and grammar. The order in which the magazine writer puts these words signals to the readers their relative importance. In sentences written in English, early words are more important than late words.

Imagine this scenario: you walk into a room. It is rectangular apart from bay windows into a garden. There are some arm chairs. There are also a few people sitting in them reading. The walls are green. With one sweep of your eyes you can see all of this. But it took 29 words to describe it. This is because visual communications are *parallel*, yet verbal and written communications are *serial*. We do not have in any language a single word for such a room: if we needed one, we would devise it.

This is why a picture is worth a thousand words. We can gaze at the picture and take in further details but to describe the whole room would take a volume of words. Was there a fireplace and exactly how many people were present? These are questions not yet answered. Yet, by observation we can see in one pass that the walls are rectangular and that they are green.

What is the most important thing about the room? That depends on the context. If we were writing a feature article on a house and that was the only green room, then the colour scheme would be the starting point. If other rooms were empty of people, then the human element may be the priority. We would pick the difference and start at this point. The task of the writer is to tell readers something different to identify. The writing should stress change not continuity. This key point is a constant for all types of writing in magazines; whether it be news, features or comment.

Five ways to improve magazine writing

1. Make the writing direct and involve the reader. For example, in instructions do not write 'the left edge has to be folded over the centre' but 'fold the left edge over the centre'.
2. Look at all verbs and strengthen them. Not 'it was deemed appropriate to put the swimming pool in the basement' but 'they decided to put the swimming pool in the basement'.
3. Linked to point two, make the language direct: have people or organisations doing things.
4. Shorten sentences. A sentence should have only one idea in it. Writers shorten sentences by hunting down and killing the word 'and' unless used in lists. 'And' shows that the writer is having another thought which should be in a separate sentence. They can also look for subordinate clauses and make them into their own sentences.
5. Keep things close to the reader. Use the word 'this' rather than 'that'. 'That' is further away; 'this' is closer.

All of these may seem to be small points when taken individually but together they help to make the copy active, accessible and relevant to the reader.

Structure and language

There are two key elements or components to good magazine writing whatever the type of article: structure and language. They should be considered as two different levels as it is difficult to work on them both at the same time. They need to be separated by a discipline. The discipline we use in my training company ContentETC is called POWER[3]. It takes the five steps in good writing and itemises them so that the structure and the language are separated.

POWER: five steps to good writing

POWER stands for: Prepare, Organise, Write, Evaluate, and Rewrite.

Prepare: Who is the article for? What type of article is it? What will its
structure be?

Organise: Arrange the characters or events in the right order. Identify the
key words which should be prioritised. Look for the 'killer quote'
which should also be high up. Is there anything in the story
which could be a box out or a side bar?

Write: Now use the appropriate language in the style of the magazine
to write the story. This creates a focus on language.

Evaluate: Read over the story – first for structure and then for language.
The key questions about structure are: is everything in the right
place; is there something missing; and is there something there
which is not needed? The key questions about language are: are
the sentences tight; are the verbs strong; and is the language
active?

Rewrite: now implement the evaluation in rewriting the story.

Initially using the POWER steps will slow the process of writing the story. It
will stop the writer going to the keyboard and 'thinking on the page', trying to
work the language and the structure together. But it will produce better copy
and, in time, become a good habit.

HOW TO CONSTRUCT THE MAGAZINE NEWS STORY

Every news story should have new information for the reader. One definition of
news is 'a fact or event not made public before'. Many topical print on paper
magazines lead with news either on their front page or in their front section.
Magazine websites are full of news.

The classic way to write a news story is in an inverted pyramid: the widest
sweep at the top of the story and successive layers of detail. The entry point is in
an introductory sentence or paragraph: the intro or lead. It must answer the
questions who, what, when and where?

Figure 5.5 graphically depicts the inverted pyramid shape of a news story.
Starting with the lead the writer quickly follows up with the How? and Why?
(which in some cases may actually be part of the lead). The reader is then taken
through less important details and out of the story into the next article.

Figure 5.5
The inverted pyramid
shape of a news story

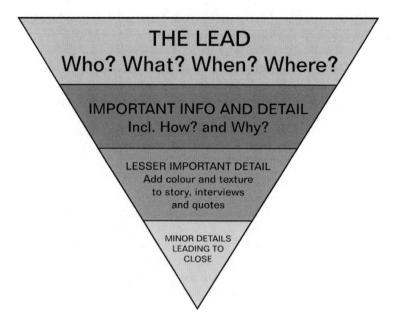

Here is the intro from an award-winning news story of the assassination of President Kennedy by Tom Wicker:

Dallas, Nov 22 – President John Fitzgerald Kennedy was shot and killed by an assassin today.
The correct questions are asked.

Who?   = The President and the assassin
What?   = shot and killed
When?   = November 22 and today
Where? = Dallas

Wicker unfolds the rest of his story in a classic structure. The characters are all introduced in the right order for the story. That order is: Kennedy and the assassin, Vice President Johnson, Mrs Kennedy, Governor of Texas Connally, physicians and nurses, Mrs Connally, Secret Service agent, two priests and the Judge who administered the oath to Johnson. The events are unfolded, not in a straight narrative form, what happened first, what second etc. That would make the reader plod through the story. Wicker sketches each scene, again in the right order, and keeps going back over them giving more and more detail each time. He also uses transitions to take the story on. For example, he follows the actions of Mrs Kennedy at one time in the story using her to pull the narrative on. (Students are encouraged to read the whole story on *The New York Times* website[4].)

For most journalists it takes a lot of practice to write in this manner. They have to be clear as to the structure of the story. Many writers make the mistake of starting the piece before they really know its direction. By using the POWER method it is possible to clarify the structure before they write.

Many writers make the mistake of starting the piece before they really know its direction

This inverted pyramid shape is used for news stories in magazines today. It has come to the fore again in writing for digital platforms where the key point needs to be made up front. We have noted that magazines online are a 'faster' medium than on paper, as it seems that we consume digital media at a faster pace than we consume content on paper. However, there is a problem today with this structure, just as there was back on that sad day in 1963: some people may already know the story's content. Certainly everybody who read the *New York Times (NYT)*, where Wicker's story was published, would have known the facts before. It had already been on radio and TV all day before the *NYT* special edition hit the streets.

News can now flow to readers over digital media so fast that this pyramid style may only tell readers what they already know. They can receive a tweet of it, read it on the internet or see blogs. As a result, the introduction with its summary of the whole story needs to be changed. Magazine writers need to find different ways to break into the story in order for the reader to be remotely interested, to stop them saying 'I already know that' and turning the page. After all, the object of the writing in magazines, on paper or online, is to retain readers as long as possible.

We can craft different intros for the Kennedy story to illustrate this. Each different intro is an 'angle': it gives the story a different 'spin' and establishes the theme of the story as it unfolds.

Here are two alternative intros for the Kennedy story:

The first focuses on the differences between the background of Kennedy and Johnson:

Camelot is dead, shattered by rifle fire in Dallas today. The French wines and string quartets beloved by President Kennedy and Jackie will give way to a different culture in the White House. It will be barbeques and a Texas Hoedown as President Johnson takes the reins of power.

The second focuses on Mrs Kennedy, the widow:

The day started well for Jackie Kennedy: groomed and adored by the Texas public. It ended horrifically: her assassinated husband's blood on her clothes and stockings and missing her hat.

In both cases these intros use more literary structures than the classic news story allows for, with its dependence on the structured summary introduction.

When is news non-news?

Some of the news in magazines today is hardly news at all: it is re-written press releases. Not journalism, but 'churnalism', the churning out of copy which has originally been generated by PR operations. In order to reduce churnalism, magazine news writers and editors can take five steps.

First, look for patterns in the news flow. A company launches a product: who has launched a similar product recently? So instead of the intro being 'Company launched a new gizmo this month ... ' it becomes 'Company is the third vendor into the gizmo market ... '

Second, obtain your own quote from some independent authority and put that high up in the story. 'Company's launch of its new gizmo this month was met with disbelief by experts.'

Third, look for what's missing. 'Company's new gizmo launched this month lacks the power of ... '

Fourth, give the story forward spin by getting experts to predict what will happen next rather than what has just happened. For example, will the gizmo market become more competitive?

Finally, use social media contributions by users as part of your news: what is the most read online story; what is the best comment or tweet?

Setting the news agenda

Magazines have specialist audiences. The news they carry needs to be tailored to their specialism. The same facts can be angled towards the targeted market of each title. Imagine this scene: a rare parrot escapes from a private aviary and is killed by the rotor blades of an RAF helicopter which is taking the Prime Minister to an audience with the Queen.

- For *Cage and Aviary Birds* the intro would focus on the rare breed of the parrot and the keeping of private aviaries.
- For *Helicopter International* it would focus on the type of helicopter and other incidents of birds in rotor blades.
- For the celebrity magazines it would focus on the fact that the Queen was kept waiting by a dead parrot.

As well as taking events in the world and angling them for specialist audiences, magazines also run news which is exclusive to their publication and for their specialism. These exclusive news stories come from running investigative journalism campaigns. *Horse and Hound,* for example, often runs investigations to expose stories about equine welfare. One concerned a man who ran a stables (Spindles Farm near Amersham) where the horses were badly neglected – he then absconded from the court where he was to be prosecuted. The magazine also ran a campaign about the trafficking of horses to the continent for horse meat and the poor conditions in which the horses were transported. This won a PPA Award. These stories may not necessarily generate significant interest outside the world of *Horse and Hound,* but they are of great interest to its readers. In fact, Spindles Farm did make the BBC and national newspapers.

Stories in this vein help the magazine make the agenda instead of just following events. They generate exclusive news and can be used to run a campaign calling for change. The magazine journalists who investigate them become specialists, thus reinforcing the magazine's brand name. Such content can generate spin offs in letters, comments and blogs – both in print and digital media. Handled well on the page and online, they can generate a volume of copy as the story can be angled in different ways with box outs. *Horse and Hound* did this particularly well in May 2010 with quotes about the neglected stables from the RSPCA, local people, the police and others.

THE FEATURE STORY AND ITS TEN OPTIONS

Feature stories are a package of words and images which both inform and entertain the reader. They are deliberately intended to be read more leisurely than news items. They are normally an in-depth look at a subject or person – there is no prescribed word count but upwards of 1,000 words is common. The shape of the feature story, unlike the inverted pyramid of the news story, is a diamond: a hook at the top in the intro or lead gets the reader into the story. Then comes the body of copy – the width of the piece – and at the end there needs to be a sharp point: perhaps a reiteration of the lead in a different form. This is depicted graphically in Figure 5.6.

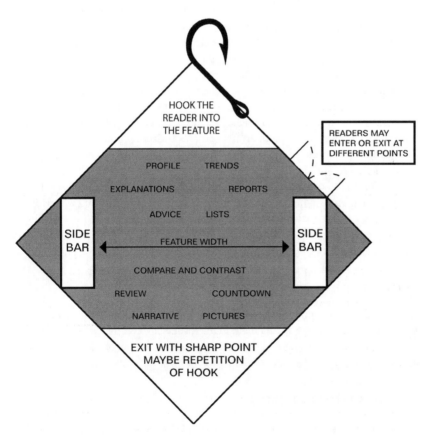

Figure 5.6 The diamond shape of features

Ten types of feature

There are many different types of feature but I will focus on the classic ten types. These are not clear cut categories, they often blur into each other, but they give a view of the range of feature structures available.

Profile

The first is the profile, often based on an interview with the subject. Here the writer needs to let the subject speak, as if a good host at a party says to the reader 'here's somebody interesting you should meet'. Then the writer steps aside and lets the subject get on with it, adding explanations when needed.

Marketing Week's Lucy Tesseras interviewed the vice president of global marketing at the *Financial Times* for the 21 March 2013 issue. She started with the fact that the *FT* was 125 years old yet was having to face the challenges of the digital age. By the fourth paragraph the subject of the profile, Jocelyn Cripps, was talking. The feature carried on over four pages with five box outs including a short curriculum vitae and a Q&A section. The main copy finished with the words: 'What happens over the next 125 years remains to be seen, but continued innovation and forward thinking remain firmly on the agenda.' By going back to the age of the *FT*, Tesseras completes the diamond structure of a classic feature.

This rule of letting the subject speak directly has often been broken by great feature and profile writers. Deborah Ross frequently breaks this rule, becoming part of the conversation and introducing the writer into the story. In the *Independent Magazine* on 11 May 2013 she wrote a profile of the singer Michael Bolton. She started with: 'I meet Michael Bolton – "Grammy-award winner" and "humanitarian", but never "crooner" or "soft-rock balladeer" according to the instructions to TV producers that somehow got caught up on my press bumpf – at a London hotel and the first thing that strikes me is how small he is.' This sentence breaks all the rules – but it works. And she finished: 'And now it is time for the photographs so he wanders off in his Grammy-award-winning way which, now I think about it, may be just that little bit humanitarian, too. Bless.'[5] She makes a perfect diamond shape of her profile feature taking the opening point and making it again in a different way as a personal observation.

Trends

The second type of feature is 'the trends' feature which takes different items which form a trend and explains them to the reader. Fashion magazines are strong on this type with the latest for summer fashions, for example, or the new colours in vogue. The same is the case for home decorating and furnishing titles.

Explanation and special reports

The extended length of a feature makes them ideal to explain and to answer the question why? Writers on *The Economist* are masters of this third type of feature, especially in their special reports. In a special report on television in May 2010 *The Economist* kick-started the piece with a feature on the changing face of TV.

The writer, Joel Budd, came into the story in a manner known by journalists as 'sideways'. A music streaming website found that its traffic fell between 8pm and 9pm on Saturdays. The reason? 'Britain's got Talent' was on TV, showing that TV still has a hold on mass audiences. The feature includes two charts and ends with the warning that the next few years will be dangerous for TV, but it will not suffer the same fate as the music industry or newspapers as a result of the rise of the internet.

Advice

The fourth type of magazine feature can give advice, particularly to specialist readers. To some extent the idea for this content is borrowed from partwork publishers. *Guitar Techniques* is peppered with advice feature stories into which it weaves profiles of great rock and classical guitarists. In the 1980s and 1990s, EMAP launched many titles in sporting and hobby markets on the back of 'how to' advice and technique. Clear step-by-step photography is normally a crucial part of the advice feature.

The big list

The fifth type of feature is the 'big list' feature. Create a long list of things to do and/or things to avoid and you make a strong appeal to readers. A classic big list feature gives a number of steps to improve. *Good Housekeeping* used this to help its readers look younger and get healthier in a 28 day step-by-step guide in its September 2009 issue. This neatly fits into the monthly publishing cycle of *Good Housekeeping*. Of course editors can use the non-rounded number as a good coverline as we have seen earlier in this chapter ... 132 Ways To ... .

Compare and contrast

Our sixth concept, compare and contrast features, are a handy way of exploring a subject. Such pieces can examine two opposing viewpoints, pitching one person's opinion against another. The *Radio Times* used this form of feature to examine the celebrities Ant and Dec. It had Ant talk about Dec and Dec talk about Ant in 19 February 2013 issue. This was supplemented with a quiz in which they were asked how much they knew about each other. Altogether, a five-page feature, both light-hearted and informative. On a more serious note, a political weekly can ask two authors with different standpoints to debate a key issue on page.

Review

The review feature – the seventh type – is a favourite of editors and readers. *BBC Music* magazine is packed with reviews of music and audio equipment. A key part of reviews is a star rating and a top choice. *Which?* magazine has the majority of its content devoted to review and recommends products or services in a factual and objective manner.

The countdown

Countdowns are our eighth type of feature. Some magazines would have a large void if they did not use the 'ten to one' feature. Who was the best Formula One driver ever? *F1 Racing* asks. But, even better, it does not present the number one first, but builds tension by starting at number ten and ending with number one. The pictures and profiles of the drivers get bigger and bigger the higher they are up the list.

These features need not necessarily revolve around humans and some of these lists can be long: *Antiques Info* magazine provided photographs and extensive captions of 66 Georgian drinking glasses in its March/April 2013 issue with an explanation by the editor of what to look out for when buying. Countdowns and lists can also pick up attendant publicity in other media, particularly the national daily press.

Narrative

The penultimate on our list of features is the classic: the narrative feature. This tells the story of an individual, a group of people or an organisation. It uses all of the narrative techniques of building suspense and including people talking about their experiences. In the continued aftermath of the events of 9/11, the USA financial magazine *Forbes* ran excellent narrative features on the effect on individuals and companies in the New York business community.

The real-life magazines excel at these narrative features. They take sometimes harrowing stories and turn them into great reading. An example from the Winter Special of IPC Media's *Pick Me Up* in December 2012 shouts the cover line 'She

 Photo 5.4 Reality magazines such as *Pick Me Up* regularly include well written narrative features

Wouldn't Leave the Man Who Killed Her'. The three-page feature opened with 'Grabbing a roll of white masking tape, I stuck it in a line right down the middle of our bedroom. I'd had enough'. The sister of a murdered woman is talking. It starts with the relationship between these two sisters, one so untidy and messy the other had to carve out her territory. It goes on to unfold the murder of this untidy sister. It ends pointing to her murderer: 'We'll never forgive him'. This is a powerful feature crafted by the writers and sub editors. If students wish to see excellent writing for their audiences, read the reality magazines and see how they develop and create a story.

Picture-driven

Last in this list of types of feature is the picture-driven feature. Photographs with the right captions tell a whole story: they give visual information and entertainment to readers. It is interesting to note that with digital editions of both magazines and newspapers such as *The Times* and the *Guardian,* the 'news in pictures' includes a slide show of many high-quality pictures to scroll through, it being physically possible to place many more photos online than in print.

HEADLINES AND CAPTIONS

Writers and editors spend a lot of time on their copy but for readers, both on paper and online, the first thing they often see is whatever image appears on the printed page spread or the screen. The order of 'reading' a page is often: image first, then caption, then the headline and finally into the copy.

Picture captions are more than just a description of what is in the picture. They should give something extra to the reader. Take a picture of the Taj Mahal, which everybody should recognise. Just having a caption 'Taj Mahal' tells us nothing we do not know. We could add that the Emperor Shah Jahan, who had it built for his dead wife, wrote this poem about it in the seventeenth century:

> In this world this edifice has been made;
> To display thereby the creator's glory.

That lifts the caption and gives the reader extra information.

The next in the sequence is the headline. Here writers love contrasts and alliteration. This is demonstrated in these two examples from *Garden News* 6 April 2013: 'Big crops small plots', and 'Best ever Baskets'. They also like to use song titles: 'Nothing like a dame' is *The Spectator* headline from 30 March 2013. They also like puns: 'Cross examination' was the head in the same issue of *The Spectator* about an exhibition of crucifixions.

CRAFTING OPINION COLUMNS AND EDITOR'S LETTERS

... people come
to magazines
for news and
stay for the
opinions

It is often said that people come to magazines for news and stay for the opinions. The readers may not agree with the opinions of the writers but they are helped to develop their own views by them: the grit to make the pearl. The two things opinion columns and features require are a clear structure and a strong point of view. I believe that many opinion and column writers on magazines start their writing without knowing that they want to say. They burble on for several paragraphs, looking for the subject and find it as they write.

Never start to write unless you know what you are going to say. You may love or hate Jeremy Clarkson, but you should know that he is a brilliant column writer because he is clear about what he wants to say and then creates a great structure for his columns. Structure depends on three things: the clear opinion, the evidence to back it up and the links between the points made. Readers will dip out of columns if they cannot understand the point – note that they do not necessarily have to agree. If they suddenly find the opinion piece going in a new direction because of poor transitions between the parts, they may well move on to the next content.

The editor's letter at the front of a magazine is also a comment column. Here the editor can start the conversation and act as a guide through the issue. One editor I know persistently writes about what is in the *next* issue, because that is what the team is now focussed on. So the whole letter is a disappointment for readers: the editor is telling them what they cannot yet see. The editor's letter needs to show passion about the subject as well as reveal something about the editor. This is especially true with specialist magazines.

THE INTERVIEW AND HOW TO CONDUCT IT

For all types of writing, news, features and columns, the journalist needs to interview subjects in order to squeeze the most out of them for readers. Background research on the subject is essential, but should be checked with the subjects every time. Sir Alex Ferguson is almost always said in profiles to have been a Govan shipyard worker: but he never worked as a shipbuilder. He was actually a toolmaker.

The interviewer wants to come away with 'notes, quotes and anecdotes'. Notes are the basics: how old, what title, what contact details etc. The interviewer should never rely on their memory: the most unreliable thing is a writer's memory. Next they want to get stories from those they interview. These stories offer the chance for the lead or intro of a feature or a background news story. Readers love stories: that's why they read magazines. A good anecdote can be a box out for a feature: they make the piece human. So magazine writers should ask the questions 'why did you do that?' and 'how did that happen?' Both of these are open ended questions which get people talking.

Look for the quotes which stand out. Magazines need the voices of many people talking to the readers. A good quote should be high up in the news or feature story. They provide the essential material for pull quotes, the short quotes pulled out of a longer piece to get the reader interested in it. They can also be used to tweet about the interview and provide material for blogs. Writers can slightly change quotes to fulfil the proper rules of grammar – but do so with care so as not to change any meaning.

If dealing with a subject who is reluctant to talk, it is a good tactic to tell them that we will first talk and later agree what can be quoted. This way the subject will start talking, may start to relax, and give the interviewer the story – then later be happy with the more formal process of agreeing to be quoted.

Finally there are two questions which are not asked often enough: what else do I need to know and who else can help me? Interviewees often say after the interview: but he did not ask me about that subject, the very one I wanted to talk about. Ask as the penultimate question – what else should I know? The interviewee can then tell you anything else on their mind. They may ramble and go over the same ground again: let them, you may get a better quote. Then try to see who else can help: plug yourself into their network of colleagues and associates and take the story further.

> ... pull quotes, the short quotes pulled out of a longer piece to get the reader interested in it.

PRINT AND DIGITAL – KEY WRITING STYLE DIFFERENCES

A theme of this chapter is that writing for print and digital media are different. This is for two reasons:

- They are different media and are consumed by readers in varying ways.
- Importantly, digital content is also consumed by search engines.

Only those highly intelligent beings who write algorithmic search engines really know the criteria of search. However, by observing what comes to the top of the generic search we can surmise the innards of these engines. They are certainly looking at content: it used to be the keywords but there is so much computing power available that engines are now delving into the content. On paper you might write about Ryan Giggs, the Welsh soccer star and winger at Manchester United, in this way:

> Ryan Giggs remains the final member of the golden academy which included Beckham and Scholes. The Welsh winger is not as fast as he was but still has a positive impact on the team, even at the top of the Premier League. The Manchester United veteran ...

You introduce more information about your subject by describing him in different ways, avoiding repeating the words 'Ryan Giggs'. But that's no good for digital content. The search engine scans the text and sees 'Ryan Giggs' only once. So is this story really about him? The software of the search engine cannot yet work out that 'Welsh winger' and 'Manchester United veteran' are the one and same Ryan Giggs. The more times the digital content mentions Ryan Giggs the better.

The same applies to picture captions and the tags pictures have in digital content. So often you click on the picture and it has a tag such as 'picoo1213'. That may be OK for your picture files but does not identify the content to the software as being about Ryan Giggs.

To summarise – the key style differences between writing on paper and for digital media are:

- Write shorter sentences for digital.
- Use more headings within the text for digital media to guide the reader.
- Use bullet point lists on digital content which can be scanned and absorbed quickly.
- Keep repeating the main subject in digital content.
- In news writing for digital media, revert to the inverted pyramid style so that the information is presented rapidly and accurately.

Magazine editors will expect industry entrants and new job applicants to be skilled across various platforms and it is important that this should be demonstrated through a portfolio.

NOTES

1.   PPA and ANMW (2010).
2.   Nielsen (2006).
3.   See ContentETC website at www.contentetc.com.
4.   Wicker (1963).
5.   Ross (2013).

REFERENCE SOURCES

Nielsen, J., 'F-Shaped Pattern For Reading Web Content', 17 April 2006 available at www.nngroup.com/articles/f-shaped-pattern-reading-web-content/ (Accessed 17 June 2013.)

PPA and ANMW, *Best practice for bar coding and issue numbering of magazines, partworks, collectables and promotional vouchers.* Updated November 2010. Available at www.PPA.co.uk. (Accessed 17 June 2013.)

Ross, D., 'Top of the crops: Michael Bolton on critics, crooning and why the mullet had to go', the *Independent,* 11 May 2013 available at www.independent.co.uk/ news/people/profiles/top-of-the-crops-michael-bolton-on-critics-crooning-and-why-the-mullet-had-to-go-8607796.html (Accessed 17 June 2013.)

Wicker, T., *The New York Times,* Saturday 23 November 1963, available at www.nytimes.com/learning/general/onthisday/big/1122.html#headlines (Accessed 17 June 2013.)

CHAPTER 6

Magazine distribution, sales and marketing

David Stam

Excellence in sales, distribution and marketing can prove to be a huge competitive advantage for today's publisher with considerable resources and expertise invested in these disciplines. Right product, right place, right person and right time have traditionally been the four cornerstones of an efficient circulation department – recessionary times have added right cost as a vital fifth dimension.

A UNIQUE DISTRIBUTION MODEL

Circulation sales or free distribution are vital to publishers. On a stand-alone basis the former is an essential source of revenue and profit provided that pricing models are set to cover all the direct cost areas such as paper, print, mailing, trade and subscriber discounts. Moreover, copies have to be targeted to deliver readers to advertisers, in the right numbers and from the relevant target market. In certain sectors, publishers may offer advertisers rate-based circulation guarantees; advertisers only invest in the certain knowledge that certain sales levels will be met.

Visibility in one sales channel can drive sales through another; research demonstrates that 74 per cent of subscription sales of consumer magazines originate from customers who have initially bought that title in a retail store[1]. In the developing digital world the paid-for print copy is still often the first contact point for future digital subscribers. As readers of this book will have discovered by now, the magazine publishing world is not without vanity or ego and many publishers and editors genuinely wish to see their titles in as many outlets as possible, despite the costs of printing and distribution together with the risk of unsold copies.

There are three other unique factors to consider. First, mass consumer and specialist consumer magazines in the UK are likely to have six or twelve monthly audits of their circulation figures. These are verified by the Audit Bureau of Circulation (ABC). Business and professional titles may also be covered either by ABC or Business Press Audits (BPA). A magazine's sales performance is often highly transparent – what the overall sale is and the annual percentage movements whether upward or downward. Advertising agencies and media

... the magazine publishing world is not without vanity or ego ...

pundits pour over ABC figures within minutes of them being released. There is no hiding place for poor performance.

Second, magazines are brands but every issue or edition has a new cover and fresh content that sit under the overall umbrella of that brand. Creative and journalistic interpretations can vary. It could even be argued that every issue is a new product. This causes special challenges for commercial teams with the two most common questions they need to ask being: 'How many copies do we distribute' and 'how do we promote to the consumer?' Magazine marketers now employ sophisticated algorithmic models to allow them to gauge the best potential for particular covers, promotions or general sales seasonality – but success or failure of that issue almost certainly sits with editorial colleagues.

Third, many magazines are highly time sensitive; they have to be in order to compete with digital information and rolling TV news. Titles such as *The Economist* will be on sale in London retailers within a few hours of the final pages being printed. This calls for speedy logistics and cost efficiency.

This chapter describes the complete spectrum of magazine sales, distribution and marketing with particular emphasis on consumer magazines in the UK.

Magazines can target their readers through three main routes to market. These are:

- retail sales
- subscription sales
- free distribution including controlled circulation and magazines to clubs and societies.

Sales of digital editions will be covered in Chapter 8.

RETAIL

If a reader purchases a magazine it will either be bought at a retailer or via a postal subscription. The majority of copies sold in the UK are still purchased from an extensive network of over 50,000 retailers.

The UK retail magazine market is valued at £1.4 billion and made up of 800 million sales per year[2]. ABC analysis reaching back to 2006 reveals that publishers who are dependent upon retail sales have had a torrid time. The overall retail market for magazines shows all years in that period to be in annual decline, none more favourable than minus three per cent and the first half of 2012 an alarming minus seven per cent down against 2011.

Customers, however, do like to buy magazines in shops. Statistics for the first six months of 2012 showed that 73 per cent of sales reported by ABC were generated in stores and just 17 per cent via subscriptions[3]. In the high circulation weekly markets, principally women's or TV listings, over 85 per cent of sales were rung up on retailers' tills. Figure 6.1 shows the retail supply chain in the UK.

ABC analysis reaching back to 2006 reveals that publishers who are dependent upon retail sales have had a torrid time

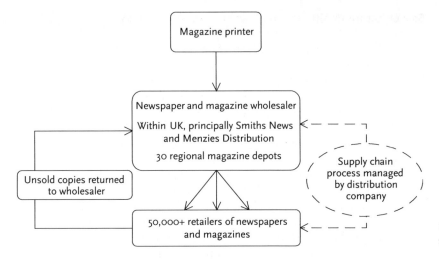

Figure 6.1 Retail supply chain

Role of the distributor

The majority of publishers employ a magazine distribution company to manage their retail supply chain. There are five main players in the UK: Marketforce (UK), Comag, Frontline, Seymour and Mail Publisher Solutions. These companies are themselves owned in full or in part by publishers and were invariably born out of a publisher's in-house circulation department. For example, Comag is jointly owned by Hearst Magazines UK and Condé Nast Publications. As well as providing sales, marketing and distribution services for those co-owners, Comag has a healthy business serving other publishers.

Distribution companies take the day-to-day hassle of managing retail sales away from publishers, allowing them to focus on content and marketing. In fact, the term 'distribution company' is something of a misnomer – these businesses rarely own their own vans and logistics is undertaken by dedicated third-party operators or by wholesalers. Activities cover five key areas: finance and publisher cash flow, management of logistics, retail sales, allocation of copies through the supply chain and data provision. The more publishers the distributor has under his banner, the greater his market share and ability to negotiate competitive prices and influence the supply chain for the benefit of all his clients.

The key to distributor success lies in management of data and, in recent years, all distributors have invested heavily in sophisticated information technology systems. These allow copies to be accurately targeted to the right retailer, thus minimising waste. Polling electronic point of sale (epos) returns from large retailers also allows distributors to give publishers vital feedback on real-time sales. This is especially useful for weekly titles as speedy and informed decisions can be made about promotions, content and covers for immediately subsequent issues. Sound data takes the guesswork out of the process.

Sale or Return (SOR)

The world over, magazines are supplied to retailers free of financial risk. Display them, sell them – and if you don't – publishers will take them back and you won't have to pay for them. SOR is one of the factors that make magazines an attractive category for retailers. It was not always that way. Until the late 1980s many leading titles in the UK were provided on firm sale to wholesalers and retailers, with perhaps some discretionary SOR during promotional periods. Sheer competition in terms of number of magazines jostling for shelf space, including a range of highly attractive SOR launches into the UK from German Publishers Gruner + Jahr and Bauer, contributed to flipping the UK market rapidly into one where the publisher takes all the risk. Today in the UK, publishers will expect to sell 60 per cent of distributed copies: weeklies performing more efficiently than monthlies, as sales patterns are more predictable for that genre and the sheer volume of copies distributed means that, in percentage terms, the volume returned is less.

Unsold or returned copies are a significant cost line in the business models of consumer publishers. Simply put, publishers have to pay for all the copies they distribute but only get paid for the ones they sell. Circulation departments talk increasingly about *optimising* rather than *maximising* sale. Copies are not distributed to all retailers. Both individual stores and multiple store groups have copies allocated to them based on their potential to sell. Larger titles are more readily available; consumer titles selling over a quarter of a million copies per issue can expect to be in some 40,000 plus newsagents. In contrast, middle-ranging titles selling between 50,000 and 75,000 copies per issue target around 15,000 stores, with titles selling under 2,500 copies appearing in fewer than 2,000 outlets[4].

Unsold copies are always returned to the wholesaler and disposed of in an environmentally friendly way, the vast majority being recycled into papermaking.

The wholesale network

Wholesalers are a vital link in the supply chain between printer and retailer and the UK prides itself in having a fast and cost-effective wholesale network for both newspapers and magazines. The key to this lies in the fact that wholesalers distribute and sell both media to their retail customers using highly time-sensitive logistics on a shared cost basis.

Two wholesale companies operate in the UK: Smiths News and Menzies Distribution. They distribute magazines to over 50,000 retailers from approximately 30 branches nationwide. It was not always so. When this chapter's author was a young publishing executive in the late 1970s there were well over 300 wholesale branches operated by both multiple and independent owners. Even in the very early years of the new millennium there were three multiples and a number of independent wholesalers. How did this significant structural change come about?

Wholesalers are appointed by publishers – or by distribution companies acting on their behalf – to distribute newspapers and magazines to retailers in a specific geographical area. Under guidance from the Office of Fair Trading (OFT) this form of media distribution has some protection from competition law. Wholesalers enjoy 'absolute territorial protection' (ATP). This means they are awarded exclusive access for a given time period to distribute to specific areas of the country. Retailers stocking newspapers and magazines cannot choose their supplying wholesaler – publishers will have nominated one for their postcode. Competition authorities have looked at these arrangements long and hard for over ten years and seem content with them for media using this unique mode of distribution. With the focus on the consumer, the OFT are satisfied with overall availability of magazines and the stability of the retail universe at over 50,000 stores. They also consider pricing to be competitive; in fact in recent years cover prices have declined in real terms.

Through acquisition, taking over failing businesses and publisher negotiations, Smiths News and Menzies Distribution have been able to grow their market shares significantly within this legal 'safe haven'. This rapid consolidation has largely benefited major publishers and distributors in terms of efficiency of working practices.

The retail view of this supply chain, however, is mixed. Larger multiple retailers, on the whole, welcome a single wholesale relationship for each store and recognise the resultant operational efficiencies. Smaller and principally independent retailers are more vocal about the need for wholesaler choice which they believe would deliver better levels of service and profitability. Retailers, large and small, desire more control over the number of copies allocated to their stores. It is an ongoing debate.

Retailers

In today's fast moving retail landscape it is strange to think that only 20 years ago wholesalers could refuse to supply magazines to a retailer, on the basis that a newcomer may damage the established business of existing retailers! A Monopolies and Mergers Commission (MMC) report in the 1990s changed that. Now the press retailing universe supports over 50,000 stores as diverse as the small street corner newsagent to a huge WH Smith or Tesco. Stop for petrol or visit a garden centre and the chances are you will be able to buy a magazine. For publishers and their distribution companies the retailer is now king and much time and cost is spent in managing these vital relationships.

Figure 6.2 shows the market share that key retailers or retail sectors enjoy of the total UK magazine market.

In looking at retail market share it is important to be mindful of two key caveats. First, share at individual title level can vary significantly from the industry norm. For example, WHS Travel has a 6 per cent share of the overall magazine market. Their share of the weekly news and current affairs magazines market, however, is likely to be four times this, as these titles are both highly sought after by the travelling public and fit the demographics of many WHS Travel stores. Secondly, in number of actual stores, the pie chart of Figure 6.2 stretches the ninety per cent/ten per cent rule. Just five per cent of all stores selling magazines have 'Tesco' over the door but that group accounts for 15 per cent of all magazine sales. WH Smith's High Street division drives eight per cent share through just over one per cent of the retailing universe.

> Stop for petrol or visit a garden centre and the chances are you will be able to buy a magazine

Convenience and
other multiple groups
15%

Other supermarkets
and dept stores
4%

Morrisons
6%

Asda
6%

Figure 6.2
Retailer market share

Source: Adapted from
Wessenden/Seymour
(Q1/2012)

Coop
6%

Sainsbury
8%

Independent
retailers
26%

WHS High St
8%

Tesco
15%

WHS Travel
6%

Photo 6.1 There are
over 50,000 retailers
selling magazines
in the UK. They
range from major
WH Smith stores
to neighbourhood
newsagents

WH Smith

WH Smith is a major force in magazine retailing. Through two operating
divisions – High Street and Travel – there are over 1,200 stores under what must
be one of the best known brands in UK retailing. Their stores are visited by 73 per
cent of the UK population at least once a year and they sell over one million
magazines per week. The divisional names are apt – the 621 High Street stores
are well located in city centres or shopping centres and focus on the core areas of
newspapers and magazines, stationery and popular books and entertainment.
Recent years have seen extensions into post office services and currency and the
business has also pioneered the Kobo eBook reader in the UK. Since the early
years of the millennium the business has raised its game considerably, under
consumer pressure from supermarkets and online sales and financial pressure
from the City. Margins have increased, costs have been strictly controlled whilst
stores and merchandising have become bright, friendly and attractive.

It is hard to make a journey in the UK without coming across one of WH Smith's 643 Travel stores in stations, airports or on the motorway. These stores offer a different proposition to their High Street counterparts; the average travelling customer has less time to browse and may require sandwiches, snacks and drinks as well as something to read. They expect to check out without a wait. In stores such as those on Waterloo or Victoria stations and in Heathrow or Manchester airports, huge numbers of customers have to be served in a very short period of time.

The British high street has changed in the last 15 years, some would say out of all recognition. With the exception of WH Smith, it is now rare to see an independent or multiple newsagent in this prime retail space. Smith's importance to publishers is underlined by their commitment to range. At the top end of their retail estate, a large WH Smith shop can display up to 1,750 magazines with additional titles available for collection through in-store ordering. Magazines are displayed at the front of the store both driving footfall and inspiring impulse purchase. Indeed, browsing customers are welcome, with a trip to Smiths a good way to fill a rainy lunchtime. In particular, for publishers of specialist titles, for example sports, hobbies, IT or transport, being ranged by WH Smith is absolutely essential.

While publishers welcome the commitment to stocking a wide choice of magazines, it has not come without cost, with many titles ranged by Smiths expected to invest in promotional space or pay fees for listing.

Case study 11

Bookazines and partworks

Retailers have taken advantage of two growth areas of publishing to help arrest the decline in sales of regular frequency, ABC reported titles.

Bookazines are an innovation of the last ten years and a growing part of the market. They are as the name depicts – a hybrid between a large format paperback book and a perfect-bound magazine. Expect bookazines to have the following characteristics:

- the look and feel of a glossy paperback but displayed in the store's magazine section for volume sales
- a retail price considerably in excess of a monthly magazine, seldom less than £8 and occasionally more
- in store for longer than a traditional monthly magazine
- popular subject matter including computing, mobile technology, health and fitness and nostalgic modern history
- a price, format, longevity and subject matter that all combine to make them attractive for overseas markets as well as UK store groups.

By comparison, partworks have been a part of the UK magazine scene for over 50 years. They follow a totally unique business model.

- A partwork is a publication, usually weekly or fortnightly, which runs for a finite time period, normally from 50 to 80 weeks. As such it is made up of parts.

- Issue by issue the titles builds up to a completed product. In times gone by after 80 weeks purchasers would have collected a full dictionary, encyclopaedia or cookery course. Nowadays the end product may even be a completed model of a ship, aeroplane or car.
- For the publisher the focus is on persuading as many people as possible to buy the early issues, to lock them into the collection. After that there is a decay curve of purchase through to the last part. Thus there is heavyweight and highly costly TV advertising for the first and early issues.
- The majority of the publisher's investment is up-front, for both editorial innovation costs and TV advertising. This can make partworks a high risk route for publishers. Risk is significantly mitigated by product testing in a limited UK TV region prior to national launch with national rollout only proceeding if profitable sales can be predicted. Partworks can be very profitable for publishers but they are not for the faint-hearted.
- The genre is owned by a small group of publishers who focus on it and is largely avoided by the large, mainstream consumer publishers.
- Despite being often very bulky to display, partworks are important to retailers as they stimulate regular visits to the store to purchase. A key launch time is January when sales of other merchandise are low. They are distributed via the wholesale supply chain.
- They are also an important source of export sales for UK-based publishers.
- Increasingly, subscription sales of partworks are growing.

Supermarkets

Before the mid-1990s very few UK supermarkets stocked magazine ranges; now the main supermarkets command an impressive 43 per cent of the market – over 50 per cent if smaller convenience chains are added. Magazines are merchandised in one of two ways – either in a 'store within a store' concept or in aisle for general shopping. This rapid growth has been mutually beneficial to publishers and supermarkets but has also been a learning curve for both partners.

There is no doubt that the opening of the supermarket channel helped fuel the overall magazine market growth of the late 1990s and early 2000s. A new and exciting world of magazines was now available to consumers – particularly women – on their regular shopping trips. Large stores made full or even double facing front cover displays possible and there was often space for imaginative point of sale. Mass-selling titles such as *What's On TV* and *TV Choice* blossomed. Initially only stocking high volume sellers, supermarket ranges started to include more specialist and men's titles to add depth to the magazine offer. No longer the preserve of women's or TV titles, a large supermarket or superstore now stocks around 600 titles catering for all topics and interests.

Magazines benefit supermarkets from both financial and merchandising perspectives. There is little stock risk with sale or return, there is a minimum 25

> There is no doubt that the opening of the supermarket channel helped fuel the overall magazine market growth of the late 1990s and early 2000s

per cent margin from cover price plus promotional vendor income (see Case study 12 below). Customers claim they add colour and enjoyment to the overall shopping experience.

Publishers have had to learn new rules of engagement: persuading retailers to stock a title became a commercial discussion and not a given right. Annual business plans now include the cost of trade marketing whilst this rapid growth of supermarket share has seen significant loss of sales for the independent newsagent.

Supermarket buyers have had to learn to work with publishers who own media and entertainment brands with no own label alternative available. Moreover, the supply chain for this category is unique and supermarkets have had to grapple to understand and come to terms with it. Instead of purchasing products direct from the manufacturer, grocery buyers have to deal with wholesalers and distribution companies – until relatively recently often more than one wholesaler per store. As SOR risk lies with the publisher, copies are allocated to individual stores, not ordered by the retail chain. The process of returning unsold copies can be time consuming. It is not a supply chain the grocery trade is used to or would have designed. Ongoing discussion with wholesalers has led to operational practices becoming more tailored to the requirements of the grocery sector.

Case study 12

Listing and ranging – selling a title into a major retail chain
WH Smith, supermarkets and other retail groups all have policies for stocking magazines whether they are launches or titles that have been in publication for some time. The objective for publishers is to get titles listed and ranged as widely as possible.

LIST – to have your title accepted by the retailer so they will buy it from wholesalers and sell it in their stores.

RANGE – to have your title just listed is rarely enough. It may only be in a handful of branches within a national group. You want it ranged as extensively as is appropriate for that magazine. In other words in as many stores as possible.

Every retailer will operate in its own way – and almost certainly say that their way is the best! They will ask four key questions:

What is the retail strategy?
WH Smith have a total commitment to large ranges generating as much consumer choice as possible, supermarkets will have smaller ranges. Different sized stores within the same group will have different sizes and layouts for display. Some groups may be more focussed on men's titles. The range needs to be balanced – if fishing magazines are sold then a store will want to cater for different types of fishing, river or sea. One title would not

suffice. Increasingly, retailers will look at research and loyalty card data to establish the right magazines to stock for their customers as well as data the publisher can provide to press his case.

How profitable?

Buyers will look at six-monthly ABC data and see which titles are up and down; they will want to have the best sellers. They will also examine the cash rate of sale per title for their stores. This is defined as the revenue created per week or per issue from each title in the range. Hurdles or thresholds per store will be set. The more profitable the title the more stores you will be in.

Is there promotional investment?

Retail profitability is enhanced by the publisher's commitment to invest in their products within a certain store group. All major retailers have a range of promotions and there is an increasing expectation for publishers to buy into them. Indeed some groups now have formal annual agreements with publishers which need to be entered into to secure listings. Small scale launches may be subject to a listing fee for being displayed or publishers have to buy off shelf promotional units to secure launch display. Different market sectors have different promotional requirements. The UK news and current affairs weeklies benefit by being positioned close to the quality national newspapers – and will pay for those positions. Mass selling titles want multi-facing displays in 'bestseller' type units at front of store.

Is it a good magazine?

Magazine retail buyers are hard commercial operators but they are also committed and enthusiastic about the category. They have to be. They will have opinions on the relevance of the target market to the store group as well as the look and feel of the title being presented. They see a lot of publishers and magazines in a working day so it is wise to listen. They will need to be convinced that a title will deliver additional sales. But they are also acutely aware of the current demise in overall magazine sales and the need to turn that around. No retail buyer wants to see his or her allocated space shrunk by the commercial director and handed over to other more profitable lines within the store group.

The latter point is especially important when it comes to magazine launches. Major launches are often only briefed out by the publisher under a confidentiality agreement as they are fearful of competitive 'spoilers'. They are sold in at concept stage or with a printed 'dummy' copy so the track record of the publisher and editor is key to the decision to list.

Major consumer launches have traditionally been a huge driver of the overall market. Since 2008, however, trading conditions have been tough and print has seen significant competition for investment from digital media. To some extent retailers have taken up this slack by ranging more bookazines, partworks and children's titles. Experienced retail buyers know that launches which are well researched, executed and marketed are the lifeblood of the magazine industry. Sell them in professionally and they will back them.

Ranges are reviewed to a timetable which the retailer will brief out; twice a year is normal. Work to these guidelines – exceptions are only made for major launches. Prepare for the buyer meeting well, it may be quite short and to the point. Stress the unique selling points of your title and how it will be differentiated from the competition. Make good use of visuals.

Independent retailers

As Figure 6.2 (page 172) shows, the share of the magazine market held by independent retailers is 26 per cent. This has declined from over 40 per cent in the last 15 years. Recent trends show that some of these traditional newsagents have become small convenience stores (C stores) but, even allowing for that, the share will barely exceed 30 per cent. As in many retail markets, life is tough for the small trader and will continue to be so.

Sales of many top selling consumer titles have moved to the supermarket sector as shopping behaviour has changed. There is also tough competition from larger C stores and petrol forecourt shops. Commentators point to a myriad of other factors to explain declining magazine sales at the smaller newsagent. These include the reduction of magazine racking as space is given over to soft drinks and food lines, the inability to park outside on city roads and the decline in smoking and regular trips to buy cigarettes.

The independent sector, however, is still a key part of the retail supply chain, especially for the publishers of women's weeklies, TV listings titles and children's comics. Here the share may be higher than the average 26 per cent. (Witness the last fact by trying to get into a newsagent near a school after class!) Membership of the National Federation of Retail Newsagents (NFRN) totals 16,500 newsagents in the UK and Ireland. Founded in 1919 this retail association represents and protects the interests of the sector and is an effective pressure group. There is an ongoing debate with wholesalers over delivery charges and operational service standards and with distribution companies on availability of magazines. The NFRN's concern is that distributors favour supermarkets when allocating supplies of magazines, with the consequence that independents lose profit by selling out by the end of the week or month.

The backbone of many an independent newsagent's business is home delivery – the NFRN claim that five per cent of magazines are still sold this way. Householders place a regular order for magazine titles with their newsagents and they are delivered on the morning of publication, almost certainly alongside a daily delivered newspaper. A well run independent store will also order any magazine that customers require from their wholesaler, often arriving the next day.

It is hard to discern a sea change in the lot of the independent retail newsagent, although with the post 2008 recession putting pressure on discretionary spending and consumers making more shopping trips but spending less, there are signs that the sector decline is arresting[5]. Innovative proprietors are always seeking new ways to serve customers: Amazon collections and returns handled by local stores is an example of this. There is no doubt that independent

> The independent sector ... is still a key part of the retail supply chain

stores also fulfil a vital social role in many neighbourhoods and for many consumers – particularly the elderly – they are a not just a place of trade but a part of the community.

The margin split

There is a relatively small magazine margin differential between large and small retailers. Both can expect to earn 25 per cent of published cover price, high volume stores particularly in the travel sector may be able to improve on that by up to a further 2 per cent. The expression 'remit' is used for the balance of cover price that the publisher keeps, that is remitted by the third party distributor. It is influenced by the size and market share of the publisher in question but an average range is 52 to 58 per cent. The balance is split between wholesaler and distributor with 13 per cent and 4 per cent respectively not untypical.

SUBSCRIPTION SALES

In 2012, close to 200 million magazines were sold in the UK through the postal subscription channel. At 17 per cent of overall magazine sales, this is the polar opposite of the US where subscriptions account for 83 per cent of the market[6]. General statistics can be misleading and there is no doubt that for certain sectors subscription has become the primary distribution channel. Subs sales have quadrupled since the early 1990s and even in the current tough publishing climate still show modest growth.

Every mainstream publisher now has a specialist team selling subscriptions, using sophisticated direct marketing techniques accessing extensive customer databases. Gone are the days when subscriptions were principally for readers who were unable or unwilling to buy their magazine at retail. Now every publisher's website will be persuading you to a buy print and/or digital sub while expensively produced mailing shots drop on the mat.

What have been the principal drivers of growth for subscriptions

The international base of many large consumer publishers and, in particular, the growing influence of US publishers in the UK, woke domestic circulation executives up to the commercial opportunities presented by direct marketing. The American cousins were leading the postal subscriptions game; it was time to import some of their ideas into the UK.

Business to business (B2B) publishers also offered best practice to their consumer colleagues. Only the largest B2B titles, such as *Farmers Weekly*, are available at newsagents, so good subs marketing has been key to success in that sector for many years. Those skills were shared and so transferred over to the larger consumer titles.

The developments in retail described earlier in this chapter started to unsettle consumer publishers – especially those creating specialist titles. Growth of the multiple retailer, the decline in independent market share, more disciplined ranging and listing policies and significant increases in trade marketing spend required to secure good displays all combined to push publishers more rapidly down the subscriptions route. With direct marketing, publishers felt more in control of their route to market.

Unlike retail sales, where wholesaler, retailer and distributor discounts have to be factored in, the publisher receives the entire subscription price paid by the consumer. Annual payment in advance is also beneficial to cash flow. Technology has been a huge driver of change in three ways. First, and doubtless modern students will smile, the introduction of desk-top computers and Microsoft programs such as Excel and Access made the sophisticated reporting used by subscription marketers relatively quick and painless. Benefits and costs could easily be presented using clear reporting – hard to do with just an office calculator and a 1980's typewriter.

Second and more importantly, the rapid growth of computing power and database management systems in the nineties and the new millennium allowed publishers, or service companies operating on their behalf, to purchase cost effective IT solutions to drive direct marketing.

Third, the huge expansion of the internet, universality of email addresses and popularity of social networking sites has opened up a myriad of economical ways to gather consumer data to spearhead subscription offers.

One of the factors that keeps the magazine publishing business relatively low in terms of barriers to entry is the ability of publishers to outsource services where high capital investment is needed. The subscription channel is no exception, with the growth of third party mailing companies and fulfilment bureaux.

> With direct marketing, publishers felt more in control of their route to market

Supply chain

The supply chain for postal subscriptions is straightforward and portrayed in Figure 6.3.

Magazines are addressed and wrapped, normally in polythene. Bulk magazines are then collected by Royal Mail or a possible alternative carrier for delivery to the customer. This process is carried out either by a third party mailing company or the printers themselves. The former is likely to be close to the print site to minimise road transport costs and to ensure copies reach the postal system as quickly as possible. Printers themselves are investing in packing technology to take over the role of the mailing companies or in some cases even acquiring these businesses to provide a 'one stop solution' for publishers. Copies for overseas subscribers are normally channelled via a mailing consolidator who will buy the most cost effective air or sea freight service to reach the end consumer.

Subscription fulfilment companies

Fulfilment companies or bureaux play a vital role in managing postal subscriptions and like their retail counterparts, the newstrade distribution companies, the name is often a misnomer – they very rarely touch the actual magazine. A modern fulfilment bureau is more likely to call itself a 'customer relationship management company' or a 'subscription marketing firm'. They manage and report on databases on behalf of their publisher clients, collect

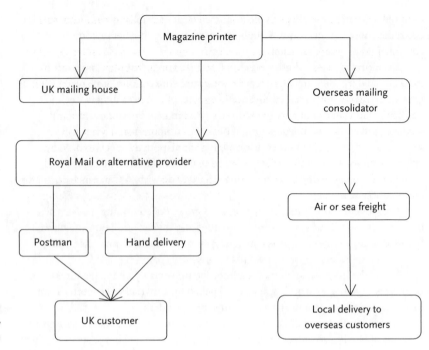

subscription revenues in differing currencies and drive complex renewal
programs. In addition, they offer extensive contact centre resources, dealing with
millions of UK and overseas subscribers by telephone, post and, increasingly, the
internet. Their operational teams liaise with mailing houses or the despatch
departments of printers to ensure the right mailing lists await copies as they pour
off the press.

It is a highly competitive market where the devil lies in the detail – good IT
systems, reporting and operational procedures are crucial. It is also very fast
moving with expertise in digital subscriptions the current hot area for investment.
There are four main players in the UK: CDS Global, Dovetail, QSS and dsb.net.
Because these service providers are critical to the publisher's business, ownership
tends to be both long term and secure. For example, Dovetail is a joint venture
business owned by Immediate Media and Dennis Publishing and dsb.net is
backed by dsb.AG, a leading specialist IT solutions company.

The financial model of the subscription bureaux is very different to their
newsstand counterparts. The latter receive money from wholesalers, deduct
their commission and remit the balance to the publisher. The subscription
fulfilment company works for a fee, normally set at an annual sum per subscriber
record and may make additional charges for services such as mailings or call
centre use.

*... a highly
competitive
market where
the devil lies in
the detail ...*

Direct marketing

The subscription relationship is unique to the magazine business and is rooted in
brand loyalty and trust. No other industry can persuade the consumer to pay
upfront, often for twelve months, for a product that has not even been produced

yet! Other entertainment sectors are highly envious, particularly computer gaming and music. It is a business model to cherish.

In its simplest form, the job of a subscription marketer can best be described as filling a bathtub with the plug out. It is an apt analogy that stands the test of time. The taps pouring water are the new subscribers signing up. The plug drain represents subscribers deciding not to renew. The level of water rises by increasing the water flow (more newcomers) or blocking the drain (stopping subscribers from leaving). Both activities are expensive, especially the former.

Subscription departments therefore focus on two principal tasks: acquiring new subscribers and persuading them to renew, normally after one year. Their mantra is code, test, cost results and report against budget. If it succeeds then repeat, if not drop the test and move on. It is a numbers intensive business with a complex array of ever-moving variables.

> ... the job of a subscription marketer can best be described as filling a bathtub with the plug out

Acquisitions

A successful subscription campaign will be delivered by:

- **Media:** using the right media to reach the likely subscriber, for example advertisement pages inside the magazine, email campaign, direct mail shot or outward telemarking.
- **Offer:** the right offer, a keen price, free issue or premium gift.
- **Creative:** a targeted, creative treatment with good copywriting and design.
- **Timing:** for example, gift subscriptions at Christmas.
- **Response:** an easy to use response mechanism, for example a reply paid card or internet landing page.

Media

Subscription offers can be made through a whole host of media but it is important to remember that the most cost effective will almost certainly be offers in the magazine itself or, increasingly, on a related website. Research shows that nearly three quarters of active subscribers were previously buying the title at retail, on an average of 7.7 times per year for a monthly[7]. Conversion to a regular sale brings convenience and almost certainly a highly attractive price or gift. When fitting together the magazine flat-plan the subscription department has to compete for free or 'house' space with paid-for advertisements and other magazine promotions, for example events. Despite this, it is vital that quality subscription promotions appear on a regular basis. Similarly, visitors to magazine websites are likely to have to navigate their way around tempting subscription offers when first accessing the site. Almost certainly, this will be the cheapest way of gaining new customers.

Magazine marketers have been quick to use the power of new media to sell print on paper 'old' media. Anyone arriving and registering with a publisher's website becomes a candidate for targeted email marketing. Publishers have also developed expertise in building and marketing to lists via email – within the remit of data protection legislation. Entering a competition, going to a reader event or simply signing up for a daily blog creates an email address for the publisher behind which lies a chance to market a subscription.

> Magazine marketers have been quick to use the power of new media to sell print on paper 'old' media

A risk-free method of selling subscriptions which is growing in popularity is pay per click. Type a magazine name or 'magazine subscriptions' into a search engine and you are likely to be presented with ads offering the opportunity to buy a subscription (via an affiliate subscription site) at an attractive price or discount. These affiliate sites are the magazine retailers of the internet. Financial models vary, but the attraction to the publisher lies in the fact that commission to the affiliate is only paid on the sale. One such site, www.magazine.co.uk is operated by Jellyfish Publishing and offers subscriptions on over 700 titles from the top sellers to the niche.

There are more ways of reaching potential subscribers than this textbook can ever do justice. When choosing, marketers need to be highly mindful of cost effectiveness and only use expensive media when the possibilities presented by cheaper communication are exhausted. They must select the right media for the market. Postal mailshots have a high unit cost but in certain markets, notably titles aimed at the professions such as teachers, doctors and lawyers, they deliver cost-effective results.

Offer

Attractive discount offers and premium gifts are essential. When asked, 28 per cent of purchasers said that price was the key reason for subscription purchase and six per cent cited a free gift as their incentive[8]. Readers are likely to have a sum in their mind that they will spend buying the title every week or month in the newsagents and discounts are expressed as a saving from this.

Increasingly popular with weekly titles are a sequence of free issues at the start of a subscription to encourage the reader to sign up. These discounts can be very significant – often more than 25 per cent and in some instances over 50 per cent. When using free gifts as subscriber incentives it is essential that the selected premium is right for the brand and the target market. Effective offers will be free golf balls as incentives for golfing magazines, music CDs for classical music titles, cosmetics for the health and beauty market and wine for the political weeklies.

Creative

Whatever the chosen medium for the promotion, be it inside the magazine, on the publisher's website or via the more expensive mail shot, it is vital to use a professional and targeted creative approach. Direct marketing copywriting differs from normal advertisement copy with the emphasis on powerful headlines, short punchy paragraphs and careful selection of typefaces. The selling proposition must be communicated readily and quickly. Every word and illustration has to work towards the end goal of making the sale; there is no space for irrelevance.

> **The selling proposition must be communicated readily and quickly**

Timing

Subscription acquisition campaigns tend to be seasonal and managed in waves; publishers are best advised not to fight seasonality and go with the flow. In the retail market there is a tendency for magazines to have strong sales in spring or autumn, therefore many acquisition campaigns also focus on those times.

Subscriptions for sports magazines are optimised at the start of the designated seasons, particularly when accompanied by an attractive pricing or premium gift offer. Christmas gift subscriptions are now an important source of circulation for publishers. Every issue of a magazine for a year can make a perfect gift, particularly for a friend or relative living far away or who has a hobby.

Response

As in any form of direct marketing, ease of reply will drive response. Pre-paid cards, freephone numbers and web subscription sites are the most common. If the latter is used, it is essential that the internet home page or landing page is user friendly and speedy to navigate. Most publishers offer satisfaction guarantees to their readers.

Renewals

The job of a subscription marketer is highly analytical with good numeracy skills a key part of the job description. The following is a brief and simple description of a part of circulation management that has rapidly developed in the last ten years.

Publishers assign a cost for acquiring a subscription in its first year called cost per acquisition (CPA). This is the unit cost of selling and servicing the subscription in Year One. The marketing cost will vary from low (off page or own website) to high (mail shot or newspaper advertisement). The weekly print, paper, postage and fulfilment bureau expenses must also be added to obtain an accurate CPA. In the monthly consumer market the average CPA is likely to be higher than the subscription revenue derived from the customer in the first year. Magazine X may have a CPA of £42 to sell a sub for £35. Thus for the publisher the renewal at a higher price is important, as it is only in the second year that he will begin to make a profit from that subscribing customer.

That makes the successful renewal of a subscription vital for publishers and they will analyse acquisition promotions very carefully, to switch marketing funds to those types of campaigns that deliver long-term customers. In the UK the direct debit (DD) is a very powerful tool for increasing renewal rates – Jim Bilton of Wessenden Marketing calls it the 'silver bullet'. A DD is effectively a mandate for a vendor to withdraw regular sums from a customer's bank account, obviously under strict rules, safeguards and permissions. However, it flips the onus for action. Instead of a customer having to act to *renew* a magazine subscription, a gym membership or any ongoing service, he or she now has to take action to *cancel* it.

Subscribers are in a positive frame of mind when they sign up in the first place and most remain so. Fulfilment bureau Dovetail states that 79 per cent of subscribers either definitely or probably wish to renew their sub when the term is due; most of the balance being indecisive. But with DD customers, according to Dovetail, an average of 85 per cent actually renew as compared to 56 per cent of customers who initially signed up through cash with order (CWO) – by cheque or credit card[9].

For this reason publishers try their utmost to persuade new customers to sign up via DD. Indeed, a handful of offers only allow for that response mechanism.

One can understand the commercial imperatives but the customer is king and the customer wants choice. Major changes in the ways by which most Britons bank have slightly blunted the DD tool: it is now much easier to cancel a DD online than it was in times gone by when a letter had to be sent to the local bank manager.

So choice remains commonplace with both DD and CWO on offer. Customers who have to actively renew are sent a sequence of renewal letters (or increasingly emails) – four is commonplace but up to seven not unknown. The last communications are likely to arrive after the subscription has expired. Between 35 per cent and 45 per cent of eventual renewals are likely to come from the first communication[10]. Renewals must focus high in the subscription department's priorities. To revisit the analogy, keep an eye on the water draining out of the fictitious bath. The cheapest renewal method can be just five per cent of the most expensive acquisition cost.

Lifetime value

Good subscription marketers have to be both creative and analytical. Their most useful desktop management tool is the lifetime value (LTV) model, a spreadsheet normally written in Microsoft Excel. The model takes into account all revenue deriving from subscribers both at acquisition and annual renewal points and all directly attributable expenses. The latter will include the first year acquisition and any renewal costs, for example mailings and renewal premium gifts. Also factored in will be production and distribution expenses. It is a multi-year performance measure with the time span under review normally three to five years. The percentage rates at which customers renew, in the first and subsequent years, are crucial. The higher the percentage renewals the better, as these drive more revenue into the latter years of the model. (The word lifetime should not be taken too literally: it means commercial life of the subscription not the mortality of the customer!)

LTV analysis demonstrates to the publisher the value or profitability of subscribers, whether as individuals, groups or as a total. At a macro level the model is used to determine the annual overall subscriptions acquisition budget and highlight the most cost effective way of maintaining and growing volumes. On a more frequent basis, at micro level each major campaign can be analysed, as can demographic purchasing behaviour. There are a range of management outputs, the most useful and common being:

- the actual lifetime value and cumulative profit from every subscriber
- the return on investment (ROI) of the marketing cost
- annual profit per year and cumulative profit over lifetime, in many cases year one will be a loss
- the breakeven point: the point in time that the subscription becomes profitable to the publisher. In the consumer market the norm will be during year two.

Table 6.1 and Figure 6.4 offer a simple example of an LTV calculation of up to five years. In this example the subscription becomes profitable during year two.

> Good subscription marketers have to be both creative and analytical

Table 6.1 Individual campaign profits over 3 years

	Year 1	Year 2	Year 3
Renewal rate		45%	71%
Subscription orders	100	45	32
Subscription price	£35	£35	£35
SUBSCRIPTION REVENUE	£3,500	£1,575	£1,120
Promotion cost	(£3,000)	(£100)	(£45)
CONTRIBUTION	£500	£1,475	£1,075
Service cost	(£1,200)	(£540)	(£384)
NET PROFIT / (LOSS)	(£700)	£935	£691
Cumulative profits	(£700)	£235	£926

Source: Alan Weaver Associates (AWA). Numbers in brackets are costs or trading losses

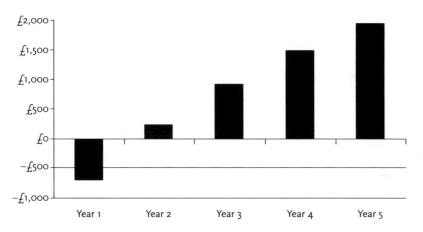

Figure 6.4 Example of lifetime value projection (cumulative profits)

Source: Alan Weaver Associates (AWA)

Use of LTV has step-changed how publishers understand the profitability of subscriptions as part of their overall circulation strategy. As retail volumes decline, the importance of subscription sales increases: future marketing campaigns will become more creative and management reporting ever more probing. As Chapter 8 shows, sales of digital publications are growing rapidly with many publishers currently offering 'bundles', often a print product and a digital product for one price. The importance and kudos of the subscription marketer, along with salary, increases accordingly.

When a publisher signs up a new subscriber it is the start of a relationship. Managed correctly, the relationship can blossom. The reader will see the publication regularly, never missing an issue. Enjoyment and brand loyalty ensue. The publisher should see the bond as long term. The customer becomes an important prospect for new and spin-off titles, attending a publisher sponsored show or outside event, or in the B2B market purchasing a report or conference place. It is a virtuous circle, with the value of the subscriber becoming greater the more they engage. No wonder other industries are jealous.

When a publisher signs up a new subscriber it is the start of a relationship. Managed correctly, the relationship can blossom

FREE DISTRIBUTION

Magazines are a highly accessible and available medium whether at home, in the workplace, while shopping, travelling or at leisure. By opting for free distribution, publishers put total dependence upon advertising and sponsorships, with freedom to set print numbers at a level which will deliver the most profitable outcome.

There are a myriad of ways to distribute a free magazine or to sample free copies of a paid-for title. Street distribution is commonplace in high traffic metro areas for example, while door-to-door delivery may be used in urban or suburban streets. Airlines are keen to take free titles which match their passenger profile, both in the terminal and in the air. This also applies to Eurostar, while free pick up at hotels, gyms and large corporate receptions are also favoured by publishers. In some instances, the venue owner may pay a significantly discounted cover price and these copies are referred to by ABC as bulk sales.

Despite these many routes to market, the free titles tend to fall into four broad categories. These divisions are not mutually exclusive, so a large circulation free title could also be a customer publication.

> By opting for free distribution, publishers put total dependence upon advertising and sponsorships

Large circulation free titles

With this model the advertiser is buying both size and a large target market defined by demographics. Half of the top twenty magazines in the UK are free[11]. They include titles produced by supermarket chains, a media and entertainment group, magazines available to society members as well as publications available principally for commuters in our major cities. Their combined circulation is over ten and a half million copies. Because of the sheer numbers involved, the distribution channel is normally free pick up or hand out but relevant account customers or members may receive a free postal copy. This growing sector is discussed in Chapter 2.

Regional specific titles

With these lifestyle titles the publisher will normally focus distribution on affluent areas of towns, cities or counties. An abundance of property, home improvement and restaurant advertisements are key to success. Examples of this will be *The London Magazine* or *SW (London) Magazine*. These titles tend to have glossy production values to reflect lifestyle aspiration.

Customer magazines

(This dynamic sector is also covered in detail in Chapter 2.) Examples are titles that are aimed at customers of a specific store group or who own a marque of car. Retailers in particular value the connection with their customers through the pages of a magazine, the objective being to increase awareness and customer loyalty. A supermarket own brand magazine will pride itself on giving sound practical advice on recipes or health and beauty tips as well as driving loyalty through promotional coupons and offers. Suppliers can advertise their wares through the pages of a title that is displayed and promoted in store.

Given increasing print costs, this media relationship will move increasingly to digital.

Controlled circulation

This sector covers titles aimed at readers who have buying power. It is almost exclusively used in business and professional markets where the targeting can be very specific and is audited through the channel of controlled circulation. Abbreviated to cc, this is defined by ABC as 'copies sent free to individuals who meet criteria set by the publisher to define the target audience'. The publisher is seeking to convince potential advertisers that the magazine is being read by key opinion formers or buyers with budget responsibility, so that the message has maximum effect.

A well audited cc title can give the advertiser a wealth of information to allow for the best possible selection of media for a campaign. For example, *Investment Week* has a total ABC of 15,274[12]: 76 per cent is attributed to the print edition and 24 per cent to the digital. The title is distributed free of charge to 16 professional groups in the investment, finance and legal professions. These job holders make up the target market of the controlled circulation and as such a breakdown of the reader's job title is included as part of the ABC certificate. In order to keep the list of free recipients relevant and up-to-date, individuals are invited by the publisher to request the title, this request being made increasingly by telephone or online. The advertiser can also see when the free distribution list was last refreshed; the more up-to-date the list the better.

Controlled circulation titles are free and as well as print, paper and distribution costs, records must be maintained and auditing paid for. The emphasis is on the quality of the reader, not necessarily their quantity. The publisher must decide on the optimum circulation level to attract the maximum advertisement sales. In the case of *Investment Week*, the ABC certificate states how many readers are under each job title, the type of funds and financial assets they have under management and what part of the country they live in. The advertiser is investing with a secure knowledge of the readership.

While society and association magazines are frequently free of charge, their readers may not necessarily perceive them to be so as they are receiving the title as part of a package of paid-for membership benefits. The *National Trust Magazine* is published three times per year and has an enormous circulation in excess of 1.9 million copies. The majority of these are sent to National Trust members. As well as an important communication medium for keeping in touch with members, the title's target market of those who enjoy active outdoor pursuits attracts considerable levels of advertising.

A magazine focussed on a professional association allows for accurate targeting and can be particularly important for recruitment advertisers. Published by EMAP Inform, *The New Civil Engineer*, the official journal of The Institute of Civil Engineers, has an ABC circulation of 50,814[13] with every UK or European member receiving a copy each week. As with many business information publishers, this well-respected brand has an extensive website including a dedicated recruitment site, special reports and digital editions.

With minimal circulation revenue and an advertisement base which is migrating to digital, controlled circulation titles are trading in a very tough climate. Print closures are not uncommon and will increase as this sector continues to move online.

CIRCULATION STRATEGY

The late John Mellon, Chief Executive and Chairman of IPC Magazines from 1986 to 1998, would chide junior publishers with a saying from his Irish homeland: 'If you don't know where you are going then any road will take you there.'

'If you don't know where you are going then any road will take you there.'

This homily is never truer than when applied to the spectrum of routes to market for a magazine as described in this chapter. How do publishers decide what is right for their title?

There are as many strategies as there are magazines in publication. Here are a range of considerations and questions to answer when drawing up the annual plan.

Consumer markets

What is the overall market climate for my title? Am I in a growth sector or one which is mature? What is the ABC performance of my closest competitors? Does my magazine need to re-focus its editorial approach to take advantage of growth opportunities?

Answer these questions and publishers can quantify their circulation targets for the next year.

Paid-for publishers should ask, is my balance between retail sales and subscription sales right for the market? In particular are the subs growing fast enough? If the target is for growth, from which revenue source is this likely to come?

Are my retail and subscription prices right for the market and in line with my growth ambitions? Is there an opportunity to raise price without damaging sales – or can I consider growing sales by reducing price?

Answers will have great influence upon the marketing plan for the title. Should we consider a free distribution model or use an element of free distribution to drive sampling and conversion to paid-for sales?

For free-to-market publishers, is the distribution efficient? If it were increased or decreased what would be the resultant effect on advertisement sales? Cost of distribution is always a key issue for this sector.

What is the interaction between digital products and the print on paper brand? At what speed do I see the sales migrating? How will this affect overall circulation targets? What are the implications for 'bundling' print and digital? How will any migration into digital affect advertisement volumes and yields?

B2B markets

As has been documented in Chapter 2, the publishing model for the business and professional sector has changed out of all recognition since the millennium. Now high-value information providers, the financial importance of print on paper has dwindled but traditional print brands often still remain at the heart of the business. There is no doubt that William Reed Business Media has strategically grown the business by launch and acquisition around the long-standing weekly *The Grocer* magazine and Informa has built digital platforms central to the world's oldest daily, *Lloyds List*.

Retail sale is rarely an available option, so how can print subscriptions be maximised profitably in the digital age? Should print and digital combined offers be made and at what price? (Marketing of digital subscriptions is discussed in detail in Chapter 8.)

For controlled circulation titles, what is the optimum distribution to maximise advertisement sales and how can best cost be achieved?

At what stage must the decision be made to close a traditional print brand? Again the focus must be on the speed of customer migration.

How can new customers be acquired? Once they have developed loyalty, how can they be moved up a chain of value to buy more products from the company, be they print, digital, data or event attendance at a conference or exhibition?

The circulation strategy for every magazine brand should be debated and reviewed once a year in the light of market and competitive conditions. Successful delivery will be a key factor in achieving the profit target set for the business. Every member of the magazine's management team should be asked to contribute in an inclusive process. A brief document should be produced and circulated so that everyone knows the key objectives.

CONSUMER MARKETING

Once the circulation strategy has been signed off, a marketing plan and financial budget can be drawn up. This is the route map for delivery and for a large consumer magazine is complex and detailed.

When interviewing marketing directors for this book, two key issues shone through. First the need to prioritise: there are many ways to market a magazine and there is simply just not enough budget to do everything. Second, it is important to focus on what works and be sure to allocate funds to those initiatives that offer the best return on that investment. The marketing budget is often the one most fought over with the finance department at the annual budget round and marketers need to be clear about which costs are driving the most benefits. For a paid-for consumer title, the following are likely to feature in the mix.

Above the line promotions

This is the name given when the magazine advertises itself in other media. Unfortunately, due to cost constraints, above the line is not used as frequently as it was in the late twentieth century. Then it was not unusual to see magazines regularly advertised on prime time TV. Now this high cost form of marketing is the preserve of mass weekly titles. National newspapers and radio are more affordable. In the former, discount coupons can be given against cover price. This type of promotion principally benefits retail sales, although newspapers can be used to make subscription offers. A drawback is the inevitable lack of retention once the advertising ends. Large-scale TV promotion remains a must for the launch of any partwork, as that business model is based on the maximum sale of issue one.

Free gifts

Free cover mounted gifts can be a highly effective way of increasing retail sales. In the children's market they have become the norm and it is hard to find a title without a gift. They are also popular with the glossy women's monthlies with cosmetic gifts of a high perceived value. Again, bear in mind that the whole retail distribution has to carry the gift, so production and distribution costs can be significant. Sales uplifts, however, can be spectacular: up to double the base issue sale is commonplace. In this scenario the gift promotion can more than pay for itself with increased sales. Again, expect little retention. The publisher will obtain the gifts at a reduced price from the producer but there is hot competition between publishers for the most attractive gifts. Logistics can be complex and lead times long, so good planning is required.

A lower cost way of offering the reader an added value gift is to feature a flash on the front cover and ask readers to telephone or apply online. This is also a very useful way of building a mailing list.

Multipacks

In the quest to improve retail sales, publishers have created the multipack: two or three titles polywrapped together. The price for the combination purchase is less than the sum of the parts. By 'piggy-backing' a more established brand, multipacks can be a useful way of encouraging sampling for new titles and good sales increases can be made. If overused it can damage the reader's perception of what represents value for money.

Despite this, they are commonplace with publishers. In the first half of 2012, ABC analysis shows that ten per cent of retail sales were made in this manner. When selecting titles to multipack it is important that there is synergy between the brands. Alternatively, a single title may make a one issue price cut. This can be a highly effective way of encouraging sampling, especially after a relaunch and if used modestly will not damage reader expectations of cover price. The disadvantage is that it requires a sizeable budget.

Customer insight

With the high penetration of loyalty cards such as Tesco Clubcard and Nectar, retailers collect a huge amount of information about consumers' shopping habits. This data is available to suppliers normally for a fee. Publishers with significant retail sales are starting to find this consumer insight increasingly beneficial for their businesses. For example, they can work out which other newspapers, magazines or convenience products are being bought with their title. Coupons printed on till receipts and discounts off the next purchase can follow as ways of stimulating sale.

Subscription acquisition and renewal costs

This chapter has described the myriad of promotional opportunities open to the subscription marketer. All have to be budgeted for, particularly if in the LTV analysis the subscription makes a loss in the first year.

Competitions

Readers' competitions in magazines normally enjoy high response rates with entry now more likely to be online or via premium phone line than by post. Publishers even believe there to be a clique of professional competition enterers at large in the UK. It is unlikely that a competition will drive significant new sales but competitions with quality prizes help keep existing readers loyal and are another highly effective way of building a mailing list.

Social media

Marketing via social media sites, especially Facebook and Twitter, is rapidly becoming a new opportunity for magazine marketers. One publisher describes it this way:

> We are content driven businesses and editorial quality is central to all of our magazines. With regular tweets and Facebook posts about what we feature in our titles we can link potential readers through to our own eco-system, i.e. our own websites or apps. At that point we can get to know them better, invite them to read more free content and hopefully tempt them into buying a digital edition or even a print subscription. It is all part of building a community with the magazine brand at its heart. Facebook and Twitter are also really good ways of getting reader feedback to what we are doing editorially.

Public Relations (PR)

TV and radio programmes will often feature a magazine editor talking about a news item, what a celebrity may be up to or commenting on a sport. If the editor comes across as lucid and credible that is reflected on their magazine brand. It is an effective way of promoting a title, it is free and most editors like the publicity.

Moreover, magazines can create their own stories which get carried by other media. Annual surveys such as *The Sunday Times* Rich List achieve huge coverage with TV, radio and competing newspapers. The value of this space can be quantified; *GQ Men Of The Year* Awards estimates its annual media coverage to be worth over £3 million per year.

THE ROLE OF THE MARKETING MANAGER

The job of the magazine's marketing manager is busy, varied and this executive plays an important role, not only in brand development but also in day-to-day operational running. This is aptly demonstrated by reading the 'Week in the Life' case study at the end of this chapter. In the ever-shifting sands of publishing company structure there is no such thing as an industry departmental norm. Nevertheless, any magazine worth its salt will have a marketing manager, who may be allocated to one title or work across a small portfolio. In the case of the large publishers, this person may be part of an overall marketing function. Students of this book will be interested to know that positions in this area are often the entry point for graduates into the world of magazine publishing. It is rewarding to acknowledge that managing directors and chief executive officers often started their careers in circulation, promotions and marketing departments.

Normally reporting to the magazine publisher, the marketing manager is often the first point of contact for third party distribution and fulfilment companies as well as for the subscription team. They will also be responsible for a whole range of outputs, both print and digital. These will be as varied as producing publicity material for above the line campaigns, in-store displays or magazine events, subscription mail shots or email campaigns, as well as organising PR appearances, sourcing free gifts and competition prizes and overseeing social media posts and tweets. An ever watchful eye must be kept on the budget to ensure that there is a focus on costs and no overspend. The marketing manager must be a good all-rounder with sound knowledge of all magazine disciplines, have a keen eye for detail and be a team player. With that combined skill set it is not surprising that the marketing department is such a good training ground for the industry leaders of tomorrow.

The working relationship between the editor and marketing manager must ideally be open, respectful of each other's viewpoint and will at times be frank. Occasionally it may be fraught and may need sensitive managing by the publisher.

Editors and their senior staff will have the overall and long-term commercial interest of their magazine at heart. Kudos and success will be rated by the circulation of their title and its rise in ABC rankings. The more profitable the magazine, the more they will be able to invest in top writers and designers. So there will be little dispute within the team over the end objectives. But that is not always the case about the means to the end.

Good editors get appointed because they have a vision for the magazine, one which will evolve and adapt to the changing demands of the readership, their lifestyles and demographics. They develop this vision by spending time with readers, on the telephone, online or through reader events. (One of the values of reader events is the face-to-face contact with editorial staff.) Having a strong opinion and point of view is normally part and parcel of the editor's job description. Try and find one without these traits. The editor sees himself or herself as the ultimate guardian of the magazine's core brand values of editorial independence and is likely to be rightly concerned if that principle comes under attack from what may be considered the short-term commercial needs of the marketing department. Particular scrutiny will be given to promotions flagged on the cover or on a prominent page. It is important that the editor is involved in the key commercial decisions at an early stage and sign off on major publicity campaigns. A sensitive magazine marketer will develop an understanding of potential conflict points and bypass them.

FUTURE PROOF

What does the future hold for circulation and marketing executives?

The route to market for magazines will continue to be dynamic with an increasing array of supply chain options available to publishers. Unfortunately there are few signs of market improvement in the mass consumer sector which, in the absence of major launches, will continue to decline in volume terms. Retailers will remain committed to magazines as they drive customer footfall and all the research indicates that shoppers like to see them in store. The large store groups will seek to maximise profitability from the category through sharper merchandising and marketing and less wasteful operational practices. With publishers committing investment monies to digital, the lack of new print products remains a cloud over the sector.

Analysis of ABC numbers reveals that growth in paid-for subscriptions is slowing but marketers in this sector seem adept at finding innovative ways to tempt new readers to sign up, particularly with the use of social media and sophisticated databases in relative infancy. Consumers may become increasingly wary of direct debits which will need careful management at renewal time. Publishers should acknowledge that this form of selling is unique to their industry and not devalue it with unsustainable subscription offers. Above inflation price rises from UK Royal Mail continue to concern but these anxieties may be allayed by the recent privatisation.

As economies climb out of consumer recession, the outlook for free distribution is positive. Advertisers and their agencies are now comfortable with mass circulation free titles and respect their sheer size and power. There seems no shortage of new products or ideas in the customer sector. Due to high production and distribution costs, the latter's rate of migration to digital will increase.

Print has already decreased in importance for business and professional publishers but it will still have a place as long as readers value that format by buying a print subscription or valuing it as an association member benefit. High print run controlled circulation magazines, however, will become a rare species with all but a few moving online.

This chapter concludes with a page from the diary of a consumer magazine marketing manager which shows the spectrum of outputs needed to stay on top of the working week.

> It is important that the editor is involved in the key commercial decisions at an early stage

Monday

9.00   Marketing Planning Meeting with Publisher. Run thru all promotions coming up over next month.

11.00   Meeting with Cosmetics Company to negotiate and plan next two free gifts. 12 weeks lead time needed for delivery and bagging.

15.00   Plan all Facebook activity for next issue with Editor.

Tuesday

Morning.   Meet with Distribution Company. Review all sales, last gift doubled sale but did not stick. Brief out marketing plans for next 3 months. Sign off on two retailer agreements. They need posters and shelf-edge strips for stores, remember to talk to designer and printer.

Afternoon.   Review marketing budget with Finance. Catch up phone calls and emails.

Wednesday

9.30.   Meet with Events Team. Major award ceremony coming up. Need to ensure that the set and all publicity material are on-brand. Long discussion about level of PR we are targeting. Take major sponsor out for lunch. GREAT NEWS! BBC rang. Want to do red carpet interviews for the awards gig. Will be great publicity and will make for great tweet from Editor.

Thursday

Morning.   Monthly meeting with Subs Dep't. Run thru all the LTV numbers for recent campaigns. Latest free premium working well and retention levels up all round since we pushed DD. As ever, subs team looking for more budgets. Need to ask Publisher.

15.00.   Meeting with Designer to look at concepts for newspaper above the line campaign. Ask for a few changes which I know Editor will want before sign off.

Friday

10.00.   Planning meeting with editorial team. Run thru all features for next 3 months. Look for great publicity/ PR angles - also how best to interact with Facebook and Twitter.

Afternoon.   Keep free to deal with phone calls, emails, write minutes of meetings and reader customer care queries. Quick drink with team on way home.

To Do List.

- Check survey results from recent reader research.
- Check next month's free gift has arrived in warehouse.
- Call PR companies to get prizes for competition.
- Start presentation for next month's strategic day-long session for next year's budget.

NOTES

1. Wessenden, *Subscriber Service Survey 2012*, p 19. An annual report commissioned by Dovetail in partnership with Demographix and Wessenden Marketing.
2. Personal communication from Seymour Distribution Ltd., 19 June 2013.
3. The balance of copies sold are export and miscellaneous sales.
4. Seymour (2011) p 8.
5. Chadwick (2012).
6. Harrington Associates (2011).
7. Wessenden (2012) p 3.
8. Ibid: p 23.
9. Faulkner, 23 April 2012, p 6.
10. Ibid: p 5.
11. ABC (Dec 2012).
12. ABC (July 2011–June 2012).
13. Ibid.

REFERENCE SOURCES

Chadwick, E., 'Convenience closing gap on supermarkets, survey says', *Retail Newsagent,* 2 November 2012, p 14.

Faulkner, C., *Dovetail subscription marketing top tips: renewals,* 23 April 2012, available at www.slideshare.net/secret/avAFF4rLnDaO8I. (Accessed 3 July 2013.)

Harrington Associates, *The New Single Copy,* 25 April 2011, XV(37) available at www.targetcast.com/news-article.php?showFile=yes&newsId=125 (Accessed 19 June 2013.)

Seymour, *Wessenden Briefing,* December 2011, 161, Godalming: Wessenden Marketing.

Wessenden (2012) *Subscriber Service Survey 2012.* Godalming: Wessenden.

CHAPTER 7

The science of advertisement sales

Andrew Scott

This chapter covers the second most important revenue stream for the majority of consumer publishers – advertising and sponsorship. Consumer publishers estimate that 36 per cent of overall turnover comes from this area and B2B 40 per cent[1]. We will look at how this has been affected by the post 2008 recession and how magazine publishers have fared against severe competition from other media. The importance of the medium's unique reader relationship will be discussed. We will also look at how a simple print advertising campaign is planned and bought, and how advertisement sales departments operate. Circulation auditing, readership research and demographic targeting are all key to the sales process and will also be examined in detail. The various revenue streams which make up advertisement turnover will be itemised and the chapter will conclude by looking briefly at some emerging trends.

The two core strands of debate running through *Inside Magazine Publishing* have been the effects of the post 2008 recession and the emerging digital technologies which are starting to transform the industry. Advertising agencies and ad departments have been in the teeth of these gales. Revenues have been under severe pressure since the recession began and there are almost daily innovations in both digital advertising techniques and the metrics with which to measure them. This also has an impact upon organisational structure in both publishers and agencies.

Elsewhere in this book a key distinction has been drawn between the three main industry sectors – consumer, customer magazines (content marketers) and B2B. For advertisers the division between consumer and customer publishers or between paid for and free titles is less relevant. Both sectors aim at consumers, deliver a highly engaged audience and can offer a great editorial environment for an advertiser. B2B remains a distinct offer with a readership defined by industry, profession and responsibility. It attracts different advertisers and types of ads. The motivation to read is the fundamental difference, as consumer magazines are most often read for entertainment while B2B magazines are perused to enhance a career or to secure important business information.

Readers may question the title of this chapter – science? The buying and selling of advertising is not simple. It involves the advertiser or client, media buying agency and of course the media owner. The process may well be monitored by a media auditor and can even have an element of barter. The trading currencies are based on detailed auditing of circulations and sophisticated readership and market surveys. From a publisher perspective, the processes and techniques require a logical and thorough approach although this chapter will argue that there is still a place for the champion of traditional selling skills.

THE CURRENT UK ADVERTISING SCENE

Mass market magazine publishing came about because of the realisation that readership has a value beyond the sums of money collectively paid to buy the magazines, in the form of sales or circulation revenue. The ability to sell ad space in a magazine, to those interested in selling their goods and services to the readership, enabled publishers to maintain relatively low cover prices. This, in turn, has led to increased audiences, hence creating a virtuous circle for the publisher by bringing in more advertisers. A classic synergy was born which has sustained the magazine market for over a century.

The current state of the overall UK advertising market – and print in particular – is shown in the next four graphics from the global agency ZenithOptimedia. As Table 7.1 shows, magazine readers were sold to UK advertisers (including the government, itself a significant advertiser) for £736 million in 2012. This represents close to 30 per cent of overall magazine industry

Table 7.1 Advertising expenditure in local currency at current prices (£ million)

	Total	Newspapers	Magazines	TV	Radio	Cinema	Outdoor	Internet
2001	10,095	4,165	1,692	3,010	414	119	575	120
2002	10,119	4,087	1,600	3,144	419	131	596	142
2003	10,409	4,135	1,565	3,173	447	127	668	295
2004	11,378	4,341	1,624	3,392	463	136	721	700
2005	11,811	4,170	1,607	3,455	521	134	762	1,161
2006	11,943	3,992	1,554	3,282	494	131	792	1,699
2007	12,711	3,978	1,494	3,380	509	144	829	2,377
2008	12,325	3,510	1,346	3,211	476	145	798	2,839
2009	10,838	2,757	970	2,858	430	153	665	3,005
2010	11,702	2,746	913	3,258	445	157	748	3,435
2011	11,985	2,513	836	3,290	452	146	753	3,995
2012	12,232	2,253	736	3,258	470	164	824	4,527
2013	12,583	2,119	677	3,258	468	167	800	5,094
2014	13,034	2,077	649	3,290	474	172	806	5,566
2015	13,446	2,036	626	3,323	482	177	815	5,987

Note: Numbers up to and including 2012 are actual. 2013 onwards are estimates.

Source: ZenithOptimedia

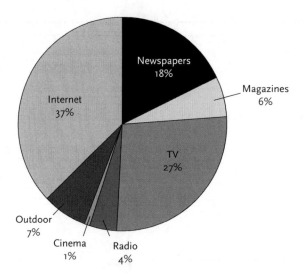

Figure 7.1 Share of
adspend by
medium 2012

Source:
ZenithOptimedia

turnover, excluding customer titles. Figure 7.1 shows this sum is, however, only six per cent of the total UK advertising market, dwarfed by the giants of TV, internet and even national newspapers. In terms of sheer numbers it is equivalent to the relatively unheralded outdoor or posters market. This magazine total sum is spread throughout a diverse industry with thousands of different individual titles – some with small numbers of readers.

The current advertising scene is defined by the change from TV, as the pre-eminent medium for ads, to digital. Having leapt into number one position, it is now widely forecasted that digital ad revenues will rise to a number which is nearly double that of TV by the middle of this decade.

This onward march of digital, combined with the post 2008 recession, has forced many magazine publishers to overhaul their ad sales structures, making them more streamlined, efficient and cheaper to run. Cost efficiency is the focus with (for example) systems being developed seamlessly, allowing advertising agencies to access the flat-plan of a title to reserve an ad and to automatically produce an acknowledgement and invoice.

The period has seen merger and consolidation of advertising agencies – this has been mirrored by large publishing companies creating groups to sell space across many magazines and their brand extensions, including digital. The days of a separate ad sales team working on each title have been supplanted by the need to offer wider, more creative solutions than simply taking bookings for display ads.

Figure 7.2 shows UK advertising expenditure since the turn of the millennium at current prices. The adage that the first casualty of a recession is the marketing budget is clearly played out by looking at the period 2008–2011. In particular 2009 was torrid for the whole advertising industry.

Figure 7.3 reveals that advertising revenue forecasts for print media (newspapers and magazines) are facing continual annual decline. This is the context which is informing decisions about changes to traditional business models in general and magazine ad sales departments in particular. The contrast with forecasted growth in other sectors is stark. Media spend continues to grow but print's share is in long-term decline, regardless of the macro economic outlook.

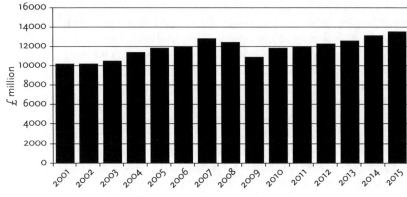

Figure 7.2
Total advertising
expenditure at
current prices

Source:
ZenithOptimedia

Note: Numbers up to and including 2012 are actual. 2013 onwards are estimates.

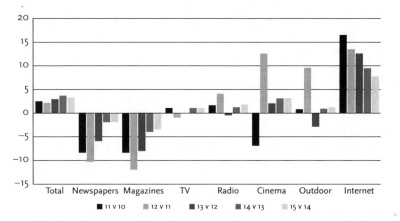

Figure 7.3
Advertising
expenditure: year-
on-year percentage
change at current
prices

Source:
ZenithOptimedia

Note: Numbers up to and including 2012 are actual. 2013 onwards are estimates.

THE UNIQUE RELATIONSHIP BETWEEN READERS AND MAGAZINES

To understand the essential strength of magazines, as a medium for advertising, it is necessary to look at the relationship that a typical reader will have with their magazine of choice. From the outset, magazines are an active media as they place the reader in control. It has been proved in research findings many times over that readers have special bonds with their favourite magazines. (One of the most useful reports, *How Magazine Advertising Works* was compiled for the PPA in 2005 by media expert Guy Consterdine. It is a thorough review of many individual pieces of research.) These bonds result in a level of engagement which puts its influence and voice on a par with a close friend or family member. Moving even beyond that high bar, magazines are said by many to act as a reinforcement of one's own self image.

Adding to this emotional engagement is a serious commitment in terms of time. A PPA survey reports that, on average, a copy of a paid for magazine is picked up 5.4 times and is read 2.5 times, lasting an average of 54 minutes[2]. Over 90 per cent of the pages are opened[3]. Moreover, according to a PPA/Kantar study of 2008, in many cases magazines are the principal offline driver of online purchase. In this regard, the genre has the unrivalled (by other media) ability to inform buying decisions in the key sectors of fashion, travel, food and healthy living[4]. In addition, specialist magazines provide the ideal environment for targeted ads with little wastage of readership. Where better to target keen photographers than a magazine dedicated to analysing and reviewing digital cameras? Such magazines are often purchased by people specifically looking for the ads in order to buy goods or services. The advertiser is aware of this audience and will often create more detailed copy for highly targeted titles. These are designed to attract this informed consumer, with a simpler message running in more general magazines.

Magazine websites, digital editions and online publishers can find a symbiotic relationship with advertisers, as they can direct readers directly to their advertisers' websites. Meanwhile, major consumer brands will utilise quotes from product reviews to provide validation of their products online and in traditional above the line campaigns. This remains the standard method of promoting movies, for example.

It is the combination of dedication shown by readers to their magazines, with the high level of expertise and knowledge that means magazines can 'punch above their weight'. In advertising terms, this means gaining more money from the overall pot of UK advertising spend than the market share of the medium, in terms of consumption time, suggests it should. This is particularly true of specialist magazines, where a high level of knowledge is presumed on behalf of the reader. A specialist consumer magazine can rival B2B titles for ability to sell a small readership for a high advertisement rate.

Not everyone sees this is as sustainable. Speaking in April 2013, Martin Sorrell, CEO of WPP, addressed this 'anomaly'.

> We [advertisers] are still investing 20% [of client ad. budgets on print] but consumers are only spending 7–10% of [their media consumption] time. This has to change.[5]

The numbers may point in one direction but the magazine industry continues to convince many to take a more holistic approach to ad spend. Sorrell may well be correct to regard giants like Google and Facebook as the prospective heirs to Murdoch and Hearst but a future with a menu of options for advertising spend remains likely. Growth rates of digital media are likely to slow as advertisers find new ways to reach an audience and stand out from the crowd.

The 2005 PPA report stated that different magazines met different needs but with readers very much in control of the 'when' and the 'where' – how they actually consumed their publications. In this way they could match the mood with the title, resulting in a highly receptive environment for advertisers.

Photo 7.1 Readers enjoy a unique relationship with magazines

The strength of this relationship lies at the heart of what publishers sell and what advertisers buy into. They crave that some of this editorial stardust be sprinkled on to their products, their brands. In fact some want increasingly to blur the line between the ads and editorial content. Display ads are designed to fit into the style of the relevant magazine to allow a seamless move for the reader between the two forms of content. This was taken to its logical conclusion by the advent of advertorials, sponsored content and competitions. This 'added value' dimension to traditional magazine advertising will be discussed later. The stronger the magazine brand, the stronger the level of endorsement an advertiser can expect to tap into. This is known as the 'Presenter Effect'[6], which Consterdine explains as how the 'interpretation of a given advertisement can be influenced by the specific publication in which it appears.'[7]

In fact, advertisements can at times be among the most sought after pages of a magazine and are integral to the overall publication. The genre of print magazines dedicated entirely to ads, however, is rapidly giving way to online offerings. Mainstay titles of the 1980s and 1990s such as *Auto Trader, Dalton's Weekly* and *Loot* have all adapted this strategy. This does not means that readers' desire to consume relevant advertising has diminished – just that their chosen medium has changed. The ability to search online for products in detail has transformed the reading experience.

> They crave that some of this editorial stardust be sprinkled on to their products, their brands

HOW A PRINT ADVERTISING CAMPAIGN IS PLANNED AND BOUGHT

How does a major manufacturer choose where to spend advertising investment? There are effectively four parts to this process:

- Decide the overall marketing objectives, the most appropriate demographic group at whom to target the campaign and the budget. This will include what percentage of the target market the advertisement campaign will reach.
- Decide the best choice of advertising medium: in this particular example we have assumed magazines.
- Evaluate the best magazines in which to advertise to achieve the objectives.
- Buy the campaign at the best price.

Let's look at an illustrative example. Volkswagen (VW) is launching a new car. They will identify a broad target market which will include demographic information (for example ABC1 men aged 25–45 years). Demographics are core to the process of advertising and essential to our understanding of media planning and buying.

Demographics

Basic demographics cover the three essentials of life and are the lifeblood of marketing – gender, social class and age. A typical lifestyle magazine will aim at a segment of the population defined in these terms. Mixed gender targets are normally achieved by advertising in different types of publications. There are exceptions, for example TV listings titles, but it is unusual to find consumer magazines which aim at both men and women.

Age and class are harder to grasp. The convention is to split the population into ten year age bands starting at 15–24 and then grouping people over 65 together. (One asks: are these splits still as relevant as the retirement age creeps up and the entry age of employment gets progressively later?) Major magazine publishers will attempt to attract women as they leave their teen years and move them through their portfolio until their dotage.

More controversial is social class. The basic A/B/C1/C2/D/E classification is standard to all marketing and provides relatively simple but useful guidelines for market researchers to be able to draw distinctions between us. Developed over 50 years ago they have stood the test of time. As long as advertisers demand access to consumers with disposable income, market research will continue to provide labels for us all to debate. Sociologists are continually reassessing these core constituents but they remain in place as basic signifiers; they are a starting point from which more sophisticated targeting can spring. For magazines they provide highly useful shorthand to describe, in the widest terms, the target market. Therefore we often hear the expression ABC1 women 15–34 years as a core target market, or for the wealthier, AB women 25–45 years.

Social grades

The classifications are based on the occupation of the head of the household.

A. UPPER MIDDLE CLASS
Higher managerial, administrative or professional

B. MIDDLE CLASS
Intermediate managerial, administrative or professional

C1. LOWER MIDDLE CLASS
Supervisory or clerical and junior managerial, administrative or professional

C2. SKILLED WORKING CLASS
Skilled manual workers

D. WORKING CLASS
Semi and unskilled manual workers

E. THOSE AT THE LOWEST LEVELS OF SUBSISTENCE
Casual or lowest grade workers, state pensioners and others who depend on the welfare state for their income

The grades are often grouped into ABC1 and C2DE and these are taken to equate to middle class and working class respectively.

Source: NRS

Marketing objectives and budget

At this early stage, a top level budget for the campaign needs to be agreed between VW (in this illustration) and their advertising agency. Once in place the next step is to analyse the marketing objectives in more detail to plan the campaign better and to refine the budget. Specific sales objectives will be set; regional differences in distribution of cars noted (this may create a bias to certain media) and importantly – what marketing are the competition using? In the case of car manufacturers, focus groups will be used to flush out the best selling points of their own and competing vehicles.

The agency, together with market researchers, will now work on the target market to find out more information. What other brands of cars does the target market consider along with VW when buying a car? How do they make their buying decisions? At this point the team will begin to access desktop market research such as National Readership Survey (NRS), Target Group Index (TGI) and Mintel, as well as in-house data from previous campaigns. For advertising likely to involve print, latest ABC trends and performance will be examined. This provides hard circulation data, with little room for the mathematical estimations and extrapolations central to readership and market research numbers.

Depending upon the size of the campaign and its international scope, the agency may also look at econometric modelling, so factors such as weather, seasonality, elections and interest rates will all determine when and where a campaign is launched. This analysis begins to put some particular advertising options on the table.

Planning the schedule

We will at this point make the assumption that VW and their agency will want to include (print) magazines in their media mix. This is not an unlikely scenario as history shows that major car manufacturers are repeat users of consumer magazines.

The media planners will now look at their print options. Any media schedule developed for a particular campaign is trying to square a circle ... how to get maximum *coverage* with optimum *frequency* but with minimal *wastage*.

- Coverage is defined as the percentage of the target market who will see the advertisement at least once. It may also be called reach.
- Frequency is the number of times that group will see the ad.
- The optimum campaign will give the right amount of opportunities to see (OTS) for a consumer to consider the product but not so many that the advertiser sees little return from a message which has run its course. Attempting to reach that final 10 per cent of the target market may be too costly.

In this example we are likely to consider titles such as *Top Gear* or *Octane,* which deliver an audience of committed car enthusiasts with a high disposable income but we also need to evaluate how often to place an ad in these titles. When does necessary reinforcement become overkill?

Using the sources of data available to them, the planners in the advertising agency will attempt to unlock this dilemma by looking at regularity of purchase within magazine circulation data and volume and frequency of readership. Again the key tools for this will be ABC, NRS and TGI. These important industry standards are explained in detail later in this chapter. They will then calculate how many insertions it will take to reach the majority of the target audience once or more. Using specialist VW titles is an option – they will generate minimum wastage but the advertising schedule will lack coverage (overall volume of numbers). With such publications the advertiser will be also be preaching to the already converted.

For a major car launch, increased coverage will be required. So the net will be cast wider to include magazines which fit the demographics. These titles will deliver large numbers but will not necessarily be 'best fit' as some of their readership will not be relevant to the chosen target market – as such there will be wastage. Titles which fit our example might be *Sunday Times Magazine, The Economist* or *Esquire.* These magazines will be seen by more prospective buyers than the specialist media can deliver. By default they will also deliver readers who are not relevant to the target market – that is inherent in more general titles. If the new car is likely to be well received by female buyers, glossy women's titles such as *Marie Claire* may be included.

When candidate media lists are drawn up, it is important to note that not all the criteria for inclusion are quantitative. Media planners and buyers will consider the overall editorial environment and other factors such as paper and printing quality.

The importance of cost per thousand/mille

In order to compare different media, and indeed different options within one medium, a standard measure is required and that is cost per thousand (CPT). This is the cost of reaching one thousand people with an advertisement in any medium. It enables comparisons to be made across TV, radio, outdoor, digital and print. It is also commonly referred to as cost per mille (mille being Latin for thousand).

Every target market will have a different CPT. For example, a knitting magazine with a readership of 30,000 women may have 33 per cent of its readership in London and the South East. If it is offering an advertiser who has craft shops in London an advertisement on the back cover for £4,000 then the CPT of Women in London/SE is £400. The calculation is:

Cost of ad / number in target market in thousands (T/M) = CPT/M

In this simple example we are offered 10,000 people, with the ad costing £4,000, therefore the CPT is £400. Every possible medium will be reduced to this formula and it is – along with coverage – a key factor in the building of a media schedule.

Cost per thousands will vary from title to title. A magazine may have a relatively high cost per thousand but if it delivers an exclusive audience, a particular environment or adds unique target market coverage points, agency planners may still decide to include it on a schedule. They will also take account of what 'added value' benefits a media owner can bring to the negotiating table – as will be shown later in this chapter. The importance of buying based on cost per thousands makes rate cards largely 'redundant' for major consumer advertising buying negotiations – it is not usually the start point.

Will the more specialist motoring press get on to the final schedule despite their modest sales? Possibly. The belief would be that this part of the campaign will generate word of mouth about the new car among VW enthusiasts. These specialist titles will also test drive and review the new range and this editorial can create content for manufacturers' websites.

Buying the advertisement space

Agency software tools provide an optimised schedule based on the budget and acknowledged criteria of coverage and frequency against that budget. At this point, however, the knowledge and experience of the agency media buying team comes into play. They sense check this optimised schedule, ensuring enough variety is included and take account of elements that a computer can never know, such as particular editorial plans which publishers may fit with the launch date. Another element which advertisers look for is whether they have the first position or similarly preferential slot in the magazine. Agency buyers place great store on

> Media planners and buyers will consider the overall editorial environment and other factors such as paper and printing quality

The First Right Hand Page or The First Double Page Spread. These will be factored into the schedule and will be a negotiation point with the media owner.

At the end of this process a print schedule is signed off by the client and the media buyer is tasked with implementing it.

HOW ADVERTISEMENTS ARE SOLD

From the perspective of the publisher it is all about the sell. Similar data is available to media departments and the ad sales teams; everyone is trying to undercut the competition on CPT for a particular target market – often it comes down to salesmanship to secure the deal.

When a new magazine launches, prospective advertisers are pinpointed by analysis of the competition. A list of key advertisers will be compiled and targeted. Experienced sales people will be aware of the idiosyncrasies of their market, such as clients who will only accept first position, or first position for certain advertising genres or right hand pages only. For example it is acknowledged that prestigious brands such as Estée Lauder will only buy pages if they can be the first beauty advertiser.

The pitch is then constructed around relevant data. For existing titles this will include ABC figures, editorial environment and marketing plans for the title plus readership and lifestyle demographics (NRS and TGI). For new launches, hard data is of course not available so agencies will make sensible projections based on experience. The sell takes place often with both the advertiser client and the agency media department. Once the decision has been taken to buy space then the actual deal is concluded by the agency buyers but typically a client will have had involvement up to that point.

As we will see later, bespoke advertising such as advertorials provide an opportunity to increase revenue and are typically sold at a premium, perhaps a third more than an equivalent ad page.

The ability to get on a media schedule when the numbers look unpromising, to up-sell where possible and to negotiate the best possible rate are all essential to a publishing company media sales executive. These skills are part of the makeup of all good sales people, who are typically highly incentivised to achieve targets. Relationships are also key, in particular the ability to build a long-term relationship with the customer. (The term 'up-sell' means to increase the title's share of space available once the initial contact has been made, for example larger size ads or greater frequency than the original media plan intended.)

Agency or direct sell

It is important for all titles, both large and small, for their sales teams to maintain close links with the marketing department of the advertiser – the client. The largest selling magazines are dealing with ad agencies on a daily basis and that is where they focus their sales efforts. The client, however, is involved in the complete decision making process – after all it is their budget. This can range from making the *inter* media decision (whether to use magazines or another media form) and the *intra* media decision (which magazines to use).

In the more specialist consumer sectors the title may not choose to be a member of ABC and is unlikely to be featured on NRS. Here it is more likely that the media sales team will be selling directly to the advertiser, not their agency. These titles will still offer a complete menu of advertising options but the sales contact comes from being embedded in the industry served, not necessarily from being part of the (London-centric) media scene.

These advertisers are less concerned with data, demographics, readership figures and market segmentation. In fact they may have little interest in corporate branding, rather they are looking for a direct response to their ad. In this way they replicate the desires of the classified advertiser. When a new type of fishing reel is advertised in *Advanced Carp Fishing* the manufacturer is hoping that the reader will visit his website or a local dealer and purchase this product – perhaps not on that day but as a direct consequence of viewing the ad.

The culture of the sales team on a specialist title is very different to that of an agency-focussed major publisher. Their sell is largely based on response and it may not make any difference if the actual sales or readership is growing or declining. A magazine may have added a band of new readers with a brilliant supplement aimed at entrants or first time users in a market, but that is of little consequence to a manufacturer of a sophisticated product aimed at experts.

Photo 7.2 Example of magazine advertisement driving online ordering

Feminisation

Women's magazines deliver the highest ad revenues of all genres. It may be a slight generalisation – and of course equal opportunities persist – but it is now relatively unusual to find men selling on the large women's brands, a change which has taken place over the past 20 years. This rather mundane observation has impacted on the culture of ad sales, which has moved away from deals being done over long, often boozy, lunches. More than one male advertisement sales director of the 1970s or 1980s was known as a 'legend in his own lunchtime'. It is now more likely that a breakfast meeting will be the key to success. Every ad sales person at *Glamour*, the biggest selling monthly in the UK, is female. Advertising is a people business but these people are increasingly likely to be women. This in turn will be reflected in the next generation of publishers and CEOs as ad sales remains, with marketing, a likely route to management.

> Advertising is a people business but these people are increasingly likely to be women

READERSHIP AND CIRCULATION VERIFICATION

In order to discover the coverage, frequency and CPT/M of any particular advertising campaign we must first establish how many people read or look at the magazines on the proposed schedule. To achieve this, media planners have an important toolkit at their disposal. The key components of this are:

- National Readership Survey and NRS PADD
- Audit Bureau of Circulation
- Target Group Index.

In addition to these three important media 'currencies', advertising investment decisions can be strengthened by examining Mintel and other surveys.

National Readership Survey (NRS)

The NRS is the UK's most important and valued source of data for print advertisement planning and buying. It covers 250 of the largest titles – 158 of them are consumer magazines.

In common with other industry bodies, NRS run as a not-for-profit organisation and its board comprises of media owner and advertising agency representatives. All fieldwork and data evaluation is contracted out to the Ipsos MORI research group.

High quality readership research is dependent upon:

- the size and quality of the sample
- the interview technique and process
- the weighting of the data to generate end results.

NRS is a continuous survey with fieldwork taking place each month of the year; 38,000 face-to-face interviews are conducted annually. Of particular importance is the fact that respondents are randomly selected from postcode data on an individual basis. This is designed to reflect the diversity of national reading habits. No substitutions are allowed and if the respondent is unavailable, a call back may occur. Internet surveying is not utilised.

The interview process takes place in the respondent's own home, lasting on average half an hour. Using two linked laptop computers, the interviewee is asked if he or she has 'read or looked at' a title – the masthead or logo of the title in question is displayed on the screen as the question is put. Timing is important – for a weekly title the notation has to be in the last seven days and for a monthly in that last month. The interviewer will also ask a range of questions about consumption of other media forms as well as general lifestyle and demographic queries.

All of the information is then collated and samples very carefully weighted to national profiles. Data is processed in a sophisticated manner and the end result is a highly valuable resource which reflects the true diversity of magazine and newspaper reading in the UK today. There are a number of outputs but a key statistic is average issue readership (AIR) – an accurate estimate of the number of adults who read an average issue of a publication within its shelf life. NRS also gives estimates on the frequency of reading, to discover, on average, how many issues of a title an average reader sees and the time spent reading them. Duplication of reading between different titles is logged. For advertising schedule planning and optimisation these factors are all key.

Readers per copy

ABC figures play an important role, alongside NRS, in the trading of advertisement space but there are major differences between them, which it is important to understand. The ABC validation process is largely carried out in the publishers' and distributors' offices where financial, sales and distribution records are checked in a manner not unlike a financial audit. NRS is dependent upon the goodwill of its large, random sample of 38,000 annual interviewees to cooperate. ABC is an audit and NRS a survey – the clue is indeed in the title.

The relationship between the two is captured in the term 'readers per copy' which is often used by media buyers. This is evaluated as follows:

- Using the readership survey we establish that the total readership of a given monthly title is (for example) 1,000,000 adults.
- In the same or similar period we establish that the circulation of the magazine – in the UK – was 200,000 copies per month.
- Therefore we can work out that the number of readers per copy of this title is simply readership divided by circulation – in this instance it is 5 readers per copy.

> ABC is an audit and NRS a survey – the clue is indeed in the title

A magazine may be seen by more people than the number of copies purchased or distributed. After all, magazines are for sharing – be it on our coffee table at home or in a hotel lobby. Some magazines can register a very high readers per copy figure of 10 plus. Men will form part of the readership of women's magazines (and vice versa). Monthly titles are likely to have more readers per copy than weeklies. Some B2B titles can be circulated internally throughout offices to groups of people.

NRS asks interviewees where the initial copy was sourced. Buyers may wish to differentiate between primary and secondary readers – the latter not reading the title in the home of the person who purchased or picked up the initial copy. They may downweight the importance of secondary readers in schedules as they consider that some of these readers do not note their advertisements as carefully as the magazine purchaser (called the primary reader).

The latter point reinforces the importance of using more than one validated data source when planning and buying advertisements. If a title does not feature on NRS, its main trading currency is likely to be its ABC figure.

Digital

NRS PADD (Print And Digital Data) is the unduplicated reach of a print publication and its website. It represents a recent innovation and estimates the level of duplication of print titles and websites – which websites do a publication's readers visit, and vice versa. Because it is an NRS initiative it offers full demographic and classification data for profiling and targeting. This is an important development towards standardisation of measurement metrics in the UK which have mushroomed confusingly across the web. Upon introduction, NRS PADD revealed that publisher websites and portals were used by 25 per cent of the population and the combined unduplicated reach of all magazine media is 77 per cent. This is a real plus for those publishers who have made very significant investments online[8].

Audit Bureau of Circulation (ABC)

ABC was established in 1931 by advertisers who wanted an independent body to check publishers' circulation claims. Since then ABC has expanded its services to become a valued 'stamp of trust' across print, digital and events platforms. It provides the industry with accurate, detailed and comparable data on which to trade advertising.

ABC is run by the industry for the industry

ABC is run by the industry for the industry. The ABC Board is composed of key media owners, media agencies, advertisers and trade body representatives, reflecting their differing interests. As the needs of each media sector (for example consumer magazines, national newspapers etc.) can also differ, each one has its own Reporting Standards Group. They work together to set the standards to which ABC data is reported. Digital media standards are agreed by JICWEBS – Joint Industry Committee for Web Standards (www.jicwebs.org). Together all these groups have a say in how ABC is run, thus representing the interests of the industry across multiple platforms.

Data

ABC is funded mainly by publishers who use their ABC figures to attract advertisement revenues.

In 2013, ABC had 559 business magazines and 573 consumer magazines in membership, this means that the vast majority of the magazine market by advertisement revenue spend is covered by ABC. All data is audited to common

Reporting Standards agreed by the industry. These standards exist for the platforms of print, website, digital editions and publications, apps, newsletters, email, social media and exhibitions.

Reporting Standards specify how often a certificate needs to be issued. Consumer magazines can report six monthly or annually and B2B magazines report annually. All members are required to make their ABC figures public.

ABC certificates detail the average circulation for both print and digital copies for all the issues of a title published over a particular time period. They also classify the copies according to type, so that buyers can make a value judgment on the strength of a particular title's circulation. There can be up to 50 different circulation or distribution types on a consumer magazine certificate. These include categories such as retail and subscription sales and various channels of free distribution.

Advertisers also want to see the percentage of a magazine's circulation which is actively purchased, as this represents the copies sold to individuals, as opposed to being made available free. Also available is a breakdown of a magazine's circulation figure by issue and multi-pack circulation figures (where two magazines are packed and sold together).

Business magazine certificates can also include highly detailed demographic data on the individuals targeted by the publication. An example of this is shown in Chapter 6 – controlled circulation. This demonstrates to media buyers the seniority of the reader and the level of budget they control. This level of detail adds to the transparency of the overall 'headline' figure and to get the best view of a publication's circulation it is essential to dig down to understand how it is comprised.

ABC consumer magazine figures are released together in a twice yearly report. The circulation comparison tables generate much media press and agency interest and can be used as a health check to see how a magazine is performing in the marketplace.

Verification

All media owners in membership submit a claim to ABC. This is then audited to ensure that the claim is correct and adheres to the industry agreed rules. The principle behind an audit for any circulation type is that the publisher must provide firm evidence of their claims which can then be verified. For instance, print copies are audited by checking a paper trail, so the media owner must provide proof from third parties that the copies were printed, received by a distributor and how many unsold copies were returned.

In order to audit a website, media owners (or companies acting on their behalf) report the behaviour of visitors to their site by analysing a set of data representing that site. The data analysed comes from the site's web server log files or from logged data captured via a tracking code inserted in a site's web pages (also known as page tags). Appropriate analysis of this data can then provide web traffic figures.

In all cases ABC's rigorous audit principles maintain its reputation for trust and are a key factor in making ABC a brand in its own right.

The future

ABC works hard to ensure that it remains relevant and adapts to meet the changing needs of the industry. Reporting Standards are constantly evolved and new metrics, products and services are developed as consumers utilise different choices of media and publishers race to meet those needs.

The growth of digital versions of print editions and widespread adoption of mobile and tablet technology has meant these are now valuable new outlets for the publisher. ABC audits to a wide range of online metrics, covering not only the number of devices connecting to a site but also measuring the engagement digital users have with a brand.

As well as verifying data for media owners and buyers, ABC works closely with JICWEBS to deliver certification for a wide variety of digital advertising trading processes. An example of this is the digital ad trading systems, where advertisers demanded reassurance that their brands would not appear on sites where offensive or inappropriate material was posted.

As the media landscape changes at a tremendous pace, with more fragmented ways for consumers to access information, ABC's role to provide transparency and trust across all channels is vital for the future health of the publishing industry.

Membership of ABC is voluntary. There are publishers who choose not to join. In these instances publishers may issue their own declarations of circulation and distribution but it should be remembered that these publishers' statements do not have the backing of this important body.

Target Group Index (TGI)

TGI is the longest established single source marketing and media survey in Britain and was established by BMRB in 1969. TGI has since expanded into more than 60 countries with over 700,000 people being interviewed every year.

In Britain, TGI collects information from a representative sample of around 25,000 adults annually; the data is released quarterly. The survey asks questions covering consumer attitudes, motivations, media habits and purchase behaviour, then links these variables. TGI is a single source survey –respondents have to fill out the entire questionnaire covering all question areas. This means any TGI variable can be cross-analysed with another TGI variable to find compelling insights.

Of particular relevance to advertisers targeting well-heeled or business people is Premier TGI. This is an annual survey of those in society who are either in the AB social grouping or earn over £50,000 per annum. It is based on a sample size of 6,500 over-20-year-olds. Use of this valuable resource can aid the planner target 'lifestyle choice' campaigns such as luxury travel.

Mintel and other surveys

Established 40 years ago in London, Mintel is a market leading business information service which is global and reaches into most major industries. Their website lists 17 key business sectors for which they provide market and business information reports. This includes the huge – in terms of advertisement spend – beauty and care and food and drink markets. The company prides itself on being 'your eyes and ears in the markets that matter'. Mintel's reports provide essential background on a given industry sector with consumer opinions, market size and forecasts, trends, company profiles and competitor analysis.

The major media owners and PPA also invest significant sums into bespoke research, to back the case for advertising in magazines as a medium and individual brands in particular. IPC Media have a consumer insight team whose role it is to give advertisers relevant data about that media group's readers. One of their studies is called AdValue – conducted by Nielsen and Mindshare. This demonstrates how magazine campaigns drive sales and reviews how magazines enhance TV campaigns.

THE MANY FACES OF MAGAZINE ADVERTISING

Advertisement revenues can be generated in many ways. The traditional forms of advertising are principally:

- display
- classified and recruitment
- inserts
- gatefolds and cover wraps.

Increasingly, agencies and their clients are seeking to engage with the magazine's readership in a more integrated way. As such, they will be looking for an 'added value' dimension to enhance traditional forms of print advertisements. Such added value formats include:

- advertorials
- competitions
- sponsorships or regular advertisement affiliation
- product joint ventures.

This section illustrates all of the above. We will also discuss how problems can arise and be resolved if the line of editorial independence is crossed.

The traditional faces

The flat-plan of a consumer or B2B title will show the following types of advertisements.

Display

A display advertisement is sold by the page (or a fraction thereof) and is commonly used to reinforce the branding of a product. Fashion brands line up to fill the early sections of *Vogue* with full page or double page spreads (DPS). Other special positions include inside front cover and the back cover. Beyond these, advertisers will also pay more to be, for example, the first car product featured or facing a particular columnist. For a launch issue one agency may be offered the option to take every site – in this way the publisher has a greater chance of keeping the new title confidential until the very last minute. Each of these ads will be offered at a particular price and will feature on the magazine's rate card, which is effectively a menu of spaces offered by the publication.

Display ads represent the bulk of the ad revenue generated by printed consumer magazines with over 80 per cent of the share – the balance being classified, recruitments and inserts. It is a similar story in the B2B sector with 75 per cent of the ad revenue generated by display advertising. As Chapter 2 shows, this revenue stream is rapidly migrating online.

Classified and recruitment

At the less glamorous end of the market are classified ads. They are sold by the line or the column centimetre and are typically offering a marketplace of goods and services which appeal to the readership of the relevant magazine. Increasingly they will have photographic content. They will almost always be clustered at the rear of the magazine, to avoid a clash with the design template of the magazine and readers know to look for them there. Classified ads have little element of branding and are a direct call to action from seller to buyer with a minimum of design and obfuscation.

Photo 7.3 Dedicated readers enjoy scanning the classified ads of specialist titles

The importance of classified advertising underpins the business model of the B2B title prior to the digital age. In this era, the key revenue for a business or professional title came from recruitment advertising. The trade press was full of job ads and that was a reason why personnel in a given industry would be happy to subscribe (or at least receive a free copy). In the late 1990s, I recall weekly computer titles so thick that printers struggled to insert staples and fold the product.

When some major employers realised that they no longer had to pay to advertise their vacancies, as they could simply put them on their own websites, this key source of print revenue started to dry up. Larger job ads boards also picked them up, increasing awareness. This revenue decline was compounded by the recession post 2008 – there were simply fewer jobs out there. B2B and professional publishers invested significant sums and worked hard to develop their own job sites, the teachers' employment site run by TSL Education being a shining example of this. In other B2B markets, where the readership was less favourable towards print, publishers took radical action and made certain titles digital only and reduced the (controlled) circulation of others.

Inserts

Subscription marketers firmly believe that they get a better response to inserted offers than they do via on the page promotional deals. This is often met with incredulity by students who dismiss 'magazine dandruff' as unwelcome and ineffective. Unwilling to argue with direct marketing experts, I take their word that inserts remain an effective marketing tactic. Objectively, it clearly is. This form of advertising is used by an array of direct mail suppliers and catalogue retailers. When supplying inserts to a publisher, it is important to remember the printer will insert in the whole print run and the advertiser must make an allowance for unsold copies. Also inserts of unusual size need to be planned in to production cycles, as they may slow binding times.

> Subscription marketers firmly believe that they get a better response to inserted offers than they do via on the page promotional deals

Gatefolds and cover wraps

Scoring well in reader awareness surveys, the gatefold cover effectively presents a 'false' cover which folds out to two DPS ads. This is clearly a premium position which the publisher will price accordingly – they will also wish to ensure that the product being advertised and the design style sit comfortably with the magazine. By securing these positions, the media buyer can improve the effectiveness of the advertising but it does need to be done in clear partnership with the chosen magazine. Large free distribution titles often sell a cover wrap – a sold advertisement cover over the editorial cover. This will be seen as a premium position, given the high visibility of these tiles in major cities, in effect a mini poster site for the advertiser.

Media packs

The rate card forms part of the media pack which magazines compile to inform (primarily) advertisers. Other key elements are the target market, editorial vision, strategy and delivery, key demographics, ABC figure, readership and contact details. This can be a glossy brochure style but increasingly is online as part of the publisher's website. TGI figures are often stressed to support the affluence and buying power of the title's audience. This is demonstrated by *Red* magazine in Chapter 4.

Photo 7.4
Reader profiling of magazines such as *Red* help the editorial team to create a well-targeted package to maximise both circulation and advertisement revenues

Added value advertising

When looking at how advertisers can achieve maximum effect from magazine advertising, it is important to discuss how commercial and editorial teams interact in a modern day publishing company.

Advertorials and the relationship with editorial

In the classic magazine model, the editorial staff are tasked with attracting readers, which they do by creating well researched, well written and well designed content: simple. The real world is, however, a little more complex for editors and journalists, as they are faced with working in a business which exerts its own pressure. The culture at certain magazines may require that editorial is moulded to ensure a positive environment for advertisers. This can create genuine conflicts of interest.

Perhaps the easiest area of cross over to understand is the advertorial, or sponsored feature. These are ad pages and paid for spaces like other advertisements but they are designed and written to fit into the magazine's style. This method of presentation is clearly designed to imply that the editorial voice of the magazine endorses the message of the advertiser. It is reasonably obvious that a line is being crossed here. PPA issue guidelines to publishers about their use[9] and the Advertising Standards Authority are prepared to adjudicate on the subject if required.

However, are advertorials really problematic? These pages are clearly labelled as 'advertisement feature' or 'sponsored feature' and as such are explicitly telling readers that they are reading a paid for ad. It could be argued that, rather than trying to 'hoodwink' readers, the advertorial is a refreshing bout of honesty, in a world where some editorial is actually created to attract advertising but this is concealed as the genuine opinion of the editor or writer. Which is the more misleading? An advertorial written extolling the virtues of (say) Ireland ('in association with an Irish tour company') or an 'independent' review of the stunning Irish countryside where the journalist was on a PR trip with everything – including the Guinness – bought and paid for. Is the latter really more trustworthy in terms of communicating a message to potential holidaymakers?

This is the line that editors and publishers have to navigate every day. A successful magazine must have the trust of its readers and demonstrate that it is striving to present a true picture of events. In addition, it must ensure that key advertisers, PR companies and commercial partners are also kept on side. What is the appropriate level of distance for editorial staff from this commercial fray?

Editorial staff are definitely expected to come up with special sections or supplements around which the ad sales team can sell. Look at the variety of holiday supplements with January issues. Do we really think the readers of men's lifestyle magazines require an in-depth analysis of the luxury watch market every year? This is an overt 'ad-get' feature which can then double as a retail promotion; a banded supplement which bulks up the overall pagination and is FREE. In reality, a supplement is unlikely to generate copy sales in isolation and does require considerable ad sales or an overall sponsor to cover costs.

The above example can be seen as sound publishing, so when does this blurring become a problem? Certainly on a commercial level it is an issue if readers lose faith in the editorial integrity of the magazine. There does appear to be an enormous level of benefit of the doubt given to magazine publishers. The entire customer magazine industry is built on the idea that editorial ideas can be presented to strengthen a consumer brand; distribution of these magazines makes them among the most successful titles in the UK. The bottom line appears to be that, once an initial level of trust is established, the public will believe a magazine (or brand) until that bond is broken and the brand starts to become 'toxic'. In the political world, this was the situation faced by the Members of Parliament after the expenses scandal of 2010. To re-establish the trust of the general public, new procedures had to be put in place.

When we look at the B2B sector, this pressure to pander to key advertisers can really be problematic for publishers and possibly for society at large. How do B2B titles maintain editorial integrity when they are constantly tasked with writing about the largest players in their industry, who are also their ultimate

> A successful magazine must have the trust of its readers and demonstrate that it is striving to present a true picture of events

paymasters via advertising? In 2010 Kit Gould, Managing Director of IDG UK, succinctly stated his position, 'If an advertiser holds a gun to my head, I say "Pull the trigger"'. Gould maintains that no advertiser could prevent his publication from publishing the truth about a company, even if they threaten to withdraw their advertising.[10] This is an admirable position and many would say an essential one for a credible B2B publisher. There is no doubt that some advertisers will attempt to use the leverage their ad budget creates to demand favourable coverage. All editors would say 'never on my watch' but is this credible? How often do B2B titles break scandalous news of skulduggery on their patch? It can be persuasively argued that the structure of the industry mitigates heavily against this being common place. These issues go to the heart of a free press.

Again we look at the role of the internet in this debate. Here there has been a change in the role of a journalist from that of attracting an audience, to being responsible for the level of interaction with that audience. Some may conclude that writing online advertorials or creating content for advertiser's microsites work against the independence of journalism. Rules must apply to online also, however, and paid for content must be marked as such; journalists must be allowed to write online editorial independently.

The trend towards cross platform advertising solutions – where publishers offer print and digital space – has also led to an increase in editorial input, as publishers dig deeper to find ways to maintain their ad revenues, in the face of decreasing print sales. To maintain both editorial independence and satisfy the needs of advertisers, it is vital that editors and commercial teams have clear lines of understanding and mutual respect. Like many things in life, it is largely down to common sense. Clive Horwood, Editor of *Euromoney* sums it up: 'It is a question of setting the ground rules and being a grown up.' When asked for his reaction if a story were to be 'spiked' for non editorial reasons, he stated: 'I would leave on the spot.'[11] Magazines are highly effective tools in establishing trust and brand loyalty – and maintaining it – if they stick to the established rules and guidelines of advertising and advertorials.

> Magazines are highly effective tools in establishing trust and brand loyalty – and maintaining it

Competitions

Competitions are popular with readers and make successful cover lines. They are a subtle form of advertising or promotion which can be part of a larger partnership between an advertiser and a magazine. Their mechanics are normally organised by PR agencies rather than their advertising counterparts. Essentially the reader is largely unaware of any form of transaction underpinning what appears as an editorial feature. It is, however, highly likely that the prizes awarded will be part of an overall marketing partnership between title and client.

Sponsorship or regular affiliation

A regular column or feature may attract a long-term advertiser who particularly enjoys the association with an individual writer or with a well-read section of a magazine. The advertising message may be further enhanced by an unusual copy size, such as a centre panel or strip along the bottom of a page. This will be particularly effective for colour dense advertisements set against a largely mono page.

There may be really special circumstances when a whole issue of a title may be sponsored. In the Spring of 2012 *Grazia* published a collector's edition to coincide with London Fashion Week. It was marked by an online documentary series and social media/marketing campaign. The project was sponsored by LG Mobile in a deal reported by *The Drum* website to be six figures. The special issue and live content gave readers an additional level of exclusive content and advertisers a greater level of interaction with this influential Bauer brand.

Joint ventures

Publishers are always looking for new ways to monetise their readers. One innovation is to find partners with whom they can use their name to produce goods and services for direct sale to readers. This is really a turbo-charged version of the traditional magazine reader's mail order offer combined with the idea of brand extension. The skill here is to find the right partnerships which will enhance the brand, be attractive to readers and sell products.

This is some distance from classic advertising in a magazine but agencies are increasingly seeing this as an opportunity to leverage their client base and be the key middle man, putting the right brands with the correct media. Taking an example from the newspaper industry, imagine the potential commercial power which the vast audience *MailOnline* can generate. It is currently the biggest news website in the world with 119 million unique browsers each month[12]. If its publisher, Associated Newspapers, could sell a product at a typical and modest iTunes price of 79p to just one per cent of that global audience, the turnover would be nearly £100,000 per product line.

Closer to home we can see the core brand values of intelligence, globalisation and design at the heart of the products offered to *Monocle*'s readers through its online shop. From iconic Japanese mugs (£20) to a Mongolian cashmere scarf (£415) the desire to offer brand compatible goods is clear. Over 70 luxury items are available – a number of them exclusively.

EMERGING TRENDS

How will the buyers of advertisement space and media owners react to the market and technological landscapes of the future?

Advertising agencies

An enjoyable experience awaits anyone interested in the development of the advertising industry from the 1960s as the TV series *Mad Men* has stretched to seven series and shows no sign of stopping. It tells the story of a full service advertising agency as it wins clients with great creative ideas and then – as an afterthought – puts together a relevant media schedule with the focus heavily on TV.

The point is that an advertising agency was traditionally a creatively led organisation. During the 1970s, media buying shops or independents started to develop. In 1988 a fundamental move took place which set the scene for the agency landscape today – by acquisition and restructure, Saatchi & Saatchi established Zenith and media buying and planning became separated from its mainstream agency. This model of locating media planning and buying in a stand-alone business unit became the template in the UK and played its part in increasing the cost effectiveness of media buying. This was achieved by leveraging buying power and the use of relatively hard-nosed negotiation tactics, backed by effective research. The rise of the media independent was in full flow.

As we enter the second decade of the twenty-first century, the media buying or media independent agency sector is a mature market which has gone through major consolidation, to the point where we now have only a handful of key agencies controlling the majority of spend. By 2011, just ten buying units accounted for 80 per cent of the money spent on British television[13]. Major advertisers are ever more willing to put their business up for tender and this, combined with the post 2008 recession and an increase in digital advertising, has resulted in a severe squeeze on agency profit margins. Agency finances are complex, with revenues coming from media owner commission rates and rebates together with the fee income. Commission rates for magazines are typically 15 per cent but some can be 10 per cent.

What does the future hold? With agencies having to fight both to hold onto existing business and win new accounts, their financial model has come under pressure. Advertising is a cyclical business and profits can surge as well as fall.

The growth of digital media is also having an effect on agency structure. Publishers have two types of digital advertisement inventory to sell – websites and the emerging digital editions. In some agencies there is a healthy but lively debate taking place between print and digital media buyers. Print buyers consider that tablet advertising is a logical extension of their client's business with publishers and therefore part of their remit. Pure digital product buying teams, however, may see it as part of their area. How this plays out is important to publishers because of the likely different cultures and methodologies employed by buyers in these two spheres. The digital buyer will have a wide brief to deliver an audience cost effectively in terms of CPT/M. In this scenario it is very difficult for magazine publishers to compete with the vast numbers delivered by web portals and news aggregators. If one takes out the element of environment or engagement (often passed over by the digital buying process) then why would publishers' tablet offerings attract high ad revenues?

The loss of added value is a concern that comes out during publisher interviews; in the PPA Publishing Futures Survey (2013) one media owner states: 'Once everything migrates from print to digital, the cost per thousands fall. And agencies trade digital like a commodity.'[14]

Experienced print buyers believe they can enhance the quality of campaigns by clever use of magazines, in their new digital form. Therefore, for the brave new world of tablets to be realised and continued downward pressure on prices to be avoided, it is important that publishers give print buyers the qualitative and quantitative tools to win any internal debate. Some agencies are moving to resolve this structural issue by allowing print teams to buy media for a given client across all platforms – rather than segmenting the buying process by media stream. Like many organisational issues in the digital world it is constantly evolving.

The quest for value – procurement and media audits

As stated earlier, an experienced media buyer will be aware of a magazine's rate card but it is likely to play only a small part in the buying process for large consumer titles. Buying agencies will be very aware of what rates are being charged in the media marketplace. The role of the advertisement sales team is to maximise revenue and prices achieved for designated ad spaces but these rates can vary. The size of the campaign under negotiation is a factor, as are circumstances like positioning, timings and overall demand. Very particular campaign needs have to be considered. Therefore advertisement space is not sold at fixed price – some clients will pay different rates than others.

Media spend for major consumer goods or service providers – and certain public sector organisations – is a hefty cost. From the point of view of corporate governance and stakeholder transparency – let alone personal pride – no one wants to pay above average market rate. In fact, it has become the requirement for procurement and finance departments in large organisations to ensure that media campaigns are bought at or below average costs. This is demonstrated by employing the services of a media auditor such as Ebiqity, Auditstar or 23 Media Audits. Their role is to improve the return on investment for an advertising campaign. This is done primarily by pooling data and benchmarking to find out what the average rate of buying is in a particular medium or title. Buying targets are then set for the agency, for a campaign to be delivered at this price or x per cent below it.

The widespread use of media auditors has been yet another factor that has led to a decline in prices paid for print media in recent years. A procurement-led buying process can create a downward spiral of rates. In this process, the low price goes into the mix and causes the 'pool' price to fall, therefore meaning the next target set will be even lower.

Being an auditor does not make one the most popular person on the block; some publishers will claim that the media auditing process is just about price points. On the other hand, the audit companies state that qualitative measures, as well as quantitative, are employed in evaluations. There seems little doubt that major advertisers value their services and they have become yet another part of a complex buying environment.

> Being an auditor does not make one the most popular person on the block ...

Media barter

Companies such as Astus, from Australia, or Active International are bringing another source of new revenue to publishers – bartering. Astus works by negotiating a deal with a media company. They then sell this space to their clients who pay them with a mixture of cash and products (or services). The client can therefore access a larger media campaign but without the associated full cash outlay. These products are then re-marketed appropriately to create value. Another positive result for the advertiser is that, as well as achieving the exposure of a media campaign, they will get a guaranteed level of return on their investment directly in the shape of chosen products. This kind of corporate bartering is only likely to increase in the digital economy. Before venturing into bartering do involve the finance team as it may throw up certain issues of taxation liability.

In the UK, media barter is currently valued at £250–£300 million per annum or around two per cent of total media billings. Its questionable reputation is changing as media companies strive to flex maximum value from ad sales. It certainly requires the barter company to be fully aware of the brand values of the advertiser.[15]

THE MOVE TO DIGITAL

The PPA estimate that the current share of advertising and sponsorship revenues of member companies taken up by digital sales is 17 per cent for consumer and 30 per cent for B2B[16]. This revenue acceleration includes packages of multi-channel advertising sold, plus generation of contacts or 'leads'. Both sectors expect this to grow by at least ten percentage points in the next two years, as the landscape for print circulations remains bleak.

'Served rather than stitched in'

As Chapter 8 shows, the tablet-based subscription is often bundled with a print sale. Digital editions of publications are important areas for development and where publishers are investing huge resources. A key part of this innovation is to move away from the print-based model of ad presentation. Here a page is sold to a particular advertiser at a fixed price and becomes part of that issue of the magazine. This is referred to as 'stitched in'.

Readers using tablet devices will currently view ads in one of three ways:

- as an exact copy of their print ad. This has no link to any 'underlying' website.
- an alternative version of a print ad that links to an advertiser's website or other branded content when the screen is tapped. Clearly an internet connection is needed. For car advertisers this can be to a clip of a fast moving car or for a new movie to a short trailer. One car advertisement depicted a different vehicle depending upon whether the tablet was held in a landscape or vertical position. This is known as rich media.

These first two types of presentation are still 'stitched in' as every reader is seeing the same ad, whether in the digital edition or the side journey into the advertiser's world.

- the third type of digital advertisement presentation which has moved to a model of each ad being served when the issue is viewed. The advertiser pays for a particular number of views which means it will be replaced by another commercial when that 'credit' runs out and the views delivered. The ads can then become a dynamic part of the magazine which can also be tailored to the individual reader profile. These are designated 'served'.

Obviously, before 'served' becomes commonplace, the nation's coverage of wi-fi needs to be complete. 'Stitched in' ads are readable anywhere, on any device but 'served' ads – which are much more attractive to digital savvy advertisers and their agencies – are only viable on devices with a live connection to the internet. For this mechanic the future beckons and it represents a positive example of how publishers can leverage the new platform.

Free – print fights back

There is little doubt that print advertising will continue to be a vital revenue stream for consumer advertisers for some time to come; the platform has had a recent champion with large circulation free titles.

Back in 1999, Associated Newspapers launched free newspaper *Metro*. Despite publishing the paid for *Evening Standard* (at the time) Associated had a very efficient crystal ball and saw that the future was free.

For advertising agencies this was a game changer for free titles. *Metro* was based in London and aimed at commuters – this meant that agency buyers witnessed its popularity daily. This increased confidence to place ads – response rates turned out to be good. The Rubicon was crossed and the time honoured argument held by some, that people would only read what they had paid for started to crumble. 'Paid for' remains for many businesses a strong selling point and ABC categorises magazines that are actively purchased yet *Metro* was delivering both an affluent audience and big free distribution numbers.

Fast forward to 2013 and *Metro* has been joined by a free *Evening Standard*, plus *Shortlist*, *Stylist*, *Sport* and *Time Out*. These are all distributed in huge numbers. *Metro* is available in all the major conurbations in the UK. The business models are discussed in Chapter 2 – they add up to a new and successful template for print which is wholly dependent on advertising.

As we have seen, ABC works hard to meet the audit needs of emerging distribution means. The methodology of verifying the distribution numbers of free titles is now trusted and they are a firmly accepted part of the new media landscape. Seemingly it is a model that is exportable – *Stylist* has successfully launched its first European edition in France, suggesting that it is thriving and demonstrating – yet again – that UK magazine publishing is world class.

THE NEW SALES ENVIRONMENT

This chapter has demonstrated that the UK advertising scene is both complex and incredibly fast moving. As *Inside Magazine Publishing* goes to press we are just embarking upon that digital journey. Ideas are being tried and tested. Some publishers sell print and digital as a 'bundled' package; others do not. The metrics for measuring sales and readership of digital editions are still being established. All publishers report a shortage of personnel with advertisement sales skills for the digital world – these disciplines representing clear training needs. But there is no doubt that the sector embraces the opportunities – and is realistic about the threats – with its characteristic enthusiasm.

Can margins of profitability be maintained? For example, 90 per cent of publisher Condé Nast's ad revenue comes from print but declining circulations across the whole industry will continue to exert pressure on that media platform. According to the 2013 PPA Futures Survey, the pace of the move to digital will intensify – the PPA estimates by 10 percentage points in the next two years. They are not alone in this dilemma. Likewise ad agencies struggle to maintain their own profits in the digital age and in the face of long-term recession.

Will Martin Sorrell's predictions as quoted earlier in this chapter prove correct? Improving processes and cost efficiency will ensure that ad sales teams and media departments can survive. Salespeople will have to become expert at cross platform selling to offer new services and to generate the new sources of revenue we have explored in these pages.

Thanks to Lucy Palmer and Jan Pitt of ABC for their help with this chapter.

NOTES

1. Wessenden (2013) p 16.
2. 'Quality of Reading Survey (QRS)' (2000) conducted by Ipsos-RSL for IPA, ISBA and PPA, cited in Consterdine (2005) pp 24, 29.
3. 'Reader Categorisation Study' (1972), JICNARS, by Research Services Ltd., cited in Consterdine (2005) p 34.
4. Kantar (2007).
5. Sweney (2013).
6. The early pioneer of this approach was Alan Smith, of IPC Magazines, in 1972.
7. Consterdine (2005) p 43.
8. Barry McIlheney (CEO of the PPA) quoted in PPA Communications (2012).
9. See PPA (1993).
10. Tripp (2010).
11. Ibid.
12. ABC (April 2013).
13. Fletcher (2012).
14. Wessenden (2013) p 20.
15. Dickens (2013).
16. Wessenden (2013) p 16.

REFERENCE SOURCES

Consterdine, G. (2005) *How Magazine Advertising Works*, 5th edition. London: PPA.

Dickens, F. (2013) 'Q&A with Frances Dickens on reinventing the image of media barter', 13 May 2013, the *Guardian*.

Fletcher, M. (2012) 'Trend report: cutting out the agency middleman', 5 December 2012 available at www.mediaweek.co.uk/News/1163139/. (Accessed 26 June 2013.)

Kantar (2007) *Magazines in the Driving Seat: research into offline drivers of online search and purchase*. London: PPA available at www.ppa.co.uk/public/downloads/Marketing/Research/MagazinesDriveOnline.pdf. (Accessed 25 June 2013.)

PPA (1993) *Best Practice Guidelines for Special Advertising Opportunities within Magazines.* London: PPA.

PPA Communications (2012) 'NRS PADD shows continued appetite for magazine media', 12 September 2012 available at www.ppa.co.uk/about/activities/ consumer-media-group/news/nrs-padd-shows-continued-appetite-for- magazine-media/. (Accessed 25 June 2013.)

Sweney, M. (2013) 'Advertisers should slash newspaper and magazine budgets, says WPP boss', the *Guardian,* 25 April 2013 available at http://www. guardian.co.uk/media/2013/apr/25/advertisers-slash-newspaper-magazine- budgets-wpp. (Accessed 25 June 2013.)

Tripp, M. (2010) 'Editorial integrity – editors need to be commercial players', 1 March 2010 available at www.trippassociates.co.uk/2010/editorial-integrity- the-need-to-be-a-commercial-player/. (Accessed 3 July 2013.)

Wessenden (2013) *PPA Publishing Futures 2013 Report.* Godalming: Wessenden.

CHAPTER 8

Publishing in the digital age

Jim Bilton

This final chapter of *Inside Magazine Publishing* explores the role of digital in the modern publishing operation and covers the industry's journey into digital and the scale and shape of this exciting new medium. We will also explore monetising new media and the organisational impacts and challenges inherent with working on this platform. In the consumer market, the majority of online magazines are being sold via Apple Newsstand and its emerging competitors so we look at how these offers are developing.

As part of its ongoing consulting work, Wessenden Marketing interviews and monitors a range of publishing companies and much of this chapter is based on this. Two key reports are also referred to in this chapter: *Business Models for a Digital World: PPA* and *PPA Publishing Futures 2013 Report*.

The core commentary is supported by a selection of case studies.

THE PUBLISHING INDUSTRY'S JOURNEY INTO DIGITAL

As an industry, you seem to have so many strengths – strong brands, real skills, deep customer insight – but you must avoid the mistakes we made. Don't give your content away. Try to limit piracy as much as you can. And be clear what value you are really adding – do people really need 'publishers' any longer? You have all the **skills,** but do you still have a **role**?

(Music publisher, commenting on magazine publishers)

> Magazine publishers have observed with some trepidation the fundamental changes experienced by the music business

Magazine publishers have observed with some trepidation the fundamental changes experienced by the music business, which have been driven by the rapid shift from physical into digital products and which have completely disrupted the business models of an entire industry. Yet each sector of the media and entertainment (M&E) industry is managing the digital shift in different ways and at different speeds.

In this textbook we have seen B2B publishing is well into this step change, far ahead of consumer magazines. Yet both lag behind gaming, music or even national newspapers. The reasons for the differences between industries are complex, but revolve around five issues:

- how transferable the core content service is across different platforms
- how receptive the end-users are to change
- how new players with new business models have changed the rules
- company histories and cultures are more deeply engrained in some industries
- other external, environmental factors which have changed the industry rules.

As part of PPA's 'Business Models for a Digital World' project, a number of companies from other M&E sectors were asked what their views of the magazine publishing industry were. Their observations included the following.

Publishers have real brands, based on engagement, authority and a deep understanding of the end-user, but that intense brand-focus is perceived to have some downsides. These include customer overchoice (there are simply too many magazines) and brand myopia (publishers can be obsessed about their own brands to the detriment of a broader view as to how they add value to the end-user's life and work).

Having customers with long-term user relationships in the form of subscriptions is a massive strength. It has helped media owners to develop special relationship and retention skills, yet these competencies are very specific. They have not helped to leverage enough revenue from 'super-users' of publishers' products and services.

Similarly, being able to manage multiple contacts with end-users is seen to be a real strength, but does all the granular activity truly fit into a broader strategy?

Brand ownership of legacy print products, especially in the consumer magazine sector, is considered to have real strength and longevity in comparison to other physical media products such as books, CDs or computer games. These have made the leap into digital more quickly than have publishers. Magazines, especially consumer lifestyle titles, are more difficult to unbundle and then repackage digitally than many other media. Yet digital products across all M&E sectors have a lower perceived value among end-users than the old legacy media.

The subscription culture is strong in traditional magazine publishing and its mechanisms are powerful tools which should not be jettisoned, but subscription thinking can limit the revenue potential of end-users, where 'super-users' can remain hidden behind a flat-rate subscription.

Is there still a need for publishers per se? Brand owners are creating their own communities and can buy in the skills to 'publish' in their own right, often with the help of customer publishers or content marketers. End-users can self–publish, blog and create their own websites; they can access and package their own information, very often for free, through the internet. Complete publisher unbundling poses an existential threat to the whole business.

Finally, ensuring that their skills continue to translate into a tangible, value-adding role is the single biggest challenge of the publishers' journey into digital.

> Having customers with long-term user relationships in the form of subscriptions is a massive strength

THE PUBLISHING COMPANY'S JOURNEY INTO DIGITAL

> We are moving from known, stable, print-based business models to an uncertain and unpredictable frontier. Despite the PR bravado of many publishers and suppliers, it could all end up being an absolute disaster.
>
> (Consumer magazine publisher)

The PPA's 'Business Models for a Digital World' project divides the publisher's digital journey into three distinct phases: legacy, bolt-on and rebuild.

The legacy phase

This is where the publishing operation was still based on legacy print products – most companies have long since left this phase behind. The company vision was clear and simple. The business model was stable and structured, based on core print products with satellite activities (for example live events, directories, books) revolving around this core.

The bolt-on phase

Here, digital has become a disruptive force, cutting across every activity and process, creating a business model which is an unstable collection of bolt-on activities. Print still dominates, but digital products have been dropped into a whirlpool with the potential for each activity to cross over and cannibalise another one. Severe cost-cutting runs in parallel with frantic development.

The rebuild phase

... digital is now seen as an enabling tool rather than a problem ...

In this phase, digital is now seen as an enabling tool rather than a problem: it is being used to achieve definite business aims in a company strategy which is clear, but complex and changing fast with business models which are constantly flexing. The core publishing products are digital with a growing range of multi-channel satellite services (of which print products are just one). Clear 'digital first' editorial – content which is created for digital platforms is a priority. Instead of content being 'publisher-driven', albeit shaped by customer insight, content is now 'user-driven', shaped from the bottom up by users.

Many consumer magazine publishers are still in the bolt-on phase. For a number of reasons, the B2B publishing sector is deeper into rebuild.

THE SCALE OF DIGITAL

> Digital is much more profitable than print. It is also much quicker and easier to engage with readers. We're saving on print and distribution costs at the same time as developing new products in new markets.
>
> (B2B publisher)

The big breakthrough will come when the market settles down – common publisher products in common formats. That will both reduce our costs and improve the customer experience. In the meantime, we're pouring money into an area which has still to prove that it can deliver any kind of long-term profit. Digital revenues are there, but they are simply not growing fast enough to balance the losses we are seeing in print.

(Consumer magazine publisher)

As Chapter 3 demonstrates, the publishing business model is in the middle of massive change with individual companies managing that change with varying degrees of success.

The Publishing Futures 2013 report provides a detailed analysis of the shape of the industry where print is still a central, though declining, part of most publishers' operations, accounting for 84 per cent of total consumer magazine revenues and 41 per cent of B2B revenues. By contrast, digital activities currently account for only 9 per cent of consumer magazine turnover. This forecast predicts a rise to 16 per cent in two years' time with digital B2B turnover forecasted to rise from 40 to 48 per cent in the same time span.

The B2B revenue map

Figure 8.1 charts two key factors for the B2B sector; each dot represents an individual publishing company. The horizontal axis shows the percentage of total revenues coming from print products: the industry average is 41 per cent. The vertical axis shows the percentage of total revenues coming from digital products and services: the industry average is 40 per cent.

In the top left quadrant are companies with very high digital revenues and very low print revenues. These are called pure play companies. For example, one is an online recruitment operation with 100 per cent of the company's sales coming from recruitment advertising. Another pure play digital publisher in the same space on the map has a very different business model – it is a research company which derives 100 per cent of its sales from content subscriptions. Most of the other companies in this quadrant have a mix of both advertising and content revenues, but each one has a distinct revenue model.

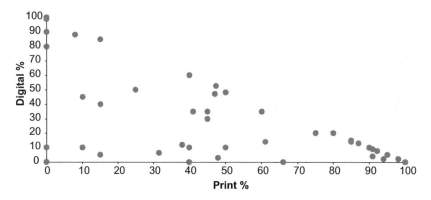

Figure 8.1 The B2B revenue map

Source: Publishing Futures 2013

> The big breakthrough will come when the market settles down – common publisher products in common formats

In the bottom right quadrant are traditional print publishers, some with no digital revenues at all, which makes them look very exposed. In the bottom left hand quadrant are companies with low percentages from both digital and print – they derive the bulk of their revenues from other non-publishing sources, most typically live events and conferences. In the middle of the map are companies many of which are more traditionally structured, but are in the process of a migration process away from print and into digital.

Eighty-five per cent of the companies surveyed have some kind of print presence. Even though their dependence on print may be reducing, it often remains an important element of the overall brand's presence in the market, giving weight and substance to online activities, beyond simple revenue.

The business model of each company is different and most are in the process of change. The balance between content and advertising revenue is another key dimension of this flexing business model.

Generally, in B2B, the more digital a publisher is, the larger, the faster growing and the more profitable the company tends to be. Being heavily digital does not automatically guarantee financial success, but this process of change often requires major re-engineering which should result in a more agile and efficient business.

The consumer magazine revenue map

This map (Figure 8.2) undertakes the same analysis for consumer magazines where the business model is much more print-biased than B2B (84 per cent of total revenues) and much less digitally-focussed (9 per cent).

In B2B there is a clear correlation between being highly digital and having faster growth and profitability. There is simply not the same linkage (yet) in consumer, which appears to be much more in the middle of the migration from print to digital, with trends and ratios that have still to settle down into consistent patterns.

In addition, consumer magazines have much less non-publishing, brand-extension activity than B2B (live events, reader services, data services) although this is growing. This accounts for the large area of empty space on the left of the map in contrast to the B2B chart.

Figure 8.2
The consumer
revenue map

Source: Publishing
Futures 2013

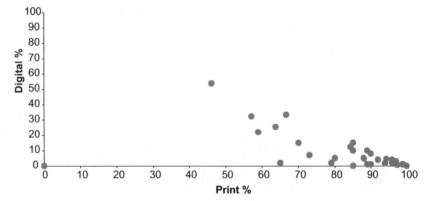

Behind these figures, there is much less variation in the business models of consumer publishers than is the case in B2B. In that sense, it is a more coherent and homogenous sector then B2B.

THE SHAPE OF DIGITAL

A few years ago, we used to have a 'digital department'. It was a separate area; a specialist hot house where people had big thoughts about our digital future. Now digital cannot be put into a box. Digital is just a way of thinking, a way of managing processes that runs through everything that we do.

(B2B publisher)

The next section gives more shape to digital by looking at the three key dimensions of activity, medium and device.

DIGITAL ACTIVITY

Look at any publishing operation and digital activity falls into five key areas:

- content delivery
- promotions and customer acquisition
- customer communications and insight
- ecommerce
- internal processes.

Content delivery

This is the most obvious and high profile area as the publishing business moves from physical, printed products to a range of digital products and services. This is examined in more detail later in the chapter under 'Digital medium'.

Promotions and customer acquisition

As Chapter 6 demonstrates, two of the most common ways of building a customer base in legacy publishing are either to send direct mail to lists of prospects and/or to use the printed magazine to draw secondary, pass-on readers into a deeper, primary relationship. Digital has added many more contact points which either replicate legacy techniques (for example replacing printed direct mail with email) or offer completely new routes (for example converting website visitors into paying customers or drawing users in from social media such as Facebook and LinkedIn).

Digital has also given a new lease of life to legacy acquisition techniques such as the phone and direct mail. Digital name generation activities can cheaply produce lists of prospects who can be contacted to convert into paying customers. As they are highly qualified leads, they can be reached via more traditional and more expensive (but still very powerful) channels.

Therefore, electronic methods can make the cost-per-acquisition of phone and direct mail much more attractive.

> Digital has also given a new lease of life to legacy acquisition techniques such as the phone and direct mail

Customer communications and insight

Being able to communicate regularly with customers through the website, emails, and social networks can build deeper relationships with customers. This activity also generates a flow of transactional data (website traffic) which can provide a mass of detail as to how end-users are behaving and are relating to the publisher's products and services.

Ecommerce

The ability to go beyond the provision of content into additional paid-for transactions and services is a major potential revenue opportunity for both consumer and B2B publishers.

Case study 13

Time Out: from content to ecommerce

A weekly print magazine was the core product of the *Time Out* cultural listings operation, which originally catered for just the London market. A series of books and guides were then launched around the magazine. International expansion started in 1995 with the launch of *Time Out New York*. Now, the *Time Out* brand is present in 37 cities around the world, through a mix of wholly-owned and licensed operations, each one with its own distinctive business model which is based on a range of products and services.

The core offering is expanding and is applied differently in different cities, driven partly by the local consumer conditions, but also by the operational background of the local licensees – some are traditional print publishers, producing print magazines, books and guides, while others are pure-play digital operators. In Tokyo, *Time Out* has just an online presence. In Paris, there is a full magazine product, but it is in digital edition format only rather than a print title.

Some of the more recent developments include apps. *Time Out London* partnered with Nokia to embed the magazine's venue information into Nokia Maps. The range of apps now extends across several mobile devices.

Yet potentially its most far-reaching development is into ecommerce, with *Time Out* acquiring and launching ticketing and booking operations. Here, having helped the consumer plan their evening through their content services, the actual event and restaurant bookings can be made through an online *Time Out* service. This can then be followed up to generate post-event consumer feedback which channels back into the content service. The ultimate aim is to engage with the audience on every step of their 'cultural journey'.

Behind all this varied activity in 37 cities, the core London weekly print product has undergone a major change in its business model by going free in London in September 2012. This radical shift is discussed in detail in Chapter two.

Internal processes

Digital processes now touch every department of a business. This ranges from the electronic trading of advertising space through to the creation of editorial product which can be repurposed for different platforms and the storage and usage of customer contacts and prospects.

Digital processes now touch every department of a business

DIGITAL MEDIUM

The four main media for the delivery of digital content are:

- websites
- emails and e-newsletters
- digital magazines
- social media.

We will examine each in turn.

Websites

Virtually every magazine, consumer or B2B, has a website. Yet the role and importance of the site varies significantly from brand to brand and from company to company.

Sources of revenue

Both B2B and consumer magazines have a broadly similar (and low) dependence on content revenues for their websites. This is shown in Table 8.1. For consumer, 15 per cent of total website revenues are from content and for B2B the figure is 18 per cent. B2B is more advertising and sponsorship driven (69 per cent of total website revenues) than consumer (50 per cent). Yet for both sectors, advertising support is critical, even though attempts are being made to develop payment for purchase of editorial. Ecommerce is more important to consumer (31 per cent) than B2B (12 per cent), but is growing for both.

Table 8.1 Website revenue split

Revenue Stream	Consumer	B2B
Content	15%	18%
Advertising	44%	57%
Sponsored content	6%	12%
Ecommerce	31%	12%
Other	4%	1%
TOTAL	100%	100%

Source: Wessenden (2013)

Charging for content

B2B publishers are more likely to charge for online editorial content (13 per cent of publishers currently charging) than consumer (9 per cent). Yet there is a wave of consumer publishers (33 per cent) who are not charging now, but who intend to in the future. There is considerable indecision in both sectors as 28 per cent of consumer and 24 per cent of B2B publishers do not know whether to charge or not. Where publishers are already charging, all are increasing the amount of paid-for content on their sites, with an annual subscription being the most common charging mechanism (used by all charging publishers), followed by pay-as-you-go based on volume of information accessed (25 per cent). Time-based passes and other subscription frequencies are not at all widespread.

Profitability

A minority of websites are profitable: 41 per cent of consumer and 32 per cent of B2B. Overall, B2B loses less money than consumer, but a significant 13–14 per cent of all publishers do not know or track their sites' profitability at all.

A minority of
websites are
profitable

Case study 14

Autosport: moving the paywall

While paid-for areas on websites have long been a feature of the B2B market, both national newspapers and consumer magazines are now looking more closely at protecting and monetising the content on their own websites, rather than give open and free access. The 2013 PPA Publishing Futures survey shows that only nine per cent of consumer publishers make any charges for online editorial content, but another 33 per cent are intending to charge in the future. *Autosport* is one consumer title which has made that leap.

Since its launch, the *Autosport.com* website has flipped backwards and forwards between free access and complete gating, dependent on the business model at the time. It became clear, however, that the advertisement funded model of free content was not financially sustainable. In 2006, the site moved to a mixed basis – most of the site was free to access (news stories, race reports and basic results) driving a monthly audience of 2.5 million unique users. A paid content area, *Autosport+*, was available to users who subscribed to the website or paid via micropayment for individual articles or features. However, the number of paying subscribers, though growing, was not enough to offset the ongoing decline in digital advertising – something more radical needed to be done.

In 2012, *Autosport* started to limit free access: 30 stories per month were made available free of charge; after that amount, access was stopped until the user subscribed or waited for their free allowance to start again in the next month. Only one per cent of the total audience has converted into paying subscribers, but that is enough to generate significant revenues. These digital subscribers are loyal readers and 15 per cent of them have upgraded to a bigger subscription which includes a PDF digital edition of the print magazine. Existing print subscribers gain free access to the site. Website subscribers have two options: £5.50 per month via direct debit (two thirds of subscribers opting for this) or £46 per year (one third). *Autosport* has also been experimenting with pay-as-you-go micropayments (89p per story) but without much success.

The experience to date is that the pricing of the digital subscription is less elastic than in print. Discounting the digital price does not drive a significant increase in volume; raising the price has not slowed the growth. The conclusion is that users are either in or out: they like the idea of digital access per se or they do not – the actual price itself is secondary. This might also explain the low take up of pay-as-you-go micropayments.

Some of the *Autosport* learnings and conclusions include:

- Paid content does not have to be complicated or high-tech (the site has no video, for example), but it has to be high quality, relevant and quickly updated. What can users get for free elsewhere and why should they pay for this? What is right for the audience?
- Trial and error is part of the process. There is no simple business model that applies to every market and to every magazine brand.
- The majority of the audience will never pay. Yet making the most of those committed and loyal 'super-users' who do pay is essential.

Writing for *InPublishing* magazine Rob Aherne, Group Publisher for Haymarket Media Group states:

> The revenues we derive from paid content are the difference between the site being profitable in its own right and being dependent on the magazine business. Without those revenues, digital development would be limited and we would probably face further difficult decisions over journalistic resourcing too. Basically, without the ability to make money direct from our digital users, our site's future would look pretty challenging. As it is, it looks altogether more appealing.[1]

Emails and electronic newsletters

There has been a big increase in publisher email and electronic newsletter activity. The applications range from delivering content which is increasingly tailored to specific segments of end-users, through to more straightforward customer contacts, in areas such as subscription renewal series and customer service notifications.

Digital magazines

There are four key types of 'digital magazine' activity and they have a hierarchy of development.

PDF replica of a print magazine

As discussed in Chapter 2 – despite being technically limited, all the research shows that a simple page-turner is sufficient for the needs of many readers. These include more cautious digital users who like the comfort of having an electronic product that is very similar to the print parent. It has the advantage to the publisher of being relatively low cost and low risk.

Enhanced replica

This is an enhanced PDF of a print magazine with links, video, web and feeds. This is the logical next step in a publisher's development, but a stage that a number of publishers are jumping over in order to create even more sophisticated products.

Fully interactive bespoke

These are either digital editions of a printed magazine or stand-alone digital publications. Although these are generally bottom-up rebuilds of a magazine, most are still based on the concept of a closed issue with a wide range of editorial content.

Fully interactive, branded application

These deliver content or data other than that offered in digital or print editions. This is very much in the smartphone area, where the screen size, mobility and functionality of the device simultaneously limit the volume of content to be delivered, while opening up more interactive applications. There are two main approaches: 'chunking' where content is carved up into smaller themed pieces rather than delivering a full issue and 'tasking' where the smartphone is a tool to do something related to the editorial of the core magazine brand (for example sourcing products and services and buying them).

Digital magazine charging policy

There are very different approaches to charging between consumer and B2B publishers. Over 80 per cent of consumer publishers, but only 21 per cent of B2B publishers are charging for their digital magazines.

For consumer, the most popular charging route (70 per cent) is as a stand-alone digital product – largely as a result of the introduction of Apple Newsstand. Only 11 per cent are charging as part of a 'premium priced print plus digital' bundle. Eight per cent are giving digital editions away free to print subscribers, although this is coming to be regarded as a transitional step before moving to a premium print plus digital bundle. By contrast, free digital access to print subscribers is the single most important approach (46 per cent) in B2B, followed by free, stand-alone or single copies (32 per cent).

Advertising and sponsorship in digital magazines

Almost 30 per cent of publishers do not sell advertising at all in their digital magazine products. Of the 70 per cent who do, the most common route in both consumer (41 per cent of publishers) and B2B (34 per cent) is special print plus digital packages. Yet a significant number in both consumer (27 per cent) and B2B (18 per cent) are still offering digital advertising as a free add-on to existing print advertisers.

Social media

Social media are cutting across every organisation with consumer publishers focussing more on Facebook, Pinterest and Google+ and with B2B skewed to LinkedIn. Twitter is widely used by over 90 per cent of all publishers. Yet the tangible return on investment (ROI) from all this activity remains a controversial question which polarises opinion as to the real benefits of having a social media presence.

The primary applications across all social media platforms are:

- building engagement with existing customers
- driving traffic to the branded publisher website.

Photo 8.1
Modern day media consumption is becoming increasingly platform neutral

The secondary applications include generating customer insight, marketing live events and selling subscriptions.

Tertiary applications, where publishers are clearly having more difficulty gaining any kind of traction, are selling other goods and services and generating advertising or sponsorship revenue.

DIGITAL DEVICE

Most publishers are active across a complete spectrum of devices and platforms at the same time, which is creating real resource issues for their businesses. These devices are:

- Desktop PCs, laptops and notebooks: these still have a core presence in most B2B markets where end-users are office-based, but most of the consumer publishers also have a presence here.
- Ereaders: there is a wider range of activity here than for any device with many local devices which have not gained a significant international presence, such as the Nook in the USA. The clear market leader in the UK is Amazon's Kindle.
- Tablets: this is clearly the core focus for the publishing business at the moment and is still dominated by Apple. Market positions are shifting rapidly however as Android tablets gain share at the expense of Apple. In particular Amazon's Kindle Fire is developing a significant presence and Windows 8 tablets are grabbing a foothold.
- Smartphones/mobile phones: this is on most publishers' 'to do' list even if they are not already active. It is an area which is clearly causing a lot of headaches as to how best to exploit their massive potential, both in terms of content delivery and monetisation. They may seem futuristic but Head Mounted Displays (HMDs) are on the horizon (such as Google Glass). They will all have their own content dynamics.

Each device has its own characteristics and functionality which shape the reading experience. The multiplicity of platforms on which content can be delivered is putting massive resource pressures and additional costs on to all publishing operations – especially those companies who consider themselves to be at the leading edge of delivery.

MONETISING DIGITAL

As we have seen throughout *Inside Magazine Publishing* a huge challenge for today's publishers – especially in the consumer markets – is how to make profits from new media platforms. This has been especially pressing as print media has been hit by recessionary times and profits from the 'old' media have been used to fund the 'new'. The key lies in how to price.

There are four key dimensions to any pricing model:

- commitment
- delivery format
- payment mechanism
- content access.

Commitment

As with a traditional print magazine there are essentially two ways of purchasing a digital product. First: ad hoc or single purchase options. In digital, these are driven by the digital newsstands and by the development of back issues, singles, and single topic or task apps. Ad hoc purchases are usually standalone, outside any subscription mechanism but can be bundled into a bigger membership package. Second is ongoing committed purchasing. This is typified by a traditional term subscription.

Delivery format

A digital magazine can be delivered as stand-alone or as part of a bundle. Pricing has to be considered in a strategic way, taking account of the prices for traditional print only titles. These are by their nature generalisations, but they set an overall structure within which a great deal of price testing is currently taking place.

Print only still remains the core channel in many markets in user perception if not in total volume sales. Print is the start point and the benchmark in the end-user's mind in terms of what a magazine subscription costs. Therefore, these subscription prices should be carefully maintained rather than heavily discounted. Some publishers are deliberately maintaining a print-only option in order to set that benchmark.

There has been a clear trend for digital-only prices to be very heavily discounted initially (sometimes to less than 50 per cent of print), moving to a softer discount (current ranges are 10–20 per cent below print). However, some publishers do operate parity between prices for the different platforms. This can be called 'channel neutral' positioning.

Initially, many publishers added digital services (website access and/or digital editions) as a free added-value element to the core print subscription. This was partly a 'toe in the water' approach to test user reaction to the new elements and their perception of their worth. Also, first generation digital offerings were generally not actually strong enough to have a clear value attached to them. The second stage is to charge a premium price for print plus digital, putting a real value on the digital elements. Prices currently out in the consumer magazine market show a premium of plus 5–25 per cent for a print plus digital bundle above a print only subscription. The third stage, already reached in a number of B2B markets, is a more subtle change in the user's psychology, where a print plus digital bundle flips over into a digital plus print bundle (where the digital service is seen to be the core and the print element is the added value). The pricing of the overall bundle usually does not change at that flip-point, but can do later in the migration.

A variant of these approaches is to drop the print only option completely as being outmoded and to have just two options – print plus digital or digital only – where both subscriptions are set at an identical price.

These observations capture publisher-direct pricing strategies. Where sales go through 'etailers' (for example Apple Newsstand, and Amazon's Kindle store) the 'etailer' has more influence on both the marketing and subscription term, where single issues and open-ended subscriptions paid monthly are standard options.

Payment mechanism

Having established the price, how do publishers get paid in this brave new world of digital sales?

Upfront subscription or continuous payment

The traditional pay-upfront mechanism with a fixed term (usually annual) remains a common charging mechanism. However, in a number of B2B markets, there is still an annually renewed relationship, but the annual charge has been broken down into regular (often monthly) payments. In consumer markets, the growth of direct debit has made a more open-ended relationship much more common. Both Apple and Amazon base their ecommerce on continuous credit card authority (CCCA) which has made this a more common mechanism for magazines.

Pay-as-you-go (PAYG)

This is an interesting innovation within the publishing world. There are two core PAYG approaches.

First, PAYG based on volume of data used which is more widespread in B2B markets, where the content can be shaped into chunks which have a more clearly defined value.

Second, PAYG based on the amount of time spent (typically on a website) which, theoretically at least, is more applicable to consumer markets. There is much less publisher experience of this approach which tends to be used as a trial tool rather than a core, ongoing payment mechanism.

There is a hybrid content offer based on a core, entry-level subscription topped up with PAYG for heavy users. This is a safe midpoint for both publisher and user.

Content access

The models for content access are three core options and a hybrid.

First: fixed access, where the content package that the user is buying into is very clearly defined, typically by a set number of issues or a term.

Second: unlimited access, where the purchase price opens up the complete content offer to be used as much (or as little) as the user determines. In a term borrowed from the late night oriental buffet it is often referred to as 'all you can eat' and is currently being used by a number of digital newsstands.

Third is metered access, where the individual user's actual usage, tracked by either volume or time, is monitored and charged accordingly. A hybrid of these options allows for a core entry-level package which is supplemented with metered add-ons.

These dimensions work together to form the basis for a pricing architecture which can be flexed for individual groups of users and for individual channels. In B2B markets, the growth of site licences has cut across and confused these broad approaches, as each major client's content package is individually tailored and priced. A site licence allows for a company to buy access to a B2B magazine or database for all relevant employees. It is a mechanism also popular with educational establishments. Whatever the approach taken, the aim of all publishers is to maintain an ongoing relationship through what may become a series of flexible purchasing occasions.

DIGITAL NEWSSTANDS: MAKING DISCOVERABILITY BETTER

A major challenge for consumer magazine publishers in selling digital editions is 'discoverability' – being able to grab the attention of the consumer in an increasingly competitive and noisy online world. Digital newsstands are a growing part of that profile-raising activity.

Apple Newsstand: the early mover

As Andrew Scott highlights in Chapter 2, the October 2011 launch of Apple's Newsstand gave the whole digital edition arena a massive boost, not least in giving publishers the confidence to charge for digital content. Yet it also brought tablet editions to a much wider audience, through Apple's integrated marketing approach of linking their hardware device sales to paid for content. This wider audience is a multinational one – 55 per cent of most UK publishers' Apple Newsstand sales are from outside the UK. It is also largely new – where publishers are able to match Newsstand buyers against their own databases, the duplication rate is very low – usually under 10 per cent.

> ... the launch of Apple's Newsstand gave the whole digital edition arena a massive boost

One common practice to date has been to allow consumers to download a shell app for free, then to offer a first, full issue free of charge before attempting the conversion to a paid sale. Publishers report that the percentage of initial free shell app downloaders who request a free issue is around 90 per cent. The conversion rate of these free triallists into paying customers ranges from a small 0.5 per cent to a very healthy 10 per cent with the centre of gravity falling at around three per cent. In terms of subscriptions versus single copies, this balance varies massively from title to title, but looks to be averaging at around 75:25 for single issue sales versus ongoing subscriptions. The standard subscription terms being offered are from three months to a year with an open-ended, monthly automatic credit card payment being a core payment mechanism.

There are a number of drawbacks in dealing with Apple, which include their significant commission, limited data about the customer and a lack of flexibility in pricing and in offering print plus digital bundles. Some consider that their early-mover presence has given Apple a worryingly high market share of consumer magazine digital editions; yet as Android devices and digital editions grow in volume, this will lessen. In addition, other digital newsstand players are becoming more creative.

Next Issue Media (NIM): publishers cooperating with each other

Next Issue Media is an ereading venture set up two years ago by five of the USA's top publishers to counter the power of Apple Newsstand. Yet it is only in recent months that it has been building up its range of titles, which now numbers over 80, based on an 'all you can eat' subscription package.

The NIM app works on iPad, Android and Windows 8 tablets with Apple and Android smartphone editions to be launched later in 2013.

The NIM website offers digital editions with a number of options:

- single issues of specific magazines
- ongoing subscriptions to specific magazines
- two unlimited 'all you can eat' plans across catalogue: the basic package can be upgraded to premium which includes an additional range of weekly titles
- free access to digital editions for existing print subscribers as part of their print subscription. However, in some cases, a small additional charge is made, usually 99 US cents per issue.

Previews and sample issues can be viewed before buying. There is an introductory 30 day free trial period for new customers.

At the time of writing, NIM has developed a user base of 120,000. Of those, 70,000 are existing magazine subscribers who are accessing the digital editions as part of their print subscriptions. The remaining 50,000 represent new customers, the bulk of whom are opting for the 'all-you-can-eat' packages. Of these, about 40 per cent have signed up for the basic package, the remainder opting for the premium offer. Single copy purchases are minimal.

Some key facts so far:

- Eighty-four per cent of users are completely new to the titles they are reading through NIM.
- Users are highly engaged with the magazines' content – basic users spend an average of 70 minutes a week with the app, while premium members spend 90 minutes per week.
- Typically, the package subscribers are reading a range of between 11 and 14 titles.
- Users are affluent, highly educated, with an average age of over 30 years.

NIM is founded on three main consumer benefits. First, most of the magazines on offer are enhanced digital editions. These are not simply page-turners or PDF replicas, but are custom designed for tablets and include added value benefits such as videos, bonus photos and interactive features.

Second, NIM offers a consistent reading experience. Magazines can be browsed, managed and read from a single app rather than through a range of title specific apps. An entire magazine can be flicked through using an animated carousel. A subscriber's entire library can be accessed from the cloud and then that customer can decide which issues to download for offline reading.

Third, the service offers smart downloading. When connected there is no need to wait to download the whole magazine before starting to read. Automatic downloading can be set up to take place when the device comes into internet connection. Also the service offers multi-device viewing with each subscription being authenticated on up to five devices.

NIM needs to mount an awareness campaign to drive up traffic and sales as well as increase its range of magazines and include more specialist interest titles. The site would benefit from the development of social features to allow more flexible content-sharing and recommendations.

A user base of 120,000 is solid, but not explosive growth. NIM claims that it will have a sustainable business when user numbers hit 250,000. The company's aim is one million users within 18 months, but this depends on the amount of marketing budget it puts behind growing awareness and increasing the discoverability of the site. NIM is an important strategic move, copied by publishers in a number of other countries. It tries to limit the power of Apple Newsstand, while at the same time learning how digital readers behave first-hand. The 'all you can eat' offer does not convince everyone, but it is an innovative idea. What many consumers seem to put high on their priority list is ease of purchase and consistent navigation across all magazine brands – these are important elements that NIM has on offer.

Zinio and PixelMags: more 'all you can eat'

'All you can eat', multi-title packages are very much in vogue and two leading digital edition suppliers are testing their own variants.

Zinio's Z-Pass allows users to mix and match three magazines from a subsection of Zinio's 5,500 titles (some premium titles are excluded from Z-Pass) for a flat monthly fee in the US of $5. Zinio will recommend titles based on customers' interests or users can make their own choices from the Zinio library.

Z-Pass, which includes a 30-day free trial, is part of Zinio's strategy to improve the digital reading experience, by making it easier for customers to find relevant content, based on what individual users have already been reading and looking at and to increase the discoverability dimension of the digital experience.

Other new enhancements include an 'explore' section, where users can access individual articles free of charge. At the end of the article, the option to buy a single issue or a subscription is offered. The data about which articles have been read also goes into the Zinio database to target specific subscription offers.

Zinio is also helping publishers integrate ecommerce into their digital editions, through a partnership with ShopAdvisor. Readers can purchase products or track prices from editorial and ad pages.

PixelMags' Readr app for the iPhone and iPad has as a key feature 20 minutes of free reading time per month, with unlimited access to the wider range of 680 titles for a flat fee. After both Apple and PixelMags have each taken their share of the subscription price, the remainder is allocated to publishers based on the time spent with each title, which PixelMags tracks.

Broad-based digital newsstands are both a valid route to market in their own right and a useful test bed, where publishers can experiment with issues such as pricing and bundling in a relatively low risk environment.

Google Play

Google has made a cautious move into digital magazine sales by recently introducing a limited range of digital editions to its Google Play entertainment area which already delivers music, film, books and games. The current strategy is to learn more about how the dynamics of the magazine market work before making a full range offer, yet it believes that the market must settle down to have a dominant, more open technological platform (possibly HTML5) before the sector really takes off. At this point Google will doubtless make a more committed move to increase share of digital magazine sales.

THE IMPACT OF DIGITAL ON THE ORGANISATION

Going 'digital first' all sounded very logical when we first discussed it, but it had a far greater impact on our company than we had ever anticipated. Going digital is not just about packaging content in new ways. It is not just about technology. It also makes you change job roles and how you structure departments; it puts new demands on the skills and knowledge that you have within the business; and how do you fill those gaps when you need new skills? Retrain or recruit new people?

(B2B publisher)

Photo 8.2
Brothers reading from a digital tablet – is this the future?

As our journey through the world of magazine publishing with *Inside Magazine Publishing* comes to an end it is proper to conclude by discussing people and structure. Magazines after all are people businesses. The main organisational issues involved in the journey into digital are:

- leading the business
- structuring the organisation
- new skills and changing roles
- changing demands on Information Technology and Customer Services (IT and CS).

Leading the business

The best senior managers are leading their organisations through rapid change with a well-articulated vision. Yet, as Tim Brooks points out in Chapter 3, it is clear that many who have been trained in more traditional publishing disciplines are feeling out of their depth. Being able to combine business acumen and managerial skills with technological knowledge is very demanding.

This also manifests itself in how a company's strategy is created. A traditional company plan used to be the product of a centralised, top-down process: senior management would lay out company goals, often formed around clear financial targets set over a relatively long period. A digital strategy is much more collaborative and iterative, with key priorities being set from the top, but with much more of the detailed implementation coming from the bottom up. This results in a more dynamic and malleable view which is constantly being flexed and refined as the external environment shifts.

Another major change is more attitudinal than structural and that is how failure is viewed. Traditionally, 'failure' was something to be avoided at all costs and to be punished. In the modern trial-and-error environment of constant testing and experimentation, failure is accepted as inevitable. It should be limited financially and used as a learning process to prompt fast reaction and change. Being able to 'fail cheaply' is the practical mantra of many senior managers in changing organisations.

Structuring the organisation

The traditional organisation structure was built around a series of departmental 'silos' (editorial, advertising, circulation, marketing and research). The digital world blurs many of the divisions both inside and between departments. The newer organisations are much more open, flat and agile. They focus more on brands, yet behind each brand there is a much more flexible, project-based approach. This often combines cross discipline teams to achieve specific goals rather than have a department that rigidly focusses on a series of repeated and unchanging processes. Some call this the matrix and this structure places much more stress on collaborative working and knowledge sharing – two things that are difficult to achieve in practice. In Chapter 4, Richard Sharpe discusses this from the point of view of an editor.

The best senior managers are leading their organisations through rapid change with a well-articulated vision

... key priorities being set from the top, but with much more of the detailed implementation coming from the bottom up

New skills and changing roles

Editorial has been at the leading edge of digital change. Again this is discussed at some length in Chapter 4. Whereas it was common for different editorial staff to write different copy for print and web products, the modern journalist must be able to write for a number of distinct channels: from long-form features through to quick tweets, as well as be comfortable creating video output and audio downloads. In addition, as digital creates more of a two-way conversation between publisher and reader, new skills such as data analysis and research are becoming part of the 'tool box' of the modern journalist. One B2B company calls its journalists 'data scientists'.

Similarly, circulation executives (the newer term is 'audience managers') need to be able to combine retail and subscriptions, print and digital into an overarching channel management approach. In the past, each channel team would work in their own silo, driven by their own targets and budgets, which could sometimes conflict with each other. The new approach is much more holistic and flexible.

The need for 'digital skills' is often quoted by publishing management in advertisements but the phrase covers a number of distinct areas: knowledge of emerging technologies, creative, marketing, commercial and analytical. One of the most sought after – and most difficult to fill – skills is data analysis: being able to sift through the masses of data created by digital media to come to practical and commercial conclusions.

Behind the whole context of changing roles and skills lies a major question. Should a company retrain and upskill its existing team or bring in new staff who have the required skills, but not always the knowledge and experience of the industry? There are practical, ethical and financial issues behind this question. It gives rise to issues which every company has to address and to which they are finding different answers.

New demands on IT and CS

While all areas of the organisation are coming under pressure, there are unique demands being made of Information Technology and Customer Services. Keeping up with technological change means understanding the delivery of content, maintaining ongoing communication with existing customers, flexing new payment mechanisms and building a single view of the end customer: these are all major challenges for IT. Customer service has changed from being just a cost centre to becoming a key element of the customer experience which needs to be invested in, as Amazon in particular has done.

In conclusion I have also identified seven points for managers to consider when a business is in transition from print to digital.

1. Establish appropriate metrics to measure the performance of this different kind of organisation. These are likely to be more focussed on sales and satisfaction levels than finance.

2. Outsource functions and partner with third parties in order to keep moving quickly, especially outside the normal skill sets of the organisation. Take care and do due diligence on whom you get into bed with.

3. There is a subtle shift in attitudes and budgets from acquisition to retention – try to hold on to existing customers for longer rather than focussing too much on constantly gaining new customers at the front end.

4. Retain some of the old skills which are in danger of being lost in the dash for new digital skills. These include commercial nous, face-to-face negotiating skills and direct marketing disciplines.

5. Develop platforms to share knowledge within the organisation. These can range from an intranet, lunchtime briefings (offer free food) or a free drinks hour in the pub after work. They are incredibly valuable experiences.

6. Invest in training, including graduate recruitment. For all the talk about upskilling and developing the potential of staff, just how serious are most publishers about really investing in people?

7. Keep life as simple as possible. There is a massive temptation to overcomplicate matters in the pursuit of perfection. This can manifest itself in over-ambitious goals, over-rapid implementation timescales, too many projects running at the same time and a final vision that is so complex and expensive that it will never deliver the required return on investment. Keep two penetrating questions in mind at all times:
    –   Do we really need to know this?
    –   What is the financial return on doing this?

In the very first chapter of this book, Christine Stam identified the start of the magazine publishing business to be 1693: over three hundred years ago. From this very early form, magazines have evolved into powerful communication tools which have affected billions of lives worldwide. New media is barely 20 years old in its website manifestations – much less in its more publisher-friendly digital edition form. Hopefully this book has given some clear indications of the speed and path of future progress for this vibrant and exciting industry.

NOTE

1. Aherne (2013).

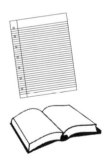

REFERENCE SOURCES

Aherne, R. (2013) 'The Autosport paywall journey', *InPublishing*, 57, March/April 2013, p 9.

Wessenden (2012) *Business Models for a Digital World: PPA*. Godalming: Wessenden.

Wessenden (2013) *PPA Publishing Futures 2013 Report*. Godalming: Wessenden.

Making print and paper buying choices

Publishers rightly attach huge importance to the look and feel of their printed magazines. Brand values and the editorial vision are enhanced by the selection of paper of the appropriate quality, printed in a suitable format (size), utilising the correct print technology. Advertisers' aspirations and requirements must also be respected. Two key questions have to be considered and traded off: How much print quality do we *need*? How much quality can we *afford*?

Printing

There are four print processes that students need to understand:

- gravure printing, known as rotogravure or photogravure
- web offset litho printing
- sheet-fed offset litho printing
- digital printing.

The selection of the correct form of printing is a key decision for the publisher and will largely be based around the size of print run, format of the magazine and quality required for the target market. The wrong choice of process can lead to increased costs, greater complexity and paper wastage.

Gravure

The method has its origins in the 'intaglio' process whereby an image is engraved onto an image carrier. The carriers are metal cylinders (hence rotogravure) there being one cylinder each for the four base print colours – cyan, yellow, magenta and black. In simple terms, the image of the material to be printed is etched onto metal cylinders which have been coated in light-sensitive copper. They are then inserted into the press and the etched surface area picks up ink – the image is subsequently transferred to paper passing at speed through the press.

The benefits of gravure are: fast print run speeds with a high and consistent quality for long print runs, which offers a low unit cost per magazine. Costs can be further saved by using uncoated paper. Print sizes tend to be more flexible than with web offset. A downside is the high start-up cost. Overall circulation decline in the UK market means that only a small number of high volume titles use gravure.

Photo A.1
A specialist works on the depth of cell of a gravure cylinder

Photo A.2 A roll of sections wound ready for binding

Web offset litho printing

The majority of titles seen on UK newsstands will be printed by web offset litho. The process borrows its name from lithography – the transfer of images to a metal plate via a photographic method. Based upon the principle that ink repels water, ink is retained by the image held on the plate whilst the remainder is cleaned by water. The inked image then transfers to a rubber blanket and in turn to paper. There are four colour plates; the colours the same as with gravure. With web offset, paper is fed through the press at high speed from huge reels – hence the expression web – with seamless paper splicing between reels.

For magazine printing, the printed page is most likely to be dried or set as the pages pass through ovens – hence the expression 'heat set' will be used. As the printed product emerges from web offset litho presses it is automatically folded into sections ready for magazine binding. A heat set process allows publishers to select coated papers. If uncoated stock is used, the ink is not dried by heaters but oxidises and is absorbed by the paper itself. This is referred to as 'cold set' – as used for newspapers.

For magazines with print runs between 25,000 and 200,000, web offset is normally the process of choice. The use of plates instead of metal cylinders allows for faster and cheaper start up time (make ready) and also greater flexibility for regional split printing. The downside is that plates do have to be replaced during high volume printing, causing delay and possible quality inconsistency.

Sheet-fed litho printing

The principal difference between web and sheet-fed litho is that the paper in the sheet-fed process is fed into the press in large sheets. It is later folded and cut to make up the printed magazine. As such the method is better suited to small circulation titles and is more flexible in terms of page size and paper stock. With sheet-fed litho, heavier weights of papers can be used – it is also easier to vary different paper types in the same publication.

Digital printing

The advent of desk top publishing in the 1980s led to the increased development of electronic transfer of typed data. The need to produce hard copy for sharing information before the internet led to an increased focus on non traditional printing techniques. These are generally referred to as digital printing, a process suitable for very small print runs.

The leading technology is called ink jet printing, this process takes a data file and configures the information into electronic pulses that drop ink onto the paper in sequence. This enables short start ups, little waste and cost efficiency in an office environment.

Binding

Most readers will be oblivious of the method whereby a magazine is printed but they will be very conscious as to its appearance through binding. There are two methods of binding a title – perfect bound or saddle-stitched. Perfect bound magazines tend to be used to target up-market readers and advertisers, as they allow for a heavy or glossy cover. The end product is sealed or glued down the spine with no staples. Most perfect bound titles will be monthly, *Country Life* being an exception.

Most weeklies are saddle-stitched with the finished product folded and stapled over a 'saddle'. This is more suited to lower pagination titles.

With many weekly saddle-stitched publications, the cover stock is the same as that for the body of the magazine. This is called a self-cover title. Publishers of glossy monthlies, however, will require higher quality covers which are printed separately from the main magazine. This adds time to the process which the weeklies are unlikely to have in their schedules.

Advertising and subscription inserts will be added at the binding stage, normally by machine but an awkward sized insert may be fed by hand. Once through the bindery, the printed magazines will be packed into an appropriate bundle size for retail sale or delivered into the subscription fulfilment chain, as described in Chapter 6.

Selecting a printer

When selecting a printer the publisher needs to factor in and prioritise the following:

- quality of product and reputation of the printer
- a company which is investing in new machinery
- price
- scheduling and distance from distribution hubs.

The publisher–printer relationship is a key partnership to manage.

Publishing textbooks will doubtless make the printing of a title appear seamless. In reality a myriad of hitches can occur, most minor but some major. Editorial and advertisement pages can be late, inserts can be delivered from advertisers to the wrong size, even the most modern or best serviced presses can break down or occasionally there may be a reel of paper with a quality fault. Mishaps can and do happen. Both parties need to understand each other's *modus operandi*. It is important to select a printer who is open to reasonable requests from the publisher but be mindful of one who is just in the business of saying 'yes'.

Producing a good quality job, on schedule and at the right price are the three most important criteria. A relationship whereby a printer just agrees to requests for late pages or unusual inserts because they are frightened of offending the client (publisher) and consequently losing the job, is unlikely to be healthy in the medium to long term. Both sides of the relationship should set key performance indicators (KPIs) for regular monitoring; good feedback is essential.

Paper

Selection of the most appropriate weight and grade of paper is another key visible statement of the title's vision and editorial position. Weight is defined in grams per square metre (gsm). For magazines, this is likely to be between 50–80 gsm: the higher the grammage, the thicker or heavier the paper. Quality is also on the checklist of advertisers when assessing the suitability of a publication – what may be called the magazine's environment.

There is a plethora of paper choice for the magazine publisher – who, of course, must be mindful of selecting the correct paper for the designated print process. These are the main categories available.

Machine finished paper

In reality, very few magazines use newsprint – some, however, will use machine finished paper. This paper is light but does contain bulk and will be suitable for classified advertising type titles. Machine finished coated paper gives more bulk but with a smoother matt surface. There is good image intensity and reproduction, making it suitable for specialist titles featuring advertisements.

Supercalendered magazine paper

Supercalendered magazine paper is an uncoated grade, making it a very cost effective choice for publishers. One industry expert likened it to 'newsprint having been sanded'. It is a smooth paper making it suitable for the high running speeds of gravure.

Supercalendered is particularly suitable for mass circulation and full colour magazines. As such it is used for TV listing magazines and magazine supplements to newspapers. Detailed information can be printed onto a paper with good brightness using this paper choice.

Lightweight coated paper (LWC)

LWC is one of the most popular types of papers used by magazine publishers. It may also be called blade coated. The paper is coated on both sides giving it a high degree of smoothness and gloss – like supercalendered paper it is suitable for the printing of detailed information on a page.

The higher the weight – gsm – the brighter the paper. There are gloss and matt versions available. LWC paper is most often used in the web offset process and will be the paper of choice for many monthly titles. It provides a quality reading experience for both the consumer and the advertiser. Presses using LWC paper have the ability to generate fast running speeds.

Opacity and brightness

The two variables of opacity and brightness must be considered by buyers when selecting the right paper for the magazine. Opacity refers to the bulk of the paper. An image printed on one side of a sheet must not 'show through' to the other. These unwanted manifestations will infuriate advertisers, who may well demand a discount or free space to compensate. Brightness refers to the level of whiteness or reflected light by the paper – too little and it appears dull, too much and readers will struggle to read it, particularly under artificial light. Papers will be categorised by mills into grades such as bright or ultra bright.

Covers

Unless printing a self-cover, magazine covers are printed separately to the main text. They will often be printed on a wood free art paper and coated with uv varnish. This paper stock is very white and will lift brightness – the varnish giving a gloss effect to enable the title to stand out at retail.

Recycling

The basic elements of paper – wood and water – are of course natural. Therefore most publishers take environmental considerations very seriously when selecting paper grades. A very large percentage of paper used in European countries is recycled – some back into the paper making process. Good quality and non contaminated recycled paper holds a value – priced per tonne.

The Forest Stewardship Council (FSC) is an international non profit organisation formed with the objective of supporting the world's forests. It will issue a logo or kite mark to papers which meet principles and criteria of forest stewardship. Buyers will look for this when making supplier decisions.

Paper buying

Paper buying is one of the largest costs in a publisher's profit and loss account. It must be the responsibility of a manager who understands the mechanics of the market. Paper will come in different reel sizes and widths for printers – make a mistake and it can be very costly. Paper may be held in stock at the printers for a stipulated number of issues: 'just in time stock holding'. Buy too much and publisher's cash flow is tied up – too little and there may not be enough material in hand to allow for issue sizes or print run increases. Larger publishers will have a dedicated executive who will buy direct from the paper mills; smaller publishers should allocate a manager and give them time to learn market complexities. Printers may also buy paper on behalf of smaller publishers.

GLOSSARY

bindery area of the print site devoted to folding, stapling and packing the end product. Inserts will also be placed into the title at this stage

coating a finish, normally enamel china clay, applied to the surface of paper to improve opacity, brightness and running speed

cold set the image is set by oxidation as it dries into the paper

digital printing image printed directly from digital material; used for short-run work

distribution hub central warehouse where copies are sorted for onward delivery to wholesalers or retailers

FSC Forest Stewardship Council: international body supporting responsible environmental management of the world's forests

GSM grams per square metre. The way of measuring paper weight and consequently quality/bulk

gravure method of printing for high volume titles using four etched cylinders. Also known as photogravure or rotogravure

heat set method of drying printed pages using large dryers or ovens as an integral part of the press

insert material inserted into a magazine after printing. Normally advertisement related or subscription offers. Can be bound in by glue or stapled but normally loose

intaglio the process of etching an image into a surface

lightweight coated paper (LWC) very popular paper for web offset printing. Coated on both sides to produce gloss and allows high print run speeds

machine finished paper paper of bulk with a smoother finish than newsprint

make ready the time taken to prepare a press for good quality copy

mill factory where paper is made

opacity expression used to describe ability of paper to avoid 'show through'

running speed the speed the printed product is completed in the print process. Normally expressed as x000 copies per hour

sheet-fed offset litho as per web offset litho but paper is fed into the press in large sheets

show through the image of one side of printed paper shown through to the other side. Must be minimised to maintain advertisers' confidence

stock expression used to describe type and weight of paper

supercalendered paper smooth paper used for high run printing

UV varnish ultra-violet varnish. Applied to printed material to create a high gloss finish. Normally used for covers of up-market titles

web offset litho method of printing whereby an image is printed by transfer onto paper from a metal plate via a blanket. Paper is fed into the press from large reels

Legal issues for magazines: a brief summary

The magazine industry is surrounded by legal constraints, far more in the UK than in almost any other publishing market within a democracy. The key laws for England and Wales[1], both common and criminal, which surround the industry are:

- competitions: what is considered a real game of skill
- contract: the obligations of the publisher to readers and other parties
- copyright: defence of the publisher's own content and the use of the content of others
- trade marks: registered marks for products or services
- libel: the defamation of subjects they write about
- passing off: looking like the magazines of other publishers
- privacy: the private life of those written about
- confidentiality: information divulged in confidence.

The publisher as a company, the publisher as a person and the editor are liable to prosecution, either through common law or criminal law.

Competitions

Competitions are a favourite feature for magazines to entertain readers. Few magazine publishers have a licence to run a lottery: a game of chance for which the player has to pay to enter. So they must run competitions which have an element of skill in them. 'Send in this coupon and the first out of the hat wins a prize' is a lottery, a game of chance which the entrant has had to pay for by buying the magazine. That is illegal. 'Write the best caption to this picture and win a prize' involves a level of skill, and so is legal, even if the entrant has to use a prime phone line to enter. For publishers to be able to run a lottery without a licence, they would have to offer entry without buying the magazine in question and via a regular channel which was regarded as non-premium.

Contract

Contracts can be implicit and explicit. Larger magazine companies have legal departments which devise written contracts. The ones that often cause problems, however, are the implicit contracts. If the magazine says it will ship a prize to the winner of a competition by a certain date, it has entered into a contract with the entrants and needs to do that. If the magazine says it will provide a prize which is coming from a third party, such as a sponsor or another supplier, it still has to ship that prize even if the third party can no longer supply it.

Many celebrities have contracts, either written or verbal, with magazines about the use of the material they provide in interviews and as a result of photo sessions. They, or their agents, want to manage or restrict the use of their image and the content they provide and magazine publishers need to track these obligations so that they do not breach them. For example, a film star may want to restrict the content they give to certain countries where their film is about to be released but hold it back from others where release is not imminent. If the magazine has a syndication deal with publishers outside its country, they will need to monitor the use of its content.

Copyright

There are two aspects of copyright to which the magazine publisher, editor and art editor need to pay attention: the defence of their own material and the use of the copyright material of others.

Copyright is created as soon as the content is created: it does not have to be registered nor have to carry the copyright sign. Magazine publishers need to look out for others who may be using their material without permission. Even a small amount of material, taken systematically from a publication, can be an infringement of copyright. This covers all the content of the publication, in whatever form, on paper or digital. It is not the volume of content taken which makes the breach of copyright but whether it is the most important part.

The copyright in the content generated by people in employment is the property of the employer, automatically. Employees may not, under this law, create the same type of content in their free time as they do in their employment and sell it on to another party or use it themselves.

The copyright of the content generated by the freelance contributor, however, is theirs. It should only be used once, for the specific media and issue for which it was commissioned, unless there is an overriding contract which says otherwise. Magazine publishers who want to use the content they commission from freelancers on the many platforms which exist today, need to have solid contracts with freelancers, giving the rights to republication to the publisher. These contracts need not deny the freelancer from also using the material elsewhere, often with an embargo of, say, six months after it appears in the magazine for which it was commissioned.

Trademarks

Trademarks are registered marks on products or services which only the trademark holder can use. It is dangerous to speculate about what a product not yet revealed by a company will look like and to put the company's trade mark on it. It is therefore unwise to put trademarks on the goods of another company. It is dangerous to change the trademark or to use it as a generic term when it, in fact, only refers to the particular product or service of the vendor. For example, people do not rollerblade, they use in-line skates. People may use Portacabins as long as they are using that brand of portable cabins.

Libel

English and Welsh libel laws have been reformed with the Defamation Act 2013, effective from 1 January 2014. This Act strengthens defences and forces claimants to prove more of their case. Libel covers all publications of a magazine: its complete content on paper and in any digital form. The only part of the magazine it does not cover is the content of a real-time chat forum, which is covered by slander.

Libels start with the claimant. The claimant has to prove under the 2013 Act:

- The content was published.
- They were by some means identified.
- It defames them according to one of the cases covering defamation.
- If the claimant is a person that they were seriously damaged or are likely to be seriously damaged.
- If the claimant is a profit-making organisation that they were seriously financially damaged or are likely to be seriously financially damaged.
- It is the right jurisdiction in which to take this action.

The content has to be sufficiently published to be damaging. A web page seen by a few people will not be considered sufficiently published.

Libel also depends on what the meaning of the content actually is. This is often contended by both parties: one side saying it means one thing and the other denoting another meaning. It is up to the court to determine the meaning of the content, not the writer, editor or publisher. This is determined by the judge, as there is a presumption against having a jury.

The test of being identified by content is whether the claimant's friends, family and/or colleagues could associate it with the party as they consumed this content. It is not whether the writer or other editorial members meant to identify them. Art editors should be careful in selecting photographs which show people or companies' logos attached to a generic article, as that will create identification.

The fact that the claimant has to show that their reputation was seriously damaged means that the defence can now question the reputation of the claimant before the publication.

Defences may challenge the fact that the claimant is taking the action in English and Welsh courts. This is intended to stop libel tourism, where people do not have a significant reputation in the court's jurisdiction but take action there.

As well as this higher hurdle the claimant has to jump to establish their case, there are also more and stronger defences as a result of the Act.

These defences are:

- that the content is substantially true
- that the content is an honest comment
- that the content is in the public interest
- that the content was in a peer-reviewed journal
- that the content was a review.

The defendant needs to show that one of the meanings is substantially true, not all of them.

With statements of opinion, the defendant needs to show that the opinion in question was honestly held by the opinion holder, the columnist. The publisher or editor need not have the same opinion. If, however, they were aware that it was not the original writer's opinion, then they could be sued.

Editors should make sure that they make it clear to the ordinary reader when they are looking at an opinion and not at factual content. Editors should check the layout of all content to make sure that the ordinary reader knows they are looking at either facts, for example headed by the word 'news', or opinion, for example headed by the word 'comment'.

The idea of the public interest has been introduced in the Act. It may be shown that the content was not true, but the defence can show that the public needed to know, so that it could make up its own mind. Public interest does not mean that the public is interested, but that there is some important issue at stake.

Magazines can review products and services of vendors as long as they stick to reviewing the product or service and do not attack the vendor or the vendor's skills.

The 2013 Act introduces terms which the courts will have to define in case law, case by case. These include what is substantially true, what is in the public interest and what is a peer reviewed publication.

Magazine publishers circulate their content on paper and digitally in Northern Ireland and the Republic of Ireland. They need to be aware that the old English and Welsh unreformed libel laws still apply there and that Belfast and Dublin are likely to become the new centres of libel tourism.

Passing off

This law tries to prevent one publisher making their publication so alike another that the buyer will be confused. Publications chasing the market leader may try to make themselves look as like this title as they can, but they run the risk of a passing off action by the other publication. In particular publishers should pay attention to front cover design and logos. In 2001 there was an out of court settlement between IPC's *Web User* and *Computeractive* (VNU Business Publications), for similar reasoning. IPC agreed not to publish any computer magazine with a front cover title in two colours (black and white) and a sloping red masthead. In addition they agreed not to feature a cover panel entitled 'workshops'.[2]

Privacy

The substantive law of privacy was introduced in the UK with the 2000 Human Rights Act. This says that each individual has the right to respect for their private and family life, their home and their correspondence. Mentioning people's health problems, their sexual activities, their private emails etc breaches this right of privacy. People wishing to divulge details of their private lives should not divulge the details of the private lives of others: so 'kiss-and-tell' stories are in particular jeopardy.

Confidentiality

Some information is given or held in confidence. If a magazine journalist is told that this information is in confidence, not for publication, then the law of confidentiality says they should not publish it or tell it to another person. Only the person who gave the information can release them from this bond by telling the world themselves or by giving permission to divulge the information. This bond of confidentially applies even if the journalist finds out the same information from a third party.

NOTES

1. Northern Ireland and Scotland are different jurisdictions from England and Wales with their own courts and judges. English case law precedent in most areas is persuasive but not strictly binding. In areas such as copyright and passing off it will be highly persuasive and will almost always be followed, as it will in the Republic of Ireland. EU Directives also apply to NI and Scotland.
2. Hodgson, J. (2001) 'The Copycats', the *Guardian: Media Guardian,* 21 May 2001, p 10.

FURTHER READING

Hanna, M. and Dodd, M. (2012) *McNae's Essential Law for Journalists,* 21st Edition. Oxford: Oxford University Press.

Crook, T. (2013) *The UK Media Law Pocketbook.* Oxford: Routledge.

Further information resources

The editors and contributors wish to thank the following organisations for their help in researching material for *Inside Magazine Publishing*. Their websites are recommended to students.

Websites

Audit Bureau of Circulation
    www.abc.org.uk
Alan Weaver Associates
    www.aweaver.co.uk
Content Marketing Association
    www.the-cma.com
Dovetail Services
    www.dovetailservices.com
FIPP
    www.fipp.com
The *Guardian*
    www.guardian.co.uk/media
Guy Consterdine Associates
    www.consterdine.com
InPubWeekly
    www.inpublishing.co.uk
IPC Media
    www.ipcmedia.com
MagLab
    www.maglab.org.uk
National Readership Survey
    www.nrs.co.uk
Professional Publishers Association
    www.ppa.co.uk
Wessenden Marketing
    www.wessenden.com
Zenith Optimedia
    www.zenithoptimedia.co.uk

Magazines and newsletters

InPublishing
Retail Newsagent
Wessenden Briefing

Essential reading

Gough-Yates, A. (2003) *Understanding Women's Magazines: publishing, markets and readerships in late-twentieth century Britain.* Oxford: Routledge.
Johnson, S. and Prijatel, P. (2012) *The Magazine from Cover to Cover,* 3rd edition. Oxford: Oxford University Press.
McKay, J. (2013) *The Magazines Handbook.* Oxford: Routledge.
Morrish, J. (2011) *Magazine Editing in Print and Online.* Oxford: Routledge.
Whittaker, J. (2008) *Magazine Production.* Oxford: Routledge.

Additional books

(Also see Notes at end of each chapter for resources relevant to that topic.)

Adams, S. and Hicks, W. (2009) *Interviewing for Journalists,* 2nd edition. Oxford: Routledge.
Biressi, A. and Nunn, H. (eds) (2008) *The Tabloid Culture Reader.* Maidenhead: Open University Press.
Clark, G. and Phillips, A. (2008) *Inside Book Publishing,* 4th edition. Oxford: Routledge.
Crewe, B. (2003) *Representing Men: cultural production and producers in the men's magazine market.* Oxford: Berg.
Crowley, D. (2003) *Magazine Covers.* London: Mitchell Beazley.
Frost, C. (2011) *Designing for Newspapers and Magazines,* 2nd edition, Oxford: Routledge.
Hicks, W. and Holmes, T. (2002) *Subediting for Journalists.* Oxford: Routledge.
Hicks, W. et al. (2008) *Writing for Journalists,* 2nd edition. Oxford: Routledge.
Kaye, J. and Quinn, S. (2010) *Funding Journalism in the Digital Age: business models, strategies and trends.* New York: Peter Lang.
King, S. (2001) *Magazine Design that Works.* Gloucester, Mass.: Rockport.
Pringle, H. and Marshall, J. (2011) *How to Spend Advertising Money in the Digital Age: how to navigate the media flow.* London: Kogan Page.
Renard, D. (2006) *The Last Magazine.* New York: Universe Publishing.
Whittaker, J. (2002) *Web Production for Writers and Journalists,* 2nd edition. Oxford: Routledge.

Glossary

Please note that a dedicated glossary of printing and paper selection terms is at the end of Appendix 1 on page 253.

ABC Audit Bureau of Circulation. Membership-funded body which validates sales and distribution figures by audit. Key industry statistic and important in the sale of advertising space

ABC1 socio economic grouping which forms the basis of the main target for much magazine advertising. It describes a range of households from high earners (A) to those in junior management jobs (C1). Based on status of head of household

ASA Advertising Standards Authority. It regulates the advertising industry. Funded by industry levy, it enforces its code of practice by investigating complaints about the content of ads

above the line an advertising term to describe the use of all types of mass media – print, TV, radio, cinema, outdoor, digital. **Below the line** refers to a more personalised strategy like PR, direct mail, email or flyers

advertisements the actual commercial content which is read, heard, broadcast

advertising ad sales, ad agencies. The business of selling and buying ad space and the delivery of commercial creative content

art editor responsible for the design and visual look and feel of the publication. May be called art director in larger titles

BPA Worldwide US organisation which audits the business press (and some consumer magazines)

bookazines high pagination format with corresponding high cover price for sale in high street multiples, often as exclusives. It is not quite a book but more expensive than a magazine

Brad Insight part of EMAP, it provides information on the media industry

Brand extensions, branding exercises magazines which embody a particular set of values can begin to act as a brand and appear in different guises but still identifiably the same entity. A brand extension could be a website, TV channel, a live event or a range of furniture. Much display advertising is to strengthen a brand

business to business (also B2B) the business press. Producing publications and associated media relevant to a particular occupation, industry, profession

CPT/M cost per thousand or mille. The cost of reaching one thousand readers, listeners, watchers. The benchmark for selling ad space against its competitors

centrefold double page spread in centre of a (saddle-stitched) magazine. Can be used as a pull out

circulation number of copies of a magazine sold. Also can be used in a broader context to describe the practice of distributing magazines, or even the total number of copies distributed. The latter is not strictly correct

classified advertising ads sold by the line or column centimetre, usually placed at the back of a title. Key classified sections include recruitment, buying/selling, motoring and personals

consumer publishing major sector of the industry describing all the magazines aimed at the general public. Sold via newsstands, subscription or free distribution

content marketing (also known as customer magazines and contract publishing) significant sector of the industry covering magazines published on behalf an organisation as part of their marketing strategy

controlled circulation distribution method favoured by B2B titles, where a free copy is sent to an individual meeting certain terms of control

cover lines used on the cover to entice readers with a brief description of the best features in the issue

cover mount a free gift glued to the cover or in a polybag as further enticement to purchase

cover price publisher determined price which is charged for a magazine

coverage percentage of a particular demographic reached by an advertising campaign. May also be called reach

CMA Content Marketing Association. Industry association promoting the interests of content marketers (customer publishers)

cross platform term used to describe ad sales offer which encompasses print and other options – for example digital, live events, TV, radio

DPS double page spread. An ad which stretches across two pages so opening out to form an enlarged feature

demographics quantifiable sections of the population used by marketers – commonly sex, age and social class

digital magazines magazines published online. Formats range from pdfs of print versions to bespoke digital editions. A growing area as market penetration of tablets increases

display ads sold by page or fraction of a page. Magazines commonly sell from DPS to one quarter page

distributors part of the magazine supply chain linking publishers to wholesalers and retailers. Responsible for arranging logistics, supply management, cash flow and trade marketing

drop cap visual device on the page which emphasises the start of an article with an enlarged initial letter, which typically will then drop down over several lines of copy

DTP (desktop publishing) refers to the process of creating documents or whole publications on a PC or Mac. Mostly used in reference to the introduction of sophisticated computers in the 1990s which revolutionised magazine production

dummy pre launch, a publisher will commission a version of the title with relevant design elements, pagination, types of feature and ads to show prospective commercial partners. Often incomplete or with Latin text

editor/editor in chief position with overall responsibility for contents of the magazine

editorial term to describe journalistic and photographic content of magazine. Most magazines will work to a particular editorial/advertising split. Increasingly becoming known as content

enewsletter popular form of electronic communication for magazine publishers to inform readers of new issue, upcoming features and to sell products

epos electronic point of sale. Barcode scanned sales of products. Gives early indication of sales of an issue to circulation teams

FIPP the worldwide magazine media association. Represents associations and companies involved in magazine publishing internationally. Head office in London

flannel panel box giving details of publisher, staff, contact details in magazine

flat plan chart showing potential layout of an issue, where each article will be placed and where each ad will go. It enables relevant departments to see an issue develop through to sign off. Controlled by production editor

free magazines without a cover price

frequency describes publishing cycle of a magazine – weekly, monthly, alternate monthly, quarterly, annual. Also **frequency** refers to amount of times an ad is seen

Google analytics key service offering from Google giving detailed statistics on users and website traffic. It is the most widely used web stat service

grid design tool template used to format pages which will enhance the reading experience and provide visual continuity in a magazine

handbag sized/compact reduced size magazine format introduced very successfully by *Glamour*. Other monthly titles offer this size in parallel with larger formats

independent newsagent traditional newsagent selling mix of tobacco, confectionary and news (newspapers and magazines). Circa. 20,000 in the UK

inserts piece of printed advertising material which is delivered loose or stitched into a magazine. Can also be used to market subscriptions

journal traditionally used to describe all periodicals, the term has evolved to refer to scholarly journals which are peer reviewed

launches term used to describe the initial issue of a magazine to be published. A launch phase may be longer as the new title is sampled by new readers after the first issue

licensing generally international brand extension which uses name, logo and some content but where magazine is published by a local publisher, with territory relevant advertising

lifetime value (LTV) subscription term to describe the amount of revenue a publisher can expect from an average subscriber, secured by a particular campaign, factoring in renewals

live events term used to cover conferences, awards, webinars, trade shows etc. which are offshoots of a magazine brand, essential to the B2B sector

M&E media and entertainment business sector

masthead name of the magazine in its particular font. Legally protected from unauthorised use. Often acts as the logo for a magazine

media agency or media buyer type of advertising agency responsible for planning and buying a media campaign

media pack collection of data about a magazine which acts as promotional material to potential commercial partners, particularly advertisers or their agencies. Typically contains readership demographic information, ABC figures, advertising rate card, key editorial features, mission statements. Largely available online

multipacks pack of magazines bound together and sold as one item at retail. Packs are created by the publisher so the titles almost always come from the same stable. Enables sampling and boosts sales. Magazines involved need to have compatible target markets

NFRN (National Federation of Retail Newsagents) trade body representing independent newsagents

NRS (National Readership Survey) Largest survey of magazine and newspaper readership in the UK. Core information to the process of trading ads

partworks a series of magazine-like products which are regularly published for a finite number of issues. Often the completed set forms a comprehensive reference work. Launched by heavy TV campaigns

pay walls barrier to web content which requires payment to allow access. Key attempt to generate revenue from provision of news online

PPA (Professional Publishers Association) Industry body representing magazine publishers in the UK, promoting the medium and defending members' interests across consumer, B2B and content marketing sectors

point of sale (POS) refers to where the transaction takes place; for consumer magazines this is in a retail environment. POS material refers to posters and stickers that may be displayed in stores

production the process of turning features and photography and advertisements into a physical magazine. Usually overseen by a production editor who manages the workflow

pull quotes section taken from an article and used as a sub heading to break up text and attract the eye of a reader

qualitative data information regarding people's opinions, feelings and behaviours gathered to inform editorial and commercial decisions. Information is observed rather than measured

quantitative data information which can be measured and delivered in numerical form: readership, sales, demographics, time spent reading a magazine etc.

ranging retailers can only carry a certain number of magazines in their stores so they go through a process of adding or deleting titles on a regular basis. May also be referred to as listings

rate card published menu of prices which a publisher intends to charge for different sizes and types of advertisement. In the UK this is more of an aspiration as prices are subject to negotiation. Also includes mechanical data and deadlines

readership a magazine will sell an amount of copies but its **readership** is likely to be greater. The link between circulation and readership is the number of people who read each sold or distributed issue. This is the **readers per copy** figure.

renewal essential to the economics of selling subscriptions is the ability to persuade a subscriber to renew their subscription which is likely to have been discounted as an incentive to initial acquisition.

RSV (retail sales value) The overall sum of money generated by sales of a magazine. For a consumer magazine this is split between the publisher, distributor, wholesaler and retailer

side bar traditionally used in page design to present extra information complimentary to the main article. Usually boxed and therefore separate. Now used online for ads and links in particular

skyline space above the masthead which may be used to highlight a special offer, gift or exclusive feature

specialist magazines magazines based on one central issue or topic

sponsorship type of advertising used to position a brand as closely as possible to the editorial values of a magazine or a particular regular feature

Stamp Duty Introduced in 1712. It was a flat rate tax levied on newspapers and magazines so had a disproportionate effect on cheaper titles. Abolished in 1855

standfirst sentence after a headline but before an article, used to sell the piece to the reader

SOR (sale or return) All consumer magazines are sold to retailers on this basis so they can claim credit for unsold copies (returns)

style sheets enables access to the content on a web page but without any of the design or visual features which that web page has or will have. Often simply text

sub editing the practice of checking text (copy) for accuracy and amending accordingly. This means ensuring spelling, grammar and facts are accurate and conform to house style. Also involves fitting to layouts and writing captions and headlines

supplement additional publication sold as free extra value with a magazine. Banded or bagged

sweet spot the top left part of a magazine's front cover which can be seen most clearly regardless of retail display racking options. Optimum position for key sales message

syndication refers to the distribution of articles, features, columns and pictures from the original rights holder to other publications who pay for the right to reprint. Publishers must negotiate syndication rights with freelancers for global and online publishing

TGI (Target Group Index). Research used extensively by media owners and agencies. Most comprehensive study into the UK's consumer behaviour, attitudes and media consumption

trade marketing refers to activity (spend) by publishers with retailers, supporting newsstand sales

unsolds copies which are not purchased by consumers from retailers which are returned to wholesalers. They represent a substantial cost to publishers

VAT (Value Added Tax in UK) Magazines and newspapers remain exempt for print editions

well editorial well is a term to describe a run of editorial pages, used to emphasise value for money

wholesaler key link in the supply chain accepting bulk deliveries of magazines and then delivering them to each newsagent

Responding to the extraordinary pace of change in media is challenging, but essential – particularly for courses looking to place their graduates with media owners in our industry. It is essential for the talent supply chain to develop a comprehensive and deep understanding of the trends in the market and the industry's evolving skills needs. Becoming a Professional Publishers Association (PPA) accredited course can help.

PPA knows the skills, knowledge and attitude students need to have to get that all-important first step on the employment ladder. We have access to more than 200 employers ranging from traditional women's weekly consumer magazines to business-to-business data and information providers, and from large multi-territory companies to smaller, local, creative teams. Our members comprise the UK's leading publishers who are committed to the future of a thriving publishing industry and the creation of rewarding, challenging careers within it.

PPA knows the industry and knows what the industry wants. Consequently, our stringent accreditation programme ensures that degrees and post graduate courses carrying the PPA Approved logo will equip students with relevant skills that are sought by employers.

PPA accreditation bestows special status on courses, and recognition to educators as partners committed to maintaining the highest standards of training and development for those seeking to join the industry.

For further details on accreditation including guidelines and courses currently accredited please visit www.ppa.co.uk/careers

Index

Bold indicates references to figures, tables or photos.